PSYCHOLOGY IN THE SOVIET UNION

PSYCHOLOGY IN THE SOVIET UNION

Edited with an introduction by
BRIAN SIMON

Papers by

B. G. ANANIEV	D. N. BOGOIAVLENSKY
E. I. BOIKO	D. B. ELKONIN
P. YA. GALPERIN	A. N. LEONTIEV
A. A. LIUBLINSKAYA	A. R. LURIA
N. A. MENCHINSKAYA	E. A. MILERIAN
T. V. ROZONAVA	S. L. RUBINSTEIN
L. A. SHVARTS	L. S. SLAVINA
A. A. SMIRNOV	E. N. SOKOLOV
B. M. TEPLOV	L. V. ZANKOV
A. V. ZAPOROZHETS	

Translated by

J. & M. ELLIS	J. McLEISH
H. MILNE	N. PARSONS

and others

STANFORD UNIVERSITY PRESS
Stanford, California

MANUFACTURED IN THE UNITED STATES OF AMERICA

CONTENTS

v

CONTENTS

PART IV

PART V

PREFACE

IN APRIL 1955, a small party of teachers and educationists visited
the U.S.S.R. at the invitation of the Academy of Educational
Sciences of the R.S.F.S.R. The chief purpose was to study the
experimental schools, where new curricula and methods of teaching
were being evolved for the development of polytechnical education,
and in preparation for the raising of the school leaving age to 17. But
it soon became apparent that such a study required knowledge of
developments in psychology, and accordingly members of the delegation had a number of detailed discussions with Soviet psychologists,
notably Professors Smirnov, Menchinskaya, Leontiev and Luria in
Moscow, and Professor Ananiev in Leningrad. It was as an outcome
of these that the idea of this book was born; that is, of a book that
would familiarize English readers with the general direction of Soviet
psychology, but designed to be of interest to teachers as well as
psychologists.

I put this suggestion in a letter addressed to Professor Smirnov,
director of the Institute of Psychology of the Academy of Educational
Sciences, and Professor Menchinskaya, the deputy-director. They
immediately responded with interest, and after discussion with their
colleagues, sent thirty papers which might be included in such a
volume; from these, twenty have been chosen for publication. Full
permission was given to edit and abbreviate the papers in any way
necessary in order to present as rounded a picture as possible within
the available space.

There is no need to underline the difficulties of translating and
editing specialized papers, particularly when the material is relatively
unfamiliar. But there has been a cooperative effort to overcome these.
Mr. H. Milne and Mr. N. Parsons, who undertook the bulk of the
translation at short notice, readily agreed to produce unabridged
translations, which were then edited and returned to them for checking; it was felt that this was the best way of ensuring accurate editing,
in particular, uniformity in the translation of key terms. In resolving
some particular problems of this kind I have had much assistance
from Mr. O. Kovasc.

Dr. Brian Kirman, Mr. John McLeish and Dr. Neil O'Connor

have been closely associated with this book from the start, and have given expert advice at all stages, not only in the task of selecting papers and general editing, but also on innumerable detailed points. Joan Simon has given constant assistance, not least in the checking of references and the preparation of the Introduction. I am greatly indebted to all those who have shared in the work in this way.

In particular I would like to express our appreciation for the prompt and continued cooperation of Professor Smirnov and his colleagues, and to make a special acknowledgment to Cadria Salimova, a member of one of the Academy's Institutes, who assisted me in the U.S.S.R., and has helped the production of this book in ways too numerous to mention. The Society for Cultural Relations with the U.S.S.R. also put its facilities at my disposal. Finally, Professor W. J. H. Sprott not only encouraged this publication at the outset, but has also followed its progress and given valuable advice.

It remains to add that the transliteration of Russian names used is that adopted by the British Museum.[1] So far as references are concerned, those at the foot of the page are to works available in English translation; Russian references are to be found listed in the bibliography at the end of the book;[2] they are noted in the text by figures in brackets [20: 200], the first of which denotes the number of the volume concerned in the list of references, the second the page number in that volume.

There is one point about translation which should be noted at the outset. After much deliberation, I have adopted, for the Russian words *psikhika* (noun) and *psikhicheskii* (adjective), the terms 'psyche' and 'psychic' These words could almost equally well be rendered as the more familiar 'mind' and 'mental'. But there are two other adjectives, *umstvennyi*, meaning 'mental' (intellectual), and *myslennyi*, meaning 'mental' (thinking). These words have been translated as 'mental' throughout. The Russian noun *um*, 'mind', however, is not used by Soviet psychologists. It seemed best, therefore, to preserve the literal translations, which have been used elsewhere, for instance, in the translations of Pavlov's works, and of other papers by Soviet psychologists.

BRIAN SIMON.

April 1956

[1] With two exceptions; for ы, y is used (as by the American Library of Congress) instead of ui, since this is more generally accepted. Y is also used instead of i (И) at the end of proper names, for the same reason.

[2] Professor Luria's article, printed as Appendix I, arrived too late for inclusion in this system. His Russian references are to be found in the notes to his article.

INTRODUCTION

VERY LITTLE IS KNOWN about Soviet psychology in this country, and terms are used in these papers which require explanation. In the first place, philosophical propositions are referred to, for Soviet psychology proceeds from the materialist viewpoint that matter is primary and consciousness secondary and derivative; these are outlined in this introduction as they are understood and applied by psychologists in the U.S.S.R. Secondly, Pavlov's theory of higher nervous activity provides one of the fundamental points of departure for research and the elements of this must, therefore, be set out briefly here. Finally, a brief summary of the present organization of Soviet psychology may be given which will serve also as an introduction to the authors whose papers are printed in this book.

I

The philosophical standpoint of Soviet psychology is dialectical materialism, as initiated by Marx and Engels and developed by Lenin; it looks back, therefore, to the tradition of materialist philosophy and psychology which had its genesis in seventeenth-century England. Psychology was, of course, initially a branch of philosophy, one aspect of either the materialist or idealist outlook. Marx and Engels traced the development of philosophic materialism from Bacon, Hobbes and Locke, through David Hartley and Joseph Priestley. Hobbes first advanced the view that it is impossible to separate thought from matter; that is, he explained mental processes as motion in the brain substance, without recourse to theories about the soul. In the eighteenth century, leadership in philosophy passed to France, where mechanical materialism was developed as a universal system, but it was in England that the first attempt was made to give a consistently materialist explanation of mental processes. Hartley, in his *Observations on Man* (1749), developed the ideas of Hobbes and Locke and made associationism into a coherent system of psychology. Like Hobbes, he held that mental processes could be subjected to scientific investigation, and he attempted to provide a physiological explanation of mental phenomena based on the latest findings of science; notably medicine, anatomy, physiology, and Newtonian

1

physics and optics. Later, associationism was developed by Priestley, and accepted by James Mill and the utilitarians as one of the two corner-stones of their philosophy, as well as the psychological foundation of their educational policies.

In the mid-nineteenth century, however, this tradition found its strongest support in Russia. It was the writings of Herzen and of the sociologist and philosopher Chernishevsky that inspired the physiologist I. M. Sechenov, acknowledged by Pavlov to have initiated the physiology of higher nervous activity and frequently referred to in the following pages as the founder of scientific psychology in Russia. In embarking himself on experimental study of the higher nervous processes, Pavlov was conscious of invading a field hitherto dominated by psychologist-philosophers; and, from the outset, he determined to adopt a rigorously scientific approach. For him, as for Sechenov before him, this implied a materialist approach; that is, acceptance of the view that mental phenomena are inseparably connected with the functioning of the brain and that they can be investigated by the same objective methods as are other phenomena of nature. Pavlov specifically referred to the reflex theory of Descartes as the essential starting point of physiological investigation up to his own time,[1] and, when enumerating the fundamental scientific principles on which his own theory of reflex activity rested, he placed first 'determinism . . . that is, a cause for every given action or effect'.[2]

In accepting the materialist view of the relation of mind and matter, and rejecting dualism in all its forms, Soviet psychology is, therefore, developing a native tradition of scientific psychology, which itself stems from the original psychological theories of materialist philosophers, the first attempts to make psychology a science. This viewpoint may be briefly summarized as follows: (1) Mental processes are the product of matter organized in a particular way; i.e. of the human brain. There are not two processes here—the material processes of the higher nervous system and the mental processes of consciousness; mental processes are simply one aspect of the functioning of the brain; there is only a single process. (2) Matter is primary, consciousness is secondary and derivative; i.e. sensations, perceptions and thought derive from an external material world that exists independently of consciousness. This means that nothing can come to birth in consciousness which is not a reflection of some aspect of the material world. It is in this special sense that the terms 'reflection' and 'reflectory activity' are used in the papers printed here.[3]

[1] Pavlov-Anrep, 4. Details of the English editions of Pavlov's works are given in the Bibliography.   [2] Pavlov-Gantt ii, 125; *Selected Works*, 421.
[3] For a discussion of sensation and perception in this sense, cf. the paper by B. G. Ananiev, 'The Basis of Spatial Discrimination', p. 131.

Soviet psychologists argue that any attempt to construct a science of the mind must involve taking a firm standpoint on the relation of mind and matter; it is impossible to leave the question open, for to do so is to open the door to unscientific theories and methods, to uncritical borrowing from philosophic propositions.[1] It is in this sense that they criticize the empirical approach, the attempt to maintain a neutral position, holding that in practice this usually means acceptance of tenets of positivist philosophy which are detrimental to the advance of science.[2]

Dialectical materialism, however, differs greatly from the mechanical materialist philosophy, which was based on the early development of natural science but failed to encompass the new scientific advances of the nineteenth century. The great defect of this philosophy, wrote Marx, is that it cannot explain the interrelation of phenomena; it cannot explain change without introducing some outside vital principle beyond the reach of science.[3] Thus it conceives of movement only in terms of *mechanical* motion, i.e. the simple change in place of particles as a result of the action on them of external forces. The mechanist approach in science, therefore, involves an attempt to reduce all events to the result of external action; to analyse every process into the sum of the movements of the several parts acting externally on each other; to explain all processes in terms of the interaction of a number of such distinct and separate factors. This approach implies a strict determinism but only within certain limits, for, when

[1] Some corroboration of this view is provided by the following summary of prevailing attitudes among Western psychologists as to the relations of mind and matter: 'Perhaps the most prevalent attitude of contemporary psychologists is to regard the problem as outside the scope of psychology as at present defined. This attitude, however, very naturally means in practice a refusal to admit that any such problem exists. This again turns out upon closer examination to mean among many psychologists that the answer to the problem is quite simple, and that philosophy has made itself much trouble over many unproductive and unreal problems. When we turn to ask what this simple and obvious answer is, we find persisting, without great alteration, a variety of answers prevalent in the nineteenth century, indeed, a number of them prevalent in the ancient world. Many of them have, however, taken on a special colouring as a result of the scientific and philosophical events of the last few decades.' Gardner Murphy, *An Historical Introduction to Modern Psychology* (4th ed., London, 1938), 391.

[2] It is in the light of this that references to the insecure foundations of much of Western psychology must be understood; cf. A. A. Smirnov's paper, 'Psychological Research, 1953–5', p. 29, and S. L. Rubinstein, 'Questions of Psychological Theory', p. 264.

[3] The best known summary of this view, as related to social development, is Marx's statement: 'The materialist doctrine that men are products of circumstances and upbringing, and that, therefore, changed men are products of other circumstances and changed upbringing, forgets that it is men that change circumstances and that the educator must himself be educated.' F. Engels, *Ludwig Feuerbach* (ed. I. B. Lasker, London, 1947), 76.

something new arises which cannot be explained in these terms, the mechanist flies to the opposite pole and talks of 'spontaneity', for example, of spontaneous 'urges' or 'drives' which motivate human behaviour. It is this that Soviet psychologists have in mind when they criticize the limitations of mechanism and say that it can easily turn into its opposite, idealism.[1]

The key criticism of behaviourist psychology is that it is mechanist; in particular, because it attempts to reduce psychological phenomena to physiological terms, while at the same time maintaining that there are subjective processes of human consciousness which cannot be studied by objective methods.[2] This narrow and one-sided approach, it is held, has paved the way for purely idealist systems of psychology, concerned only with the subjective world, which tend to make a mystery of mental events and processes; this is the chief criticism of Gestalt psychology.[3]

What was new about the philosophic views of Marx and Engels was that mechanism was replaced by dialectics; Marxism is materialist dialectics, or dialectical materialism. It also differs from all earlier philosophical systems in that it does not set out to construct a finished world picture, but rather to generalize past knowledge and point the way to new. It is, therefore, not a closed system but one that is itself open to development and change. Thus Engels maintained that the old philosophy, the attempt to construct a universal system, came to an end with Hegel:

> As soon as we have realized—and in the long run no one has helped us to realize it more than Hegel himself—that the task of philosophy thus stated means nothing but . . . that a single philosopher should accomplish that which can only be accomplished by the entire human race in its progressive development—as soon as we realize that, there is an end of all philosophy in the hitherto accepted sense of the word. One leaves alone 'absolute truth', which is unattainable along this path or by any single individual; instead, one pursues attainable relative truths along the path of the positive sciences, and the summation of their results by means of dialectical thinking.[4]

The dialectical method involves, therefore, a view of the world, not as a complex of 'ready-made things', each with its own fixed proper-

---

[1] Cf. Rubinstein's paper, p. 264, and that by B. M. Teplov, on 'Objective Method in Psychology', p. 246.

[2] Cf. Teplov's references to behaviourism, p. 258; and also that of E. I. Boiko, p. 236.

[3] For Pavlov's spirited criticism of Köhler and Kurt Lewin, cf. *Selected Works*, 569 ff.; the point is referred to by D. N. Bogoiavlensky, p. 71, and in Appendix II.

[4] *Ludwig Feuerbach*, 18.

ties, but as a complex of processes in which all things arise, have their existence and pass away; it insists that all phenomena must be studied in their movement and change and in inseparable connection with other phenomena.[1] It does not, therefore, separate matter from motion, from space and time, but regards matter in motion as fundamental and inseparable from space and time.[2] Finally, it does not reduce all movement to mechanical motion, but conceives of a range of forms of movement of matter, from simple change of place to complex changes in the thought processes; within this range one form of movement derives from another, one form of movement may be transformed into another, giving rise to new qualities of matter in motion—as the expression of differences in the form of motion. This permits of the conception of quantitative change being succeeded by qualitative change, a transition to a new level. The relevance of this conception to problems of the relation of body and mind, of the transition from sensation to thought, for instance, and to detailed questions concerning the relation of practical activity and mental processes is obvious.[3]

On a wider scale, this conception is the operative one when the subject matter of psychology is defined and the place of psychology among the sciences discussed. As the sciences develop the nature of their interrelationship requires clarification; for instance, the relationship between biology and physiology, between physiology and psychology. Soviet psychologists see this question primarily as one relating to the emergence of new forms of movement of matter, which are manifested in new qualities, new kinds of objects and new potentialities of movement. So psychology has a specific sphere of investigation in which psychological laws may be discovered which differ from those of biology and physiology.[4] By contrast, it is one of the chief criticisms of psychoanalysis that, while depending on subjective methods of inquiry and creating a psychological system entirely on this insecure foundation, it tends to reduce all human behaviour to dark, inexplicable, biological urges expressed through the 'unconscious'.[5]

---

[1] *Ibid.*, 52–3.

[2] The bearing that this has on psychological investigation is made clear by Ananiev, p. 135.

[3] Cf. the approach to the development of mental actions in the papers by P. Ya. Galperin and others.

[4] This problem is referred to by Smirnov, p. 30, and forms the main subject of Rubinstein's paper.

[5] Psychoanalysis is only referred to indirectly by Teplov; for use of the term 'unconscious', cf. p. 260. But reference may be made to an article by E. T. Chernakov, 'Against Idealism and Metaphysics in Psychology' (1948) (Society for Cultural Relations with the U.S.S.R., 14 Kensington Square, London, W.8).

In this connection, Soviet psychologists also lay great stress on the historical approach to the study of phenomena. They hold that, by applying the dialectical method to the investigation of human society and history, Marx and Engels overcame the dichotomy between man and nature. There was inanimate matter on earth before there were any living beings. Life itself is a new mode of existence of matter, developing at a certain level; society and history begin when a new species of animal, man, begins to use tools and to produce his means of subsistence in cooperation with other men. Human labour is a qualitatively new form of social activity, which gives rise to the qualitatively new phenomenon, articulate speech, and integrally related with this, to a new characteristic of the mind—the conscious reflection of objective reality.

Men create their own environment by their own labour and actions. There is, therefore, a constant interpenetration between man and his environment; the two cannot be opposed as discrete objects, which only interact mechanically as a result of *external* collision. On the contrary, development takes place as a result of internal contradiction.

An example may make this viewpoint clearer. Consciousness and speech, it is argued, are prepared for in the animal world but arise uniquely in man with the development of social forms of life based on labour. Labour, a qualitatively new form of activity, gives rise to a qualitatively new characteristic of the mind—the conscious reflection of objective reality. This new characteristic corresponds to the needs and conditions of the new form of social life. As the labour process becomes more complex and society develops, therefore, this new characteristic also develops and comes to take a predominant position; whereas, by contrast, other characteristics which were predominant in the animal world cease to develop and sink into the background. It is a process of internal contradiction, between the new and the old, taking place *in dependence upon* the conditions of life.[1]

Here, the dialectical materialist theory of knowledge is also of key importance. Most theories of knowledge take sensations or ideas as their starting point and tend to abstract these from the context of men's activity; whereas Marxists hold that knowledge must be studied as it actually develops in the course of human activity, and that it can be so studied because all human knowledge, in fact, arises, develops and is tested in social practice. This is illustrated in the whole history of the development of science and technique, of social institutions and ideas.

It is this approach that accounts for insistence upon the integral relation of consciousness and activity. This is a key conception which

[1] Cf. Smirnov's article on 'Child Psychology', p. 184.

has much influence on research methods; for, if consciousness is inseparably connected with activity and changes with changes in the form of activity, then it follows that (1) mental processes can be investigated objectively, as they are manifested in activity, (2) changes in the form of activity can influence changes in the organization of mental processes. It is this conclusion that prompts acceptance of the key importance of education, in determining mental development. An essential aspect of many research projects, especially with children, is, therefore, that active educational measures are introduced in the attempt to modify mental processes and so to discover their nature and the laws governing their interrelations and development.[1]

Soviet psychologists are also much concerned with the question of speech; in particular, the development of speech in children in its relation to the development of more complex forms of thought.[2] In such investigations they attempt to study how knowledge arises and develops in dependence upon concrete conditions of life and activity. The phrase 'conditions of life' will frequently be met with in this connection, and it usually implies 'form of existence', in the sense that it does not refer to an unchanging environment acting on a child, but rather to the whole content of the child's life—including his relations with other people, his own activity and his attitude towards this, his place in society and so on. In all this work, the goal is never that of reaching final judgments, of seeking, for instance, the ultimate elements of mind, or of personality; but rather that of discovering processes, and the laws governing these. Here is one of the reasons for the decisive rejection of mental testing, or psychometry.[3]

Finally, Soviet psychologists regard materialist dialectics as an important instrument for the development of psychology. The dialectical method arises out of, and generalizes, the achievements of science in different fields, and continually finds confirmation in those achievements. Thus, it is held, Pavlov's work confirmed and developed the materialist theory of reflection. All scientific investigation is guided by theory, but in many scientific theories there are embedded philosophic preconceptions which hold up the advance of science; the more so, when their existence is unsuspected and they are applied unconsciously. Use of the dialectical method in criticizing and analysing theories and research methods can assist psychology to

---

[1] Cf. A. N. Leontiev's experiments with 'tone deaf' children, described in 'The Nature and Formation of Human Psychic Properties', p. 228; and the structure of the experiments conducted by Galperin, L. S. Slavina, A. S. Liublinskaya.

[2] Cf. A. R. Luria, 'The Role of Language in the Formation of Temporary Connections'; A. S. Liublinskaya, 'The Development of Children's Speech and Thought'.

[3] Cf. Smirnov, 'Child Psychology', p. 189.

shed these preconceived ideas and to maintain a strictly objective, scientific approach in both theory and practice.[1]

This accounts for the very critical attitude of Soviet psychologists, critical both of other schools of psychology, which they find insufficiently rigorous, and of their own achievements. They consider it necessary, in the interests of scientific advance, to keep a constant watch on formalism and one-sidedness in theory or practice, in order to make sure both that achievements are solid and secure, and that the next steps towards more profound investigation are clearly indicated.

The general principles informing Soviet psychology may, then, be briefly summarized as follows:

(1) Mental processes are properties of the brain, the highest form of organic matter; it is impossible fully to understand mental processes without a knowledge of the cerebral processes which underlie mental activity.

(2) Consciousness is a reflection of the objective world; in explaining mental processes, therefore, the psychologist must take into account the objective reality they reflect.

(3) Neural-mental activity is conditioned by the form of existence of living beings and changes with changes in the form of existence. Therefore, the development of human consciousness is conditioned by changes in the material life of society and must be studied, not in the abstract, but in a concrete historical setting.

(4) Consciousness is formed in practical activity and revealed in the course of activity. Changes in the content and form of practical activity can, therefore, influence changes in the organization and development of mental processes.[2]

These principles, so formulated in 1947, have only been arrived at as a result of a long period of discussion and experiment. There was no outright rejection of other schools of psychological thought in the early 1920's, but rather a gradual working towards the goal of a single, unified science of psychology. It was in the course of this trend of development, and as a result also of new demands made upon psychology, that the theories of various different schools of psychology were examined and found wanting. So, for instance, mental testing was first severely criticized in 1931, after the first Five Year Plan had begun and new developments had taken place in education. But it was not until 1936 that the whole system of mental testing,

[1] Cf. Ananiev's criticism of theories of perception. One method whereby Soviet psychologists re-examine their assumptions is by careful analysis of the categories of psychology: cf. E. I. Boiko, 'A Contribution towards the Definition of "Skill" and "Habit" ', p. 233, and E. A. Milerian, 'Involuntary and Voluntary Attention'.

[2] B. G. Ananiev, 'Progress of Soviet Psychology' (Society for Cultural Relations with the U.S.S.R., 1948).

which had become grafted on to individual schools, was abolished. The outcome of many years' discussion was then summed up in the statement by the Communist Party that mental testing was unscientific and held up educational advance, that it had been found to be in conflict both with dialectical materialism and with the practical experience of Soviet society. It was at this period, when a completely new approach was called for, that psychologists developed new methods of research, of the kind already described, relating the development of mental processes to activity.[1]

Today there are suggestions that these investigations, though very valuable, may result in a one-sided view unless they are supplemented by other methods of approach.[2] Discussion on other points also continues, and there are a number of indications of conflicts of opinion on certain vital questions. While insisting on the importance of adhering to the materialist standpoint and the dialectical method in resolving these conflicts, Soviet psychologists also point to another important influence affecting the development of psychology as a science. This is the traditionally high level of development of Russian physiology; in particular the elaboration by Pavlov of a theory of higher nervous activity which, if properly assimilated, can provide a new point of departure for psychological investigation. To this subject we may now turn.

II

Experimental psychology began with the new developments in physiology in the early nineteenth century, and it is held that the Pavlovian theory of higher nervous activity, which represents the crowning achievement of physiology, has now, for the first time, provided psychology with a firm scientific basis.

Great attention has always been accorded to Pavlov's work in the Soviet Union, as also in other countries. The Soviet Government made large grants for the provision of laboratories and the furtherance of research from 1921, continued to provide generous financial support up to Pavlov's death in 1936, and has since maintained this support for the work of his successors. Nevertheless, the full implications of Pavlov's theories have only recently been appreciated by psychologists. The importance of revising earlier conceptions of mental and neural processes was forcibly brought home during the war, when many psychologists worked in hospitals for those suffering from injuries to the limbs and brain and gained practical experience

[1] This point is made by D. B. Elkonin, p. 47. The decree abolishing the practice of intelligence testing in schools is printed in full in *Soviet Psychiatry* (1950) by J. Wortis. [2] Cf. Teplov's criticism, pp. 251–2.

of the plasticity of the higher nervous system.[1] It was partly as an outcome of this work that some psychologists began to modify their ideas about the neural mechanisms of mental activity, and to appreciate that Pavlovian physiology, which had not formerly been considered significant in relation to the higher thought processes, was relevant to all spheres of psychological investigation.

This trend was greatly accelerated after the Scientific Session, called jointly by the Academy of Sciences and the Academy of Medical Sciences in the summer of 1950, when the two main contributions were made by Pavlov's pupils, K. M. Bykov and A. G. Ivanov-Smolensky. The primary function of this conference was to assess the significance of Pavlov's work and to discuss how it could most fruitfully be developed. Leading research institutes were criticized for their failure to develop the physiology of higher nervous activity, and the relevance of Pavlovian theories to other sciences—notably biology, medicine, psychiatry and psychology—was strongly emphasized. So began a wide discussion and application of Pavlovian principles, which is still continuing and is reflected in nearly every paper printed in this collection.

Pavlov's discovery of the conditioned reflex, which he contrasted with the inborn (or unconditioned) reflex already known to physiology, provided him with an objective method of studying the dynamics of higher nervous activity. This discovery was made when, in the course of studying the activity of the digestive glands in dogs, he observed certain 'psychic' phenomena which constantly participated in the mechanism of physiological processes. These phenomena had always been referred to in terms of subjective psychological categories; that is, they had been named but not explained. Pavlov explained them in terms of the conditioned reflex.[2] During the thirty years that followed his work extended to cover a much wider range but Pavlov reached the conclusion that all higher nervous activity is effected through the mechanism of unconditioned and conditioned connections. Ivanov-Smolensky summarizes his views as follows.

An unconditioned connection is a relatively constant, inherited connection between an organism and its environment, formed in the course of phylogenesis; a conditioned connection is a temporary and highly variable connection between the environment and the organism, acquired in the course of ontogenesis. But Pavlov expressed the view that conditioned connections, if repeated through a series of generations, may be 'converted hereditarily into unconditioned connections'. He found that the cerebral cortex of the higher animals

---

[1] For instance, Professor Luria was director of a hospital devoted to treatment of brain injuries, and Professor Leontiev directed a hospital for the rehabilitation of the disabled. [2] Pavlov-Gantt i, 47 ff.

possesses a coupling, or linking, function, that is, the function of acquiring, forming, creating, new connections between the organism and its environment, the function of evolving new vital experience, the function of ontogenetic adaptation, which adjusts the organism to the conditions of its environment and the environment to the requirements of the organism. In the basic concepts of the theory of higher nervous activity, therefore, are to be found expressed, in a brief and synthesized form, all the major biological problems: the theory of evolution, the interaction between the organism and its environment, adaptability and variability, heredity and acquired experience, ontogenetic and phylogenetic development and the inheritance of acquired characters.[1] By showing the dominant role of the cerebral cortex in controlling the relation of the organism and the external world, Pavlov was able to overcome the dichotomy between organism and environment, and so to cross the boundary from the mechanistic idea that the phenomena of nature are predetermined for all time to the historical conception of the development of the animal world.[2]

Ivanov-Smolensky added that Pavlov's theories are equally significant for psychology. In his work, mental activity, which philosophers and psychologists have studied for hundreds of years, and which has latterly been studied in the light of the psychophysiology of the sense organs and the theory of localization of mental functions, is subjected to systematic study by a new scientific method; and as a result, important laws governing the higher nervous processes, which are the material basis of mental activity, have been disclosed. Pavlov considered that the concepts of psychology must be explained by data obtained from strictly objective investigation of higher nervous activity. It was in this way that he conceived of the superimposition of mental activity on physiological facts, the 'amalgamation' of the psychological and the physiological; he conceived of the higher functioning of the brain, which is called mental activity, as a unity of subjective and objective.[3]

A brief account may be given of the terms used by Pavlov, as they are understood by those now carrying on his work, in order that subsequent discussions of his theory may be understood by the general reader.

The conditioned reflex represents a new class of reflex, one which arises and develops in the course of the organism's life and embraces all the reactions of animals and man, from the primitive salivary reflex in response to a stimulus associated with food, to human speech and writing. The process whereby a conditioned reflex is formed in

[1] *Scientific Session on the Physiological Teachings of Academician I. P. Pavlov* (Moscow, 1951), 77–8.   [2] *Ibid.*, 28.   [3] *Ibid.*, 90–1, 120–1.

11

the laboratory is well known. It is formed on the basis of an unconditioned reflex, such as salivation in response to the insertion of food
into the mouth. If an *indifferent stimulus*, the ticking of a metronome,
for instance, is associated sufficiently frequently with the introduction
of food, the dog will salivate when he hears the metronome tick. This
is a *conditioned reflex*; the mechanism of its formation, according to
Pavlov, 'has its seat in the cerebral hemispheres; . . . the unconditioned reflexes being functions of the lower parts of the central
nervous system'.[1]

Pavlov explained that the mechanism whereby a conditioned reflex
is formed is elementary, but that its relations are extremely complex.
'These are, even in animals, highly intricate. A great mass of various
stimuli act upon this reflex incessantly.' The complexity of the conditioned reflex consists, therefore, in its 'extraordinary dependence . . .
on the phenomena of the internal condition of the organism, as well
as on the phenomena of the surrounding outer world'.[2] It was this
consideration that led Pavlov to use the term *conditional* reflex. 'As
these reactions are dependent upon a multitude of conditions, it
appeared logical to us to designate them as conditional, as *conditional
reflexes*.'[3]

Here Pavlov introduced the conception of the *signalling system*. In
the case of the unconditioned reflex—salivation in response to the
presentation of food—those properties of the substance to which the
saliva is physiologically adapted act as a stimulus; for instance, the
hardness or dryness of the food. But, in the case of the conditioned
reflex, 'those properties which bear no direct relation to the physiological role of the saliva act as stimuli, for example, colour, form and
the like. These last properties evidently receive their psychological
importance as *signals* for the first ones, i.e. for the essential properties.'[4]

Pavlov went on to note that 'the mechanism of stimulation of the
salivary glands through the signalizing properties of objects, i.e. the

---

[1] Pavlov-Gantt i, 215.   [2] *Ibid.*, i, 215.

[3] *Ibid.*, 226. Or, again, 'The term "conditional" is becoming more and more
generally employed, and I think its use is fully justified in that, compared with
the inborn reflexes, these new reflexes actually do depend on very many conditions, both in their formation and in the maintenance of their physiological
activity . . .' Pavlov-Anrep, 25. The operative word is *ouslovny*, the exact translation of which is 'conditional'. In French and German this original term has been
preserved, but in English it has always been rendered as 'conditioned'; this usage
has, therefore, been retained in these pages. But the point is of great importance,
since the term 'conditioned' implies the determined quality of the reflex, whereas
'conditional' puts the emphasis on the dependence of the reflex on *varying* circumstances and conditions, a very different matter. It was precisely this latter point
that Pavlov wished to stress in his terminology.

[4] *Ibid.*, 79.

mechanism of *conditioned stimulation*, may be easily conceived of from the physiological point of view as a function of the nervous system'. At the basis of each conditioned reflex there lies an unconditioned reflex. It must, then, be assumed that

> the point of the central nervous system which during the unconditioned reflex becomes strongly stimulated, attracts to itself weaker impulses arriving simultaneously from the outer or internal worlds at other points of this system, i.e. . . . thanks to the unconditioned reflex there is opened for all these stimulations a temporary path leading to the point of this reaction.[1]

In brief, a conditioned reflex is formed when excitation occurs simultaneously at two points of the central nervous system and a connection arises between these two points; there is a coupling, or linking, of the two sites of excitation. So Pavlov summarized the physiological role of the cortex as 'either (1) a connecting, combining or coupling function (according to the mechanism), or (2) a signalling function (according to its significance). And the signalization is adaptable in strict correspondence with external agents.'[2]

In the example given above, the ticking of a metronome constituted the *conditioned stimulus*; but Pavlov found that any natural phenomenon could be converted into a conditioned stimulus, and that a conditioned reflex could be established on the basis of all kinds of unconditioned reflexes.[3] This indicated the enormous importance of the conditioned reflex which constitutes a *temporary connection* between external stimulus and response; a connection which has as its basis a connection between the relevant areas of the cerebral cortex.

> Obviously conditioned reflexes favour enormously the safety and welfare of the organism. Thanks to these temporary connections, diverse and complex agents become conditioned stimuli, which evoke conditioned reflexes. Centres become related functionally and synthesis of stimuli occurs. Probably the site of this coupling, combining activity is to be sought for in the points of union, the synapses of the neurones, especially in the cortex of the cerebrum.[4]

Why is a conditioned reflex regarded as a temporary connection? Pavlov found that conditioned reflexes are only maintained so long

---

[1] *Ibid.*, 80.   [2] *Ibid.*, 354.
[3] 'A conditioned reflex is formed on the basis of all unconditioned reflexes and by all possible agents of the inner and outer world both in their elementary form and in their largest complexes,' Pavlov-Gantt ii, 171. Among unconditioned reflexes, Pavlov attached particular importance to what he called the orienting-investigatory reflex; this is discussed in some detail by Elkonin, pp. 55–6, and frequently referred to elsewhere.   [4] Pavlov-Gantt i, 297.

13

as the conditioned response is *reinforced*. For instance, if a dog is repeatedly fed after presentation of the given stimulus this is reinforced and the reflex is evoked; but if the dog is not fed the conditioned reflex disappears, is *extinguished*, though it may be re-established. It is precisely the temporary nature of the connections formed that gives these their importance in explaining the adaptive, learned behaviour of the organism. Temporary connections of all kinds are formed during an organism's life history; those which have a stable significance in maintaining an equilibrium between organism and environment are consistently reinforced, those formed to more transitory stimuli cease to be reinforced and become extinguished.

'Obviously it is highly important for the animal under the circumstances of his life to be physiologically connected thus distantly and variedly with the favourable conditions which are necessary for his existence or with the injurious influences which threaten him,' wrote Pavlov. And again:

> This temporary relation and its law (reinforcement by repetition and weakening if not repeated) play an important role in the welfare and integrity of the organism; by means of it the fineness of the adaptation between the organism and its environment becomes more perfect. If the temporary relations to some object are of great significance for the organism, it is also of the highest importance that these relations should be abandoned as soon as they cease to correspond to reality. Otherwise the relations of the animal, instead of being delicately adapted, would be chaotic.[1]

So Pavlov established that the conditioned reflex is the mechanism of the relationship between the organism and the external world, providing 'the most delicate equilibration with the surrounding medium', and indicated how greatly the activity of the organism depends on its form of existence.

The other mechanism with which he was primarily concerned was that of the *analyser*.

> The temporary connection proves to be necessary as soon as the relation of the animal to the external world becomes complex. But this great complexity of relations presupposes the ability of the organism to decompose the external world into separate parts. And in fact every higher animal possesses manifold and delicate analysers. They are what until now have been called sense organs.[2]

Pavlov dispensed with the term sense organs because it had a subjec-

[1] Pavlov-Gantt i, 56, 372.　　　　　　　　[2] *Ibid.*, 126–7.

tive content, as a result of attempts to describe animal behaviour in terms of subjective judgments about human sensations and conceptions. His term 'analyser' covers the whole analysing apparatus of the nervous system.

For example, the visual analyser selects the vibrations of light, the acoustic analyser, the vibrations of sound, and so on. With regard to the structure of the analysers, each includes, on the one hand, the peripheral receptor with all its afferent nerves, and, on the other hand, the nerve cells which lie at the central termination of the nerve fibres ... the highest and most subtle analysing activity of which an animal is capable can be obtained only with the help of the cerebral cortex.[1]

The cerebral cortex, then, has an analysing function based, in the first instance, on the peripheral endings of the various afferent nerves.

Each single afferent nerve fibre, running from some definite element of the peripheral receptive field, must be regarded as a conductor to the cortex of some definite element of one or other form of energy. In the cortex a special cell must stand in connection with the fibre, the activity of the cell being related to some definite element of one or another definite form of energy.[2]

Following up this hypothesis, and using the method of studying conditioned and unconditioned reflexes, coupled with the old method of surgical extirpation of parts of the brain, Pavlov sought to work out a new dynamic theory of the localization of functions in the brain. As a result of many experiments he came to the conclusion that

each peripheral receiving apparatus (the sense organ) has in the cortex a special central territory, its own terminus, which represents its exact projection in the brain. Here—thanks to the special construction of this area ...—can be effected highly complicated stimulations (the highest syntheses), and also their differentiation (the highest analyses). However, the given receptor elements transcend this central area, extending out over a great distance, probably through the entire cortex, but the farther they are from their centre, the more unfavourably they are disposed (in regard to their function). In consequence of this, the stimulations become more elementary and the analyses less refined. In conformity with this view, the motor region, too, must be considered as a receptor one, as

[1] Pavlov-Anrep, 110.　　　　　　　[2] Pavlov-Gantt i, 383–4.

a projection of the whole movement apparatus; the receiving elements of this system, however, may be farther distributed from their central territory.[1]

Describing the results of the first experiments that led to this conception of the motor area, Pavlov noted that the results obtained suggested that

> the motor area of the cortex must be thought of as an analyser of the impulses from muscles and joints (proprioceptive) exactly as other areas are analysers of impulses from stimuli acting on the organism from outside (exteroceptive). From this point of view the entire cortex represents a complex system of analysers of the internal as well as of the external environment of the organism.[2]

The fact that the path, or arc, of the conditioned reflex passes through the cerebral cortex made possible a study of the whole dynamics of higher nervous activity by this means and it is precisely in the results of this study that the full significance of Pavlov's work lies. It was by use of the conditioned-reflex method that he discovered the interrelationship of the processes of inhibition and excitation and the laws of irradiation and concentration. The method of formation of a conditioned reflex may be recalled, in order to contrast inhibition with its opposite, excitation (stimulation).

> If a new, formerly indifferent stimulus, entering into the cerebrum, meets in the nervous system at the moment, a *focus* of strong excitation, this newly arriving stimulation begins to concentrate, and to open a road, as it were, to this focus, and through it onward to the corresponding organ, becoming in this way a stimulator of that organ. In the opposite case, i.e. if no such focus of excitation exists, the new stimulation is dispersed without any marked effect in the mass of the cerebrum. Such is the formulation of the fundamental law of the highest parts of the central nervous system.[3]

There are, however, many kinds of conditioned reflexes and their properties and speed of formation vary. Since they are

> in the highest part of the central nervous system, in which there is a constant collision of innumerable influences from the external world, it is comprehensible that among the different conditioned reflexes there is an incessant struggle, a choice among them at any

[1] Pavlov-Gantt i, 302.   [2] Pavlov-Anrep, 360.   [3] Pavlov-Gantt i, 124.

given moment. Consequently there are constantly arising cases of inhibition among these reflexes.[1]

Pavlov finally distinguished two main inhibitory processes: *unconditioned, or passive (external) inhibition, and conditioned, or active (internal) inhibition.* It is the second process that is important for psychology, and an example may be given of internal inhibition.

> If a strong conditioned reflex is repeated several times without being accompanied by the unconditioned reflex by help of which it was formed, it immediately begins to lose its strength, and more or less quickly, but gradually, falls to zero; i.e. if the conditioned reflex as a signal of the unconditioned signalizes falsely, the former immediately and steadily loses its stimulating effect. This loss of effectiveness of the conditioned reflex comes about not by its destruction, but by its internal inhibition; for a conditioned reflex which has been extinguished in this way, after some time becomes restored *per se*.[2]

Pavlov regarded excitation and inhibition as two active, contradictory processes, both of fundamental importance in the functioning of the organism; he demonstrated that they are in a state of continuous interaction and that, under certain conditions, one can be transformed into the other.

The dynamic nature of excitation and inhibition is shown by the fact that they irradiate from the point of formation to other regions of the cortex, interact with local processes, and then leave these as if receding to the initial point of origin.

> The irradiation of the nervous processes forms . . . one of the fundamental phenomena of the activity of the cortex of the brain. Related to this process is its counterpart—the concentration and collection of the nervous processes at a certain point. . . . The separate phenomena of the nervous activity of the cerebral hemispheres are subject to two general laws (or they may be spoken of as one law)—*the law of irradiation and of concentration* of the nervous process.[3]

Irradiation corresponds to generalization (i.e. the capacity of the organism to react not only to the particular stimulus, but also to other

[1] *Ibid.*, 125.
[2] *Ibid.*, 125–6. Inhibition is discussed in lectures IV–VI, XIV, XV, Pavlov-Anrep; but for Pavlov's latest findings, cf. Pavlov-Gantt ii, 87–9, 172 ff., *Selected Works*, 252 ff., 275–7.   [3] *Ibid.*, 218–19.

similar objects) and concentration corresponds to differentiation (i.e. the capacity of the organism to discriminate more and more precisely between stimuli). The interrelations between these two processes are governed by *reciprocal induction*; i.e. if a cortical centre is in a state of excitation, adjacent and even remote centres are inhibited by negative induction, and *vice versa*. Induction can also occur in one and the same nervous centre; that is, after strong excitation, inhibition will set in, and conversely. So Pavlov conceived of a very fine definite localization of processes of inhibition and excitation, as a result of which

the whole cortex becomes reduced to a huge mosaic of points of excitation and inhibition closely intermingled. This mosaic is formed and reinforced partly by the reciprocal crowding in of the opposed processes of excitation and of inhibition, directly evoked by the corresponding external agents; partly, however, by internal relations, in particular by reciprocal induction, when one process leads to the strengthening of the other.[1]

It is these processes that make possible the analysing activity of the cortex. But closely combined with this is the function of synthesis. Pavlov pointed out that the very fact of the formation of a simple conditioned reflex is proof of higher synthetic activity, since thereby the cortex does not merely sum up two phenomena but synthesizes two inborn reflexes (e.g. an orienting reflex to the sound of a metronome and a salivary reflex to food) into a reflex of a new, higher nature.

But, in addition to the simple conditioned reflex, Pavlov later established second-order conditioned reflexes; that is, instead of elaborating a conditioned reflex on the basis of an unconditioned one he established it on the basis of another conditioned reflex which had already been elaborated. He also successfully established third-order conditioned reflexes. This advance was of great importance in that it enabled him to postulate that single stimulations become linked together in a chain, are associated; and that association is the basis for the development of thought, of understanding.[2]

[1] Pavlov-Gantt i, 355.

[2] *Ibid.*, 337. Pavlov held that the 'temporary connection' disclosed by physiology and 'association' as conceived of by psychologists are 'fully identical; they merge in and absorb each other'. He noted a growing acceptance of the view that conditioned reflexes provide a solid foundation for associationist psychology and added, 'This is all the more true since it is possible to form a new conditioned stimulus with the help of an elaborated conditioned stimulus; and recently it has been convincingly proved on a dog that two indifferent stimuli repeated in succession can also become interconnected and evoke each other' (Pavlov-Gantt ii, 171; *Selected Works*, 251). Nevertheless, Pavlov considered association (which he likened to Locke's conception of synthesis) as only half the process of thinking; in his view analysis was equally important (*Selected Works*, 588).

These are examples of the synthetic activity of the cortex. But the cortex has also a systematizing function. The chief proof of this was the uniting into a single dynamic unit of a series of stimuli and responses; that is, the automatization of a variety of forms of activity in the form of a *dynamic stereotype*.[1]

Pavlov, therefore, maintained that there was a functional unity of all levels of the central nervous system, with the cerebral cortex playing the dominant role, and established that the functions of the sense organs are naturally connected with the functioning of the brain. These findings applied, not only to the interrelations between organism and external environment but also to the internal environment, for Pavlov expressed the view that 'the entire organism and all its component parts are able to report about themselves to the hemispheres'.[2] This view has since been upheld by experimental investigation; in particular, research has shown that there are nervous mechanisms which perform the function of internal 'sense organs'; these, like the external 'sense organs', serve as receptors and analysers which maintain connection between the cerebral cortex and the organism's internal environment.[3]

Pavlov, therefore, regarded the organism as an integral whole: (1) Because all its parts and their functions are interconnected, because it is a system which functions as a single whole, a system, moreover, which is constantly and continuously interacting with its external environment in a process of mobile, fluid, ceaselessly fluctuating and unstable equilibrium. (2) Because of the functional unity, achieved mainly through the nervous system, between the organism's internal and external vital activity; that is, between the activity going on within its internal environment and the activity which connects the organism with its external environment. (3) Because of the unity of the mental and somatic.[4]

Pavlov engaged in many controversies with psychologists who challenged his findings, but always himself adhered steadily to methods of objective research, refusing to use concepts embodying subjective interpretations. As early as 1900, he had noted that 'the dualism which regards the soul and the body as quite separate things is still too firmly ingrained in all of us; for the scientist, of course, such a differentiation is impossible'.[5] He was always careful to insist, however, that his findings could not automatically be applied to human beings. Towards the end of his life, however, he himself began

---

[1] Pavlov-Gantt ii, 98 ff.; *Selected Works*, 448 ff. A reference to the experiment that established this point is made in L. V. Zankov's paper, pp. 157–8; here also the trace reflex is described.

[2] Pavlov-Gantt ii, 119; *Selected Works*, 412.

[3] *Scientific Session*, 29 ff.   [4] *Ibid.*, 28–9.   [5] *Ibid.*, 92.

to embark on the study of higher nervous activity in man as a result of work in neurological and psychiatric clinics; and it was at this stage that he developed his theory of the *second signalling system*.[1]

The first signal system has already been referred to; this covers the mass of stimuli from the external world which signalize its properties to the organism. But for man, as an articulate and social being, words also act as stimuli; stimuli that differ qualitatively from any others because they comprehend, generalize and 'stand for' the multitude of separate stimuli of the first signal system. In other words, man's cortical processes differ qualitatively from those of the animals because of the predominant influence of speech—the second signal system.

When the developing animal world reached the stage of man, an extremely important addition was made to the mechanism of higher nervous activity. In the animal, reality is signalized almost exclusively by stimulations and the traces they make in the cerebral hemispheres, which directly lead to the special cells of the visual, auditory or other receptors of the organism. This is what we too possess in the shape of impressions, sensations and ideas of the world around us, both the natural and the social—with the exception of oral and written speech. This is the first system of signals of reality, common to man and the animals. But speech constitutes a second system of signals of reality which is peculiarly ours, and is a signal of the first signals. On the one hand, the numerous speech stimulations have removed us from reality. . . . On the other, it is precisely speech which has made us human. . . .

Pavlov added, however, 'It cannot be doubted that the fundamental laws governing the activity of the first signal system must also govern that of the second, because it too is activity of the same nervous tissue.'[2] At the same time, he stressed that the first signal system in man differed from that of the animals precisely because of the existence of the second; there is an integral relation between these two systems.

Pavlov's work in this field was carried further by his pupils, in particular by N. I. Krasnogorsky and Ivanov-Smolensky who embarked on direct research with children from 1907. There are frequent references in the following papers to the relevant researches which are particularly significant for psychology.[3] In his investigations of patho-

---

[1] This is foreshadowed in the last of the series of lectures delivered in 1924, 'The Experimental Results obtained with Animals in their Application to Man', Pavlov-Anrep, 395 ff.

[2] Pavlov-Gantt ii, 179; *Selected Works*, 262.

[3] They are discussed in some detail by Elkonin and Bogoiavlensky.

logical conditions, Pavlov also elaborated his theory of types of higher nervous activity, which has had much influence on methods of treatment of neuroses;[1] this theory, also, has inspired psychological research.

In his well-known work, 'Reply of a Physiologist to Psychologists' (1932), Pavlov joined issue with the psychologists. He argued that use of the words 'purpose' or 'intention' merely hindered research, that it was, in fact, the task of research to disclose the laws underlying conscious purpose and free will, not simply to give these labels to particular forms of activity. In other words, it was inadequate merely to give a description of man as one of the systems of nature; what was necessary was a profound study of the inner processes of this system, its mechanism.

Man is, of course, a system (more crudely, a machine), and like every other system in nature this system is governed by the inevitable laws common to all nature; but it is a system which, within the field of our scientific vision, is unique for its extreme power of self-regulation. The chief, strongest and most permanent impression we get from the study of higher nervous activity by our methods is the extraordinary plasticity of this activity, and its immense potentialities; nothing is immobile, intractable, everything may always be achieved, changed for the better, provided only that the proper conditions are created. A system (a machine) and man, with all his ideals, aspirations and achievements—at first glance, how terribly discordant a comparison it seems! But is this really so? Even from the generally accepted point of view, is not man the pinnacle of nature, the highest embodiment of the resources of infinite nature, the incarnation of her might and still unexplained laws? Is this not rather calculated to enhance man's dignity, to afford him the deepest satisfaction? And everything vital is retained that is implied in the idea of freewill, with its personal, social and civic responsibility.[2]

This statement provides an example of Pavlov's ability to combine humanism with science, and shows how far removed he was from the mechanist and behaviourist standpoint. In fact, though Pavlov's name is most frequently associated with behaviourist psychology in this country, the development of behaviourism has been relatively little influenced by his theories.[3]

[1] Cf. Pavlov-Gantt i, 370 ff.; ii, 162 ff.; *Selected Works*, 313 ff.
[2] Pavlov-Gantt ii, 144; *Selected Works*, 446-7.
[3] This is indicated in an interesting account, written by Professor K. S. Lashley in 1946; B. P. Babkin, *Pavlov: A Biography* (London, 1951), 319-22.

Only a brief outline of Pavlov's work has been given here, one designed primarily to explain terms and methods which are referred to later. Most of the points raised are developed further, in their application to psychology, in the following papers by Soviet psychologists.

III

The study of psychology in the Soviet Union has been greatly extended during the past two decades, in particular since the war. The chief centres are special research institutes, but research is also undertaken by university departments of psychology and at the larger educational institutes (four- or five-year teachers' training colleges). Psychology, of course, forms part of the course for teachers in training at both college and university, but it is also taught as a subject to all pupils during the final year of the ten-year school.

The central research institute is in Moscow. It was originally founded in 1912 by Chelpanov, but now forms part of the Academy of Educational Sciences of the R.S.F.S.R. which was set up in 1944 and has in all nine institutes. The Institute of Psychology has a full-time staff of fifty and three main departments: (1) General psychology, concerned with problems of perception and sensation, the thought processes and speech, individual psychology and the psychology of labour and industrial training. (2) Child psychology, covering children of pre-school (3 to 7 years) and school age (7 to 17 years). (3) Educational psychology, comprising child development and the psychology of learning. The institute is also concerned with the history of psychology, and methods of teaching psychology in school.

The inclusion of this institute in an academy devoted chiefly to the educational sciences indicates the close relation between psychology and education in the Soviet Union. But the institute is not confined to educational work; it has responsibilities in the whole field of psychology. Psychologists are also members of some of the other institutes belonging to the academy, and so participate in the particular approach of each. For instance, among the authors of these papers, Professor Zankov is on the staff of the Institute of Methods of Teaching, and Professor Luria heads a group of psychologists working in the Institute of Defectology; this institute also includes doctors, physiologists and educationists, and is particularly concerned with research relating to the diagnosis, care and education of children suffering from defects of sight, hearing, speech, or intellect for whom special schools are provided. Professor Ananiev directs a further research institute, at Leningrad, with a combined staff of psychologists and educationists.[1]

The Academy of Educational Sciences is connected, through the Academy of Sciences of the U.S.S.R., with research institutes and departments working in related fields such as medicine; and this relation finds expression in the form of joint conferences on particular questions of mutual interest. The institutes themselves are entirely concerned with research and not with undergraduate teaching, but there are close connections with particular schools for experimental purposes. Outside the R.S.F.S.R. there are two other Institutes of Psychology, at Kiev in the Ukraine, under Professor G. T. Kostiuk, and in Georgia. In each of the other thirteen republics, departments of psychology form part of combined research institutes of education.

Psychology is taught in the relevant departments of the universities and colleges and there is no sharp division between these and the research institutes. Thus, Professor Leontiev, who is secretary of the Academy of Educational Sciences, is head of the Chair (Department) of Psychology at Moscow University; again Professor Rubinstein and Dr. Zaporozhets, who belong to the Academy's Institute of Psychology, and Professor Luria of the Institute of Defectology, are members of the same department and participate in undergraduate teaching. The psychology departments of both universities and colleges, of course, undertake their own research projects. The head of the department at the Lenin Educational Institute, the largest teachers' training college in the U.S.S.R., is Professor K. N. Kornilov who has played a leading part in the development of psychology since the early 1920's. This organizational structure assists the unified approach to psychological questions, characteristic of Soviet psychology, and expressed in many of the papers that make up this book.

The papers themselves come from various sources. A number were originally contributed to journals,[2] three are speeches summarizing trends of research, three, which cover a fairly wide field, were contributions to the Fourteenth International Congress of Psychology, one is an introductory chapter from a book giving the results of research in a particular field, and one was specially written for this book. In order to present a reasonably comprehensive picture of the state of psychology within the limits of a single volume, every contribution has been rigorously edited; where sections of papers have

[1] Some details of the Institute of Defectology and of the Leningrad Institute are given in: B. Simon, *Some Aspects of Research in Educational Psychology in the U.S.S.R.* (1955) (Society of Cultural Relations with the U.S.S.R.).

[2] Chiefly *Sovetskaya Pedagogika* (Soviet Education), a journal concerned with all aspects of education, and *Voprosy Psikhologii* (Questions of Psychology), a specialist psychological journal, founded in January 1955. The journals appear monthly and bimonthly respectively.

been omitted, however, these are replaced by a summary, printed inside square brackets [ ], so that the omission is clearly indicated.[1]

So far as the arrangement of the book is concerned, the report by Smirnov, reviewing research during the years 1953–5, provided a natural introduction. Here there is both an assessment of work described in succeeding articles, and an indication of other work undertaken which could not be reproduced here. It is interesting to note the severe criticisms with which this paper concludes; this is the method used in the Soviet Union not only to draw attention to deficiencies that must be remedied, but also to ensure that there is an equal development of different branches of psychology, that progress is not held up by lack of attention to some key problem. In this connection, psychologists are keenly aware of the links that psychology has with other sciences, and with the practical tasks of education and training.

In the second section are grouped a number of papers concerned with the bearing of Pavlovian physiology on psychology and with direct research into higher nervous activity. Those by Elkonin, Bogoiavlensky and Milerian (and also the paper by Zankov in the next section) may be regarded as the first fruits of the reconsideration of psychological theory and practice in the light of the theory of higher nervous activity. While Elkonin is particularly concerned to summarize experimental evidence relating to conditioned reflexes in infants and young children, the other three articles are, rather, theoretical reassessments; thus Bogoiavlensky attempts to break new ground in the analysis of the complex process of understanding.

The remaining papers in this section are concerned with detailed research projects. That by Sokolov is of interest in that it demonstrates anew the unity of the organism in its relations with the environment; while Shvarts shows that sensitivity to visual stimuli is greatly increased when the subject is given a set task which involves considerable mobilization of his resources, and that this increase can be transferred to other conditions. The papers by Zaporozhets and Luria, dealing with the orienting reflex in children and the particular influence exercised by speech in the formation of conditioned reflexes, are interesting researches derived from the Pavlovian approach.

The third section groups three papers on perception and memory. That by Zankov has already been referred to. The paper by Leontiev and Rozanova has been included as an example of direct research into processes of memory; the design of this research project derives from the principle of the unity of consciousness and activity, and illustrates the conception of learning as the formation of temporary

[1] In the interests of preserving continuity, no indication is given of the omission of short passages.

24

connections. Unfortunately, owing to lack of space, it has been impossible to include further examples of researches on memory undertaken, for example, by Smirnov and by P. I. Zinchenko, of the Teachers' College at Kiev. Ananiev's contribution consists in the introductory chapter of his book, *Spatial Discrimination*, published at the close of 1955. Here there is a new approach to the problem of spatial discrimination based on Pavlovian methods and theories, which constitutes a challenge to certain accepted views.

Since the rejection of mental testing as irrelevant to psychology and harmful to education, Soviet psychologists have turned their attention to elucidating the mental processes involved in learning. Some of the researches undertaken are described in the papers included in the fourth section. Here again, the influence of Pavlovian theories is evident. The relevance of these to education has been summarized by Smirnov as follows: (1) The decisive influence of education on child development is underlined; (2) The extreme plasticity of higher nervous activity and the connection between structure and function is demonstrated, so discrediting theories which ascribe inherent defects to normal children who fall behind in school; (3) The view that the child is a passive product of external influences is rejected, and it is shown that development takes place in the process of active 'equal weighted' interaction with the surrounding world; (4) The importance of conscious learning is emphasized since, as Pavlov discovered, connections can only be formed and retained to those stimuli which possess a definite meaning and importance for the organism.[1]

While the papers by Smirnov and Menchinskaya set out the general approach to child development and the psychology of learning, and that by Liublinskaya is concerned with the interrelation of language and thought in children, Slavina and Galperin deal with a series of investigations bearing on stages in the development of mental actions. In each case the method used is that of systematic formation of mental abilities in children who have been diagnosed as backward in school. The essence of the findings is well summarized by Leontiev where he suggests that mental processes, reflecting external reality, are formed as a result of the transformation of practical, external operations into internal mental operations; in the course of this transformation, as a process becomes automatized, so it is abbreviated; 'many links of the process become superfluous, are not consolidated', and so fall out of consciousness. As a result the final operation appears to be a momentary 'psychic action', which 'seems to be the manifestation of a special capacity of the mind', an inborn ability. In reality, however, 'these actions are nothing but the product of past experience reflected and transformed in the mind of the individual'.

[1] *Deutsche Lehrerzeitung*, Nos. 52 and 53, 1955.

These investigations have shown that, when an otherwise normal child has not developed a certain ability, it means that he has failed to consolidate a necessary link, or stage; if he is taken back to the initial stages in the particular process, and the necessary connections are systematically formed, he develops the requisite ability. Slavina and Galperin advance fruitful hypotheses relating to the necessary stages of development of mental abilities; as Smirnov points out these have considerable importance for educational practice, both as regards general teaching practice and remedial measures for those who have fallen behind. In this connection it should be noted that there is a single common school in the U.S.S.R. with a common curriculum, and that there is no streaming or selection of any kind. The compulsory leaving age is seventeen in the cities and urban areas, and it is planned to extend this to the countryside by 1960.

Lack of space has prevented the publication of other papers bearing on education, notably the researches of Bozhovich and others on the formation of personality and the development of specific qualities under the influence of the collective. This work derives from the teaching of Makarenko, recognized as the greatest of Soviet educationists. Another related topic which could not be included concerns types of higher nervous activity and temperament, a subject which has inspired much research.[1]

The closing section consists of three theoretical articles. Boiko deals with the confusion of the categories 'skill' and 'habit'. The articles by Teplov and Rubinstein are placed here rather than at the beginning of the book where they might more properly have found a place, because it seemed that they could more usefully be read with the preceding work in mind. Teplov is concerned to elucidate the vexed question of the use of introspective methods in psychology, and to emphasize the significance and scope of objective methods. Rubinstein poses and discusses some fundamental questions; the chief of these being the extent to which psychology can, and must, be based on physiological findings without losing its own identity. Both these articles are, once more, critical. This, again, seemed a good note upon which to end. The papers included in this book bear witness to concrete advances, to a considerable rise in the status of psychology and, in spite of what is said about deficiencies, to some notable services to education. But Soviet psychologists tend to regard every advance as a stepping stone to the next rather than as a final achievement in itself. So Rubinstein surveys the field of psychology, underlines what he finds to be mistakes in emphasis and gaps in knowledge, and suggests the lines for a comprehensive series of research projects to remedy the position; these researches are already under way.

[1] Cf. Smirnov's paper 'Psychological Research, 1953–5', pp. 39–40.

Finally, there is included in Appendix I a paper specially written for this book by Luria, summarizing the main features of psychopathological research in the U.S.S.R. To place these Soviet papers in a wider setting, a brief report of the Fourteenth International Congress of Psychology by Zaporozhets and Sokolov is included as Appendix II.

PART I

PSYCHOLOGICAL RESEARCH, 1953–5 [1]

BY

A. A. SMIRNOV

URING THE TWO YEARS which have elapsed since the last Psychological Conference, Soviet psychologists have carried out a considerable amount of work which has contributed towards the development of psychology as a materialist science. But we must not overestimate the degree of success achieved. The recent advances have not yet yielded sufficiently tangible results to justify the claim that gaps in theory and in its application to practice have been closed. Psychology is still not satisfying the demands made upon it.

I

A review of work undertaken must touch first on theoretical questions. Here the primary problem is the nature of the psyche. It might be supposed that there could be no significant difference of opinion on this question since all Soviet psychologists start from the premises of dialectical materialism. But several articles have recently appeared which clearly deviate from the only correct view, that psychic processes are a function of the brain;[2] these aroused keen opposition from the general body of Soviet psychologists, as was clear from subsequent discussion in the press.

---

[1] Report prepared for the Third Psychological Conference in the U.S.S.R.; published in *Voprosy Psikhologii*, No. 5, 1955, pp. 38–53 (translated by N. Parsons).

[2] E.g. those by B. V. Beliaev and V. M. Arkhipov, *Sovetskaya Pedagogika*, No. 9, 1953, and No. 7, 1954.

Another important theoretical issue is that of the place of psychology among other sciences. With which sciences should psychology be grouped? Psychologists undoubtedly differ on this fundamental problem.[1] An open debate in the press is needed, a broad discussion as to whether psychology is a natural or a social science, or whether it occupies a special position as one of the human sciences, since man is a product both of natural and of social development.[2]

Other notable theoretical questions now under discussion include the problems of human needs and of human abilities. Is the presence of a specific need a prerequisite of human action, or can social necessity be a sufficient motive, requiring man to act in a certain manner irrespective of any personal need? Again, what part do innate tendencies play in the development of abilities? Can we speak of predispositions in this connection, and what is to be understood by the term? What are the relations between the typological characteristics of higher nervous activity and human abilities?

Solution of these problems has both practical and theoretical importance. Moreover, profitable theoretical discussion requires the support of concrete investigations; it must not, as is too often the case, consist merely in abstract statements savouring of personal opinion and lacking a factual basis.

II

What has been done during the past two years in the main departments of psychology?

Direct study of the material substratum of psychic processes may be considered first. Investigation of the physiological basis of psychic activity is a vital corner-stone in the building of a materialist science of the human psyche. Soviet physiologists are studying man's higher nervous activity, but their achievements, both in extent and speed, still fall far below what is needed. All the more essential that psychologists should take part in this work and that the two sciences should find an effective meeting-place.

Soviet psychologists have made an extensive study of higher nervous activity; in particular, attention may be drawn to researches on the work of the analysers and the reflex nature of reception and its mechanisms. E. N. Sokolov has studied the reflexes involved in the regulation of sensitivity, above all the orienting reflex, as one that

---

[1] This question was touched on in an editorial in *Voprosy Filosofii*, No. 4, 1954, which summed up a discussion of philosophical questions in psychology; and in general methodological articles in the same journal by S. G. Strumilin and B. M. Kedrov, relating to classification of the sciences.

[2] Cf. Rubinstein, 'Questions of Psychological Theory', p. 267n. (Ed.).

plays an essential role in the 'tuning' of the analysers. Among the many components of this reflex, particular attention was given to the vascular and the related skin-galvanic responses and to changes in the electrical activity of the brain.[1] These investigations showed the characteristics of the orienting reaction both to indifferent and to conditioned stimuli. At the same time, and this is especially important, they threw light on the character of the reaction to verbal stimuli. They also indicated the exceptional stability of the vascular reactions evoked by new direct stimuli acting with a verbal stimulus which creates a 'set'[2] to these stimuli. S. V. Kravkov carried this work further in his study of interaction between analysers; that is, of conditioned-reflex connections formed not only in one analyser but also between different interacting analysers. Such research rests on Pavlov's view that higher nervous activity is a constituent part of a much broader problem, that of the reflex nature of sensation.

Among other studies of conditioned reflexes underlying sensation, mention may be made of B. G. Ananiev's investigations into functional asymmetry, observed in the operation of *twin* receptors. Investigation of the 'leading eye', the 'leading organ of hearing', the 'leading hand as organ of touch', showed that the same receptor was not always preferred for different functions. Functional asymmetry, that is, the different results obtained when twin receptors are taken separately, is specific not only for each sensory system (such as sight, hearing or touch) but also for different functions within each system. Even within the limits of a given function (such as the eye's power of accommodation) one receptor or the other may be preferred to a greater or lesser extent according to the experimental conditions. This and other data led to the conclusion that 'functional asymmetry in twin receptors arises not so much from the receptors themselves as from the twin activity of the cerebral hemispheres'. It develops from conditioned reflexes and is the 'manifestation of complex processes of interaction of the hemispheres in the reflex activity of the cortex'.[3]

Conditioned-reflex variation in sensitivity has also been the subject of research by L. A. Shvarts. He studied how a conditioned increase in sensitivity, produced in one set of conditions, is transferred to other conditions and to the action of other stimuli. This question is of great theoretical significance, since research may throw light on the problem of the permanent development of sensitivity, by contrast with temporary, phasic improvement.[4]

[1] Cf. Sokolov, 'Higher Nervous Activity and the Problem of Perception', p. 92 (Ed.).

[2] *Napravlennost*, literally 'direction', 'tendency', 'set' (of a current) (Ed.).

[3] Cf. Ananiev, 'The Basis of Spatial Discrimination', p. 131 (Ed.).

[4] Cf. Shvarts, 'Raising the Sensitivity of the Visual Analyser', p. 100 (Ed.).

A group of studies by E. I. Boiko on the physiological basis of psychic processes is concerned with the dynamics of nervous processes in the visual analyser. Motor reaction, speed and latent period are studied and used as indices of the processes evoked by the action of a visual stimulus. The results show the changes in the state of a single point of the visual analyser, observed for differing periods of time after the application of the stimulus, and the duration of the excitation remaining after the action of the stimulus has ceased. Further, the spread of excitation from one point of the visual analyser to others is traced, information obtained about the speed of irradiation and concentration of excitation in the visual analyser, and a study made of the inductive relations between different points of an analyser. Changes in the irradiation and concentration of nervous processes are shown to depend upon how often the action has been practised and how far it has become automatic.

Boiko has recently tried to discover the mechanism of creative mental processes, i.e. those which lead to the establishment of something new. He proposes, as a physiological explanation, an hypothesis that involves functional combination: that interaction of conditioned-reflex processes occurs as a result of partial spatial coincidence of excitation in the cerebral cells. A partial sharing of structural elements—as observed when different systems of connections function simultaneously and cause redistribution of nervous impulses entering the brain—such, broadly, is the material basis of creative, productive mental processes according to this hypothesis.

Another group of studies under the direction of B. G. Ananiev has been directed to bio-electric phenomena, such as those which accompany the so-called ideo-motor actions and spatial conceptions. Results show a variation in the electrical activity of the motor area of the cortex, even when movement is only conceived. Data were obtained on the resemblances and differences between bio-electrical phenomena recorded during the perception and during the conception of stimuli. Investigation of the electrical activity of the brain during attention to aural stimuli has been undertaken by E. A. Milerian at the Institute of Psychology of the Ukrainian Ministry of Education. At the Institute of Defectology of the Academy of Educational Sciences (A.P.N.), L. A. Novikova has compared the EEG's of oligophrenic and normal children; she has also studied the special nature of bio-electrical phenomena in the visual areas of blind persons, and shown that bio-electrical activity takes place in the eye-muscles of those who have lost their sight when they visualize objects.

The method of formation of temporary connections in man is an important aspect of the study of the physiological foundations of mental activity. Investigations directed by A. R. Luria have demonstrated the special way in which new connections are formed with the help of the second signal system, and how sharply this process differs from the mode of their formation in animals; immediate or sudden formation of a connection in man, its rapid stabilization and striking stability, and the ready alteration of the system of connections, etc. They also throw light on the gradual development of the role of language in the formation of temporary connections in children, and indicate the peculiar features of this development in mentally retarded children.[1]

To sum up, these researches are undoubtedly of value as a first practical attempt by psychologists towards creating a materialist psychology. The work is closely linked with that of physiologists. Psychologists and physiologists do, in fact, frequently work hand in hand. Close creative cooperation between them is an indispensable condition for the successful solution of these problems.

III

Important work has been devoted to the complex cognitive processes, though attention has not been equally distributed among the several related processes. Relatively little attention has been paid to the complex processes of perception and observation. The investigations by L. V. Zankov and others into the interrelations between language and visual presentation in teaching are welcome, but these are concerned with only one aspect of perception and ignore all other aspects of this process. Much still remains to be discovered about the laws of perception.

Memory has also been insufficiently studied of late. The few isolated investigations into related questions (at the A.P.N. Institute of Psychology and by Ukrainian psychologists) do not constitute a reconstruction of this field on the basis of Pavlov's teaching. Mention may be made of initial attempts in this direction,[2] but these achievements do not measure up to the requirements. The relative elaboration of the problem of memory which has already taken place is no grounds for relaxing efforts to study the many unsolved problems. This is the more essential since the physiological mechanisms of psychic processes may be discovered in this field more easily than in any other.

[1] Cf. Luria, 'The Role of Language in the Formation of Temporary Connections', p. 115 (Ed.).
[2] Researches by D. G. Elkin, on forgetting as a conditioned reflex, by D. I. Krasilshchikova, Sokolov, and others, and also the well-known researches of Zinchenko.

Little attention has been given to the study of imagery. Only isolated investigations, mostly concerned with spatial images, have been carried through.[1] Yet this study is essential to a knowledge of the laws whereby sensation becomes thought. The study of spatial imagery is of particular importance in relation to polytechnical education.

Psychologists have made a broader study of the thought processes, this closely coincides with research in educational psychology, especially the psychology of learning.

One of the key problems under investigation is that of the interrelation between the sensory and the verbal-logical (or abstract) in thinking, between the visual image and the concept; a question basically concerned with the interaction between the two signal systems in thought processes.[2] Results show how the interrelation between the two signal systems changes during growth, and the complexity of the dynamics of their interaction. This is shown in various aspects of children's school work. As children grow older, images not only play less part in thought processes but also undergo a certain qualitative change and begin to fulfil a function other than their original one. At about 7 to 9 years of age, images appear as the condition and foundation for generalization, and so for the full understanding of verbal material (e.g. a text). At this stage it is by means of images that verbal material is understood in a generalized form; images serve as a support for the verbal formulation of the essential points of the text.

Much research is being devoted to overcoming the negative role of images in thought processes. The visual image, which usually furthers understanding, may sometimes have a negative effect, hindering correct generalization and limiting it to the particular examples illustrated by a given image (e.g. a sketch or diagram). Investigations show that variation of visual material, designed to overcome the limited nature of the image, only has a positive effect when it provides the basis for twin kinds of generalization, that is, generalization of both the essential and the inessential. In this connection the guiding role of language is shown to be necessary when a concrete image (e.g. a given diagram) is produced. In such cases language is the prerequisite for developing a generalized understanding of those special instances which illustrate the general concepts or general laws to be learned.

A prominent place among investigations into thinking is taken by its study as analytic-synthetic activity: the character of the concrete

[1] Researches of F. N. Shemiakin, A. Ya. Kolodnaya and others.
[2] This question has been studied under N. A. Menchinskaya at the A.P.N. Institute of Psychology, under G. C. Kostiuk at the Institute of Psychology of the Ministry of Education of the Ukrainian S.S.R., and elsewhere.

processes of analysis and synthesis according to the conditions in which they take place. This extremely important question is only now beginning to be understood.

The researches of S. L. Rubinstein at Moscow University are concerned with the concrete processes which lead to a particular outcome of thinking activity.[1] In addition, N. A. Menchinskaya's researches aim to clarify the laws governing the formation of concepts, that is the transition from undifferentiated, unformulated knowledge to knowledge that is both formulated and differentiated. This transition comprises simultaneously the processes of analysis (disentangling of the separate features of a concept), and synthesis (bringing the separated features together into a defined system and generalizing them). Results have indicated broadly how different concepts are mastered in the process of learning, but have not yet adequately clarified the processes of analysis and synthesis themselves, nor the basic content of the thought processes involved in mastering concepts.[2]

M. N. Shardakov's investigations at the Herzen Institute have illuminated several aspects of children's understanding of causal relations, as well as the special nature of their understanding of the functional interdependence of mathematical quantities. The results open the way to improving methods of teaching, but have contributed little towards discovery of the actual content of that analytic-synthetic activity which occurs during school learning. The same must be said about Yu. A. Samarin's study of the formation of systems of connections in the course of school activity. Nevertheless, this work is closely linked with an extremely important problem, that of the system of instruction in school. Taken together, the investigations indicate considerable gaps in children's knowledge, requiring special remedial measures. The fact that the thought processes themselves were inadequately studied does not lessen the significance of these investigations as a first attempt to study an extremely important problem.

Special mention must be made of the extensive research under P. Ya. Galperin on the formation of mental actions during instruction and, inseparably connected with this, the formation of generalized images and concepts.[3] This has established the basic stages in the formation of mental actions and concepts: the regular transition from

[1] These are based on the views advanced by Rubinstein in his article in *Voprosy Psikhologii*, No. 1, 1955 (see p. 264—Ed.).

[2] Cf. Menchinskaya, 'Some Aspects of the Psychology of Teaching', p. 190 (Ed.).

[3] Carried out at Moscow University; considerable research has also been carried out by other investigators, especially in the Ukraine. Cf. Galperin, 'An Experimental Study in the Formation of Mental Actions', p. 213 (Ed.).

external to internal action, and the role and characteristics of speech in the carrying out of actions at different stages of this transition. Basic 'parameters' are given by means of which a mental action can be described at each stage of development. These investigations suggest the proposition that mental images and concepts, as phenomena of individual consciousness, are the product of action, the automatized and abbreviated execution of which constitutes the psychological mechanism of images and concepts. The investigations cover a wide range of actions and concepts learned in school, and are of great practical interest, indicating the most effective methods whereby schoolchildren can acquire knowledge, skills and habits. The theoretical conceptions arising from these investigations require wide discussion.

Recently there have been a series of investigations concerning the application of knowledge in practice. These have dealt with schoolchildren's difficulties when faced with new material, as a result of failure to distinguish between features which are similar to the old material and those which are new.

Research on thought processes, therefore, covers a wide range of problems of theoretical and practical significance, nevertheless there remain important questions which have not yet been thoroughly studied. These are, above all, the concrete operations which go to make up the content of thinking: comparison, abstraction, generalization and classification, judgments, inferences and proofs. There is very little of the genuinely psychological material required for a *psychological*, rather than a logical, description of these processes, and it is no coincidence that the treatment of this subject in textbooks is meagre and chiefly concerned with proofs borrowed from logic. It is important to remedy this deficiency, since it hinders the study of other allied questions, and, in particular, makes a comprehensive psychological description of the process of acquiring knowledge impossible. At present, such studies are usually concerned with the results obtained from different methods of instruction rather than with the rich psychological content of the learning process.

Investigations concerning thinking have been concentrated on children, especially schoolchildren. These are clearly important, both for their enormous theoretical interest and for their practical significance in working out the psychological bases of teaching methods. But there is no justification for limiting such investigations purely to these stages of development. The thought processes of older children and adults are scarcely ever the subject of research, though it is essential to study thinking at the higher stages before a general theory of thinking and its development can be built up. This deficiency must be remedied.

IV

Considerable attention has been given during the past few years to the study of speech. Research has been concerned with its phonetic, semantic and expressive aspects, with grammatical correctness, the mechanisms underlying speech and its general effect on man. Both spoken and written speech and the learning of native and foreign languages have been studied.

Comprehensive work in this field is being carried out under V. A. Artemov at the Moscow Institute of Foreign Languages—in the Faculty of Psychology and the Laboratory of Experimental Phonetics and the Psychology of Speech. There must be due recognition of this laboratory's valuable organization for studying speech sounds with modern technical equipment, and for analysing linguistic material. But it would be better if these departments were more closely concerned with the problems facing psychology, and produced material of value for their solution as well as data bearing on methods of language teaching.[1]

A series of studies on the perception and understanding of speech, and the development of active speech in children, is being carried out in Moscow, Leningrad, the Ukraine and Georgia. Mention must also be made of investigations begun in recent years into speech kinaesthesia as a fundamental component of the second signal system;[2] these will throw light on the nature and laws of internal speech which is inseparably connected with thought. A group of studies of real significance for school practice deals with the learning of spelling and the grammatical forms of language.[3]

In spite of the considerable range of this research, many important questions in this field still require study. In particular, there has been insufficient research into the development of oral and written speech in children of school age; an understanding of this is basic to the construction of a psychological groundwork for the development of speech in the course of school instruction.

V

Questions connected with polytechnical education have now acquired urgent significance, and study of them has begun. Investigations into the practical application of knowledge have already been

---

[1] The same must be said of the study of speech-mechanisms which has been carried out by N. I. Zhinkin.

[2] By A. N. Sokolov, L. A. Novikova, and others.

[3] Some of these are under the direction of Rubinstein, others are directed by Bogoiavlensky and his collaborators at the A.P.N. Institute of Psychology.

mentioned; in addition, work on the application of technical knowledge and the mastery of technical skills has been initiated. There has been a series of studies on the processes of spatial imagery and on the skills required in designing, and E. V. Gurianov has made a beginning in studying the ways children master elementary operations during practical lessons at school. These are, of course, only the first steps in tackling the wide range of problems raised by polytechnical education.

Considerable attention has also been given to studying how actions are formed and learned in the course of practice; that is, how skills and abilities are acquired. The development of children's voluntary actions is the subject of a group of studies by A. V. Zaporozhets. These deal with the orienting activity of pre-school children in the formation of motor skills and abilities. They show the importance of preparatory orienting investigation in carrying out specific tasks, in forming and strengthening the skills involved and subsequently in changing them; above all, they show how speech gradually acquires an increasingly important role as the child develops, indicating the interrelation between speech and visual, motor, motor-tactile and other means of orientation at different levels of the pre-school child's development. Further, they revealed the conditions and form in which language evokes an orienting reaction in the child.[1]

Studies of motor skills in manual work and sport have concentrated on the role of different analysers in the development of skills, notably the motor analyser, at different stages of human development; and the effect of motor ideas and of motor sensations.[2] The interrelation between language and visual presentations in the mastery of skills and regularities in the transfer of skills have also been studied.

VI

What is the state of research into the problems usually grouped under the heading 'psychology of personality'? This field has always been given less attention than others for two reasons; first, the tenacity with which intellectualism has survived in psychology, and second, the methodological difficulties of research. However, there has recently been a certain revival of this work. The formation of interests has been investigated as one of the essential elements in personality tendencies. The formation of different character traits has been studied: e.g. susceptibility to discipline, endurance, self-control, self-

[1] Cf. Zaporozhets, 'The Development of Voluntary Movements', p. 108 (Ed.).
[2] Undertaken at the A.P.N. Institute of Psychology by V. V. Chebysheva and S. N. Arkhangelsky, A. Ts. Puni and P. A. Rudik.

confidence, self-discipline, and sense of responsibility. Research has been undertaken on the growth of moral understanding, and on honour as a motive of conduct. A. G. Kovalev and V. I. Selivanov have written doctoral theses on the development of volitional personality traits; studies of the role of society in the formation of personality have continued. We should express our appreciation of the efforts of those who have worked persistently and enthusiastically on these complex problems.[1]

But we have not yet reached a decisive turning-point in the study of personality, especially as regards the formation of the character and moral qualities of Soviet man. It is significant that the chief workers in this field are young and that few experienced psychologists are involved. Research on abilities and aptitudes is also inadequately represented. Much is said about this problem, especially in relation to polytechnical education, and much of what is said is correct, but practically no research is being done. A. N. Leontiev's researches on the formation of man's psychic properties and processes, though positive, are only partly related to this problem; he has shown the conditioned-reflex nature of the system of connections underlying several elementary abilities, especially aural functions, and has advanced several important hypotheses relating to the systematic formation of psychic functions.[2]

A brighter state of affairs is found in the field of typological differences where B. M. Teplov continues his thoroughgoing researches. New data have recently been obtained on mobility of the nervous processes which shows that the two basic indices—the speed with which the meaning of a stimulus is transmitted, and the duration of the after-effects of excitation and inhibition—give results which are not always in agreement with each other. These facts are of fundamental importance, because they imply that the properties of the nervous system may be more varied and should be more finely differentiated than is the case at present. It has been suggested that such properties of nervous processes as weakness and a low level of activity should not necessarily be regarded as negative and harmful; weakness of the nervous system in man should be understood, not simply as a deficiency, but as a qualitative peculiarity of the work of the nervous system, which has its positive aspects. The hypothesis advanced by Teplov is that the weak nervous system may be marked by particularly high reactivity (sensitivity), so that, in appropriate

[1] In Moscow at the Lenin Educational Institute under the direction of Kornilov, and at the Department of School Education of the A.P.N. Institute of Psychology, under the direction of L. I. Bozhovich; in the Ukraine, and in Leningrad, under the direction of V. N. Miasishchev and A. L. Shnirman.

[2] Cf. A. N. Leontiev, 'The Nature and Formation of Human Psychic Properties', p. 226 (Ed.).

conditions of work, individuals of the weak type may achieve things of great value. This hypothesis has already received partial confirmation in an investigation showing that visual sensitivity varies inversely with the strength of the excitatory processes (in the same analyser) and with the typological nature of nervous activity.

Finally, the search for methods of studying typological differences in human nervous activity has continued. A new method has been found for defining the strength of the processes of excitation which is particularly valuable, since earlier methods made no attempt to define this important property.

Parallel with the laboratory investigations under Teplov (and at the Ukrainian Institute of Psychology) there have been many studies of types of higher nervous activity under natural conditions, in a real-life environment.[1] What is valuable here is the attempt to find living examples of types, as exemplified by behaviour in natural conditions, even though the examples found have not yet sufficient authenticity. There is still much work to be done in this direction: laboratory facts must be studied side by side with observations from life. This is important in assessing the significance to be attached to indices of typological differences, as manifested in defined conditions, and the extent to which a given typological feature appears under *different* conditions and in different aspects of activity. We can then considerably deepen our knowledge of typological differences in higher nervous activity, and clarify their interrelations with the systems of nervous connections which develop under the influence of living conditions and education. Wide perspectives open up in this whole field.

VII

Special attention must be given to the problem of purpose or 'set'[2] studied at the Institute of Psychology of the Georgian Academy of Sciences. These investigations cover a wide range of diverse questions, united by their common origin in D. N. Uznadze's earlier teaching on this subject. Much new work has been devoted to the role of 'set' in sensory processes, especially in the rise and succession of images, but also in the processes of memory, imagination, thinking and speech, the mastery of skills, and in various aspects of school work. Research into the relation between fixed 'set' and various personality traits both in the normal subject and the mentally ill has been continued. A wide discussion of the theory of 'set' advanced by Georgian psychologists is necessary.

[1] E.g. by Yu. A. Samarin and other Leningrad psychologists, and by V. S. Merlin in Kazan and Molotov.
[2] *Ystanovka*, literally 'setting', 'fixing' (Ed.).

Important work has been carried out on the thought processes of mentally backward children (L. V. Zankov and I. M. Soloviev) and on the interrelations between word and visual presentation in their teaching (L. V. Zankov). R. M. Boskis's doctoral thesis on the development of speech in deaf-mute children is a valuable piece of work, giving a comprehensive description of the way deaf or partially deaf children learn to speak. This is of theoretical importance in the struggle against the false view that the deaf-mute is unable to achieve full psychic development. Data obtained by Boskis and T. A. Vlasov refute the theory that the deaf-mute's brain is deficient, show how richly he can develop in the course of organized verbal intercourse, and how he can learn to speak using those analysers that have been preserved. A study of the language used by these children during instruction at school has been made by Zh. I. Shif.

V. S. Sverlov's doctoral thesis gives new data on the functioning of analysers in the blind, and on blind people's conceptions of the people surrounding them. The new work by O. I. Skorokhodova, 'How I perceive and conceive of the surrounding world', is most valuable.[1]

Work in psychopathology has continued, though on very restricted material, under V. N. Miasishchev, A. M. Shubert, B. V. Zeigarnik, and others.

No survey of the work of Soviet psychologists during the past two years would be complete without mention of some of the many general books published or prepared during this time; for example, the description by the late M. N. Volokitina and N. D. Levitov of the development of schoolchildren, *The Psychology of the Mastery of Reading* by T. G. Egorov, *The Psychology of Learning Arithmetic* by N. A. Menchinskaya, *The Psychology of Learning Spelling* by D. N. Bogoiavlensky, and *Generalized Associations in the Schoolchild's Work* by P. A. Shevarev. Mention must also be made of the considerable amount of psychological work carried out in the preparation of text-books and aids, and there have been a number of symposia on given subjects.

VIII

This analysis does not cover everything that has been done during the past two years; N. N. Ladygina-Kots' interesting animal studies, for instance, have been omitted. But it offers some evidence of the considerable amount of work carried out. Nevertheless, important

---

[1] Skorokhodova, a blind deaf-mute, was educated at the Institute of Defectology, and is now a research worker on the staff. She has written several books of this kind, and has published a book of poems (Ed.).

gaps and deficiencies have been referred to, the chief of which may be summarized as follows:

(1) Theoretical work is still inadequate. There has been no thorough discussion of many essential theoretical problems, and certain articles have displayed gross errors. In others, factual material has been inadequately assembled, or conclusions have been limited to a description of the data obtained without theoretical elucidation.

(2) Research with a bearing on general psychology is not so extensive as it should be. The study of needs and abilities, emotions and feelings, is unsatisfactory and voluntary actions and voluntary personality traits have been neglected. Work on complex forms of perception and on memory has dried up lately; nor is research on the thinking processes entirely satisfactory, being chiefly confined to questions of educational psychology.

(3) The number of psychologists, and the amount of research, in developmental (child) and educational psychology is greater than in any other field. But in developmental psychology, a serious deficiency is the small amount of work devoted to the upper age-ranges; such work as there is relies more on isolated observations than on broad factual material, systematically collected and leading to further investigation, and there is very little research into the psychological characteristics of these age-groups. Again, hardly any attention has been paid to the earliest ages and there has been no study of the new-born infant.

In educational psychology, questions of teaching and learning have occupied a central position. But these are investigated one-sidedly; there are studies of learning in this or that school subject, but practically none concerned with the whole process of teaching at a given level, involving interrelations between skills, their *systems*, their order and the sequence of learning. The Leningrad Institute of Education is now making a combined educational, methodological and psychological investigation into these questions. But, as yet, psychology has not assembled the kind of material necessary for the solution of root problems such as the planning of teaching and preparation of textbooks; not enough is known about the relevant psychological questions.

No study has been made of one of the most important problems in child and educational psychology: the interrelation between teaching and development, the operation of laws of development in the process of teaching. Little attention has been paid to the *actual process* by which different aspects of psychic activity develop under the influence of teaching; to studying *exactly how* these new mental activities develop, how the transition to a new level of development is effected, and in what way schoolchildren's thinking becomes active and independent in the process of instruction. The lasting influence of teaching on the child's mental activity, the shaping of new forms of this activity and its qualitative reorganization—all this calls for research.

Work on the problems of polytechnical education is still at an embryonic stage, though the new tasks of the schools pose fresh problems for research: the mastery of technical knowledge and skills, the psychology of polytechnical work for children, the development of their inventiveness and creativity in the technical field, the interrelations between theoretical knowledge and practical skills, and so on. All these important questions arise in the schools, and psychology must take a direct part in their solution; what is at present being done in this direction is negligible.

Another important school problem requiring more attention is that of pupils' discipline, or, more broadly, developing the moral qualities of the schoolchild. Isolated investigations of this question, though valuable,[1] have hardly begun to fill this gap; the schools, faced with this crucial task, can only be helped by extensive and thorough research. We must also extend the valuable efforts to create an experimental methodology for studying the psychology of personality.[2]

The same applies to the question of the school as a community or the collective. Isolated studies have been confined to outlining what it is that is formed under the influence of the collective without elucidating *how* personality is formed under this influence, by what actual process a particular personality trait is formed, what are the forms of social influence, and how the collective itself develops. These questions have not yet been given detailed study; indeed, the process of formation of permanent human qualities is, in general, inadequately studied, though a first attempt in this direction has been made by L. I. Bozhovich.

Research is also needed into questions connected with children's work outside school; what artistic and popular scientific books or works of art should be available, how the artistic sense may be developed—in general, the psychology of artistic education and socially useful work, which is at present neglected.

(4) There is an almost complete lack of studies of the psychology of labour, though the tasks facing industry and agriculture call for special attention to this question. Success in raising productivity depends not only on providing the best technical equipment, but also on its skilful use, the correct organization of labour and the efficiency

---

[1] Especially those undertaken at Leningrad University under Miasishchev, at the Ukraine Institute of Psychology, and at the A.P.N. Institute of Psychology under Bozhovich.

[2] Recently instituted at the Department of Educational Psychology at the A.P.N. Institute.

of methods of work. Many relevant psychological problems call for wide and thorough research. A closely related matter is young people's choice of professions on completion of ten-year general schooling.

(5) There has been a significant reduction in work on psychopathology. Former nuclei have virtually disappeared, and this represents a real loss; not only must this ground be regained, but the work must also be considerably extended. While prominent psychiatrists have recognized this, there has been little outside support. Yet the progress of such work is extremely important, since it often opens the way to new understanding of normal development and discovery of general laws of psychic activity.

(6) Work on the history of psychology gives little cause for satisfaction. There is none on the history of world psychology; apart from drawing up university courses, psychologists have not embarked on a Marxist treatment of the subject. M. V. Sokolov is working on the history of Russian psychology from the eleventh to the seventeenth centuries; and some research, by Ukrainian psychologists, is now being published. Otherwise, practically nothing has appeared in print.

(7) In general, the amount of work published is considerably less than that done. The fault lies with the institutions concerned; even the A.P.N. Institute of Psychology does not 'convert' all its scientific work, the Ukrainian Institute is slow in publishing its studies, while such strong faculties as those of Moscow University and the Lenin Institute (the largest educational college in the country) have no journals for publishing their work. Further, the research work of many peripheral faculties must be extended; several have quite adequate facilities, but the limited amount of work done at present hinders the development of psychology.

(8) The scientific level of research is not always satisfactory. Some investigations have no relation to either theoretical or practical tasks; others are superfluous; certain conclusions sound rather like well-known truisms. Sometimes, instead of a fundamental analysis of assembled material, an author gives an assortment of examples illustrating his theory; in such writings it is impossible to judge whether the theory has been upheld. The relation of an investigation to established research is not always made clear, former work not being sufficiently taken into account. Foreign experience is neglected; serious study of the literature is essential to discover what there is of value in foreign science; it is wrong to study scientific problems without considering the relevant work in world science.

(9) Practical application of the findings of research is insignificant by comparison with the extent of this work and its potential use. One

of the most important tasks is to remedy this; although some steps have been taken towards coordinating the work of psychologists and educationists, even here the situation remains unsatisfactory. There must be a definition of the nature and of the organized forms of psychologists' participation in practical work; they must not be confined to pure research. There are now enough qualified specialists to allow for work in both fields.

This report has been concerned to make a careful assessment of the work of Soviet psychologists. Fundamental criticism and self-criticism helps in evaluating the direction of our work, its theme, methodology and results. Joint efforts will enable us to open up perspectives for further research, and to direct our work towards the most important current tasks. Our chief concern must be the further development of a materialist psychology which can play an active part in the great cause of building communism in our country.

PART II

THE PHYSIOLOGY OF HIGHER NERVOUS
ACTIVITY AND CHILD PSYCHOLOGY [1]

BY

D. B. ELKONIN

SINCE THE DECREE of the Central Committee of the Communist Party of July 4, 1936, which exposed the pseudo-scientific conception that a child's destiny is fatally determined by heredity and an unchangeable environment,[2] child psychologists and educationists have done much to discover how development is determined by the child's conditions of life and his activity, and how it can be guided by education. Nevertheless, the actual process whereby the conditions of life influence development is often understood in an over-simplified mechanical way. One of the reasons for this is an inadequate grasp of the basic physiological mechanism of this influence, as outlined by Pavlov.

The processes of excitation and inhibition, irradiation, concentration and reciprocal induction, the whole complex dynamics of the cortical processes, reflect the struggle between old connections which are already well established and new connections which have only just arisen because of a change in the conditions of life.

It was Pavlov who discovered that any element in the external environment which is indifferent for the organism may, under certain conditions, become a factor acting upon its central nervous system, through the receptors, and that, under these conditions,

---

[1] *Sovetskaya Pedagogika*, No. 11, 1951, pp. 51–75 (translated by N. Parsons).
[2] Cf. p. 9, n. 1.

47

the actions of neutral elements of the external environment may produce profound changes in the organism.[1]

The determining influence exercised on the child's psychic development by his conditions of life, the content and nature of his activity, his schooling and upbringing, cannot be explained unless there is a full understanding of Pavlov's theory that the brain alone is the organ through which this influence is effected. By revealing the mechanism whereby this determining influence is exercised, Pavlov prepared the way for a scientific solution of the basic problem in child psychology, the problem of development.

Pavlov's greatest contribution was the discovery that the basic function of the cortex is to acquire and create new connections between organism and environment. He treated the cortex essentially as an organ of ontogenetic behaviour. Where there is no coupling activity of the brain, there is no ontogenesis of behaviour, no childhood; for childhood is the period in the life of the organism when, on the basis of the connections formed between organism and environment during phylogenesis, there is intensive building up of a structure of temporary connections, that is, of connections acquired in the course of individual life. The period of childhood becomes increasingly important the higher the organism stands on the ladder of evolutionary development, the more variable the conditions of its existence, and the more complex its interaction with them.

At the human level the environment acquires a particularly dynamic character because men live in a society and create their own environment and history. This means, not only that the cortex plays a more important part as the organ creating new connections, but also that its role as the organ of ontogenesis is greatly strengthened. Child psychology as the science of child development—or, more precisely, of the ontogenesis of the child's psyche and consciousness—cannot develop fruitfully without a full and exact knowledge of the laws governing the activity of the basic organ of ontogenesis, the cerebral cortex.

The social character of man's environment led to the development of a type of connection more complex and mobile than any found in animals. Pavlov wrote that 'when the developing animal world reached the human stage, an extremely important addition was made to the mechanisms of nervous activity'.

This addition is the function of speech which signifies a new principle in the activity of the cerebral hemispheres. If our sen-

[1] K. M. Bykov, *Scientific Session on the Physiological Teachings of Academician I. P. Pavlov* (Moscow, 1951), 57.

sations and ideas caused by the surrounding world are for us the first signals of reality, concrete signals, then speech, especially and primarily the kinaesthetic stimulations which proceed from the speech organs to the cortex, constitute a second set of signals—the signals of signals. They represent an abstraction from reality and make possible the forming of generalizations which, in turn, constitute our extra *specifically human, higher thinking* . . .[1]

It is essential to a full understanding of the development of the child's psyche to know how the second signal system operates in its connections and interrelations with the first signal system. In this connection, the physiological data obtained from children are particularly important.

The first research into higher nervous activity was initiated by Pavlov's oldest pupil, N. I. Krasnogorsky. Referring to his motives for studying the physiology of children's higher nervous activity, he writes:

> Pavlov's school achieved brilliant results and discovered important laws governing the central activity of animals. But the question naturally arose how far the facts derived from animals could be applied to man. If in other fields of natural science results derived from animals could be applied to man only with great caution, then might this not be even more significant when dealing with the activity of the human brain? Obviously the difference here was so great that the problem of the activity of the human brain could only be solved scientifically by investigating its physiological functioning directly in man. The first attempt at systematic investigation of the physiological activity of the brain in children was carried out by myself in the summer of 1907. I was led to this line of research by Pavlov's inspiring lectures on conditioned reflexes in animals, which I heard for the first time as a student at the Academy of Military Medicine [33: 8].

Since that time, Krasnogorsky and his collaborators have gathered much varied material on the physiological activity of the child's brain, both normal and abnormal, but Krasnogorsky has not set himself the task of studying how the features of higher nervous activity arise. Several studies of the early stages of ontogenesis were later initiated by N. M. Shchelovanov, who collected a great deal of material describing the origin and growth of brain functions, chiefly for the first year of life. These studies demonstrated that the child's cortex is ready to exercise the functions of coupling and analysing

[1] *Selected Works*, 262, 285.

exceptionally early. It was established that 'conditioned reflexes with all the organs of perception were formed from the end of the first month and throughout the infant's second month. There was precise experimental evidence for this' [59: 21].

In 1917, Ivanov-Smolensky initiated research designed to clarify specific features of conditioned-reflex activity in man, and since 1926 he has been making a systematic study of cortical functioning in children by his own original methods, drawn from previous studies of the human cortex. Many important data have been obtained on the features and types of higher nervous activity in children of different ages. It has been shown that new types of connections can be produced in children and special researches have been concerned with the interaction of the first and second signal systems.

A considerable amount of material has, therefore, been accumulated. But this has not yet been used so that the reconstruction of child psychology is proceeding very slowly. One reason for this is that many of the relevant works are difficult to obtain and there are still no symposia collating all the investigations. This article is concerned to give a brief critical review of research into the physiology of higher nervous activity in children, and to raise the chief problems that await solution in three selected fields: the early ontogenesis of higher nervous activity, the specific features and age characteristics of children's higher nervous activity, and the development of interconnections between the first and second signal systems in children.

I

The Early Ontogenesis of Higher Nervous Activity

The basic problem is to determine the earliest moment when conditioned reflexes appear. In one of his first works, published in 1913, Krasnogorsky wrote:

In the normal new-born infant the cortical innervations are developed to such an insignificant extent that conditioned connections cannot yet be formed. In the second half of the first year the formation of conditioned reflexes with all the organs of perception (eyes, ears, nose, skin) is possible, but takes place more slowly than at a later age. The mechanism of conditioned reflexes only becomes fully developed and functionally complete during the second year [33: 16].

Many attempts have since been made to define more exactly when the first conditioned reflexes appear, and how they are formed. Their appearance is, of course, directly connected with the degree to which the analysers are functionally ready.

Detailed investigations have established that the earliest conditioned reflex is that expressed in sucking movements when the child is in the lactation position 'at the breast'; this appears at the age of 3 to 4 weeks.[1] No definite conditioned reflexes, natural or experimental, have been found at an earlier age than this. The conditioned reflex obtained is a reflex to a complex stimulus with many components: visual (sight of the breast and the mother's face), aural (the mother's voice), kinaesthetic (position of the body), etc.

Analysis has shown that the basic (strong) component of this complex stimulus is the bringing of the child into a certain position. According to Denisova and Figurin [7], the conditioned reflex was obtained earliest (at 21 to 27 days) when this component was isolated. M. M. Koltsova [28] obtained a slightly earlier date and also established that the separate components of the complex stimulus, such as position of the body and the sight of the breast, were gradually separated out, and that a conditioned reflex appeared to the isolated action of each of these in a definite order. She connects the appearance of the first conditioned reflexes to artificial stimuli with the development of the brain's analysing function, which is indicated by the isolation of a separate component from the complex stimulus. A considerable amount of material has been obtained on the formation of artificial conditioned reflexes with different analysers; this shows that the first conditioned-reflex connections are formed at the end of the first or the beginning of the second month of life. Conditioned reflexes are formed with all the organs of perception during the second month. These are found to form in a certain order: first, reflexes with the vestibular canals, then to aural, visual, and tactile stimuli.

Research on the formation of conditioned reflexes in premature infants is of fundamental importance. Kasatkin [26] has shown that conditioned reflexes form during the first half of the second month of post-natal life, irrespective of the degree of prematurity (up to two months) or the age at which experiments began. For example, a conditioned aural-reflex could be formed in premature infants during the period between the actual date of birth and the time when pregnancy would normally have been terminated. It is evident, therefore, that the functional maturity of the cerebral cortex depends upon its actual functioning; this alone can explain its earlier maturity in premature infants. Shchelovanov refers to this when he points out that:

If external stimuli are absent or insufficient the organization of the work of the cerebral cortex . . . is arrested or goes astray, even

[1] Investigation by N. M. Shchelovanov and his collaborators, N. L. Figurin, M. P. Denisova, N. I. Kasatkin, Ts. P. Nemanova and others.

when the cortex is anatomically ready to function. Upbringing must accordingly begin at the right time, since its 'deficit' may grow from the first months of the child's life [59: 21].

The appearance and nature of the mechanisms of higher nervous activity during the first year of life have been less thoroughly studied, but important data have been collected of particular significance in the case of the work of the analysers. Making a differentiation is an objective criterion of this work. The process may proceed in two ways: either the differentiation occurs immediately, or it takes place gradually by way of a preliminary stage of generalization. Again, differentiation by the child during the first months of life shows individual variation, both in the time it requires and in its degree of permanence. 'Impermanence of differentiation is characteristic of children in their first months, when the processes of excitation and inhibition are marked by extreme instability' [26: 178].

Data from various investigations may be summed up as follows:

(1) two qualitatively different light-stimuli can be differentiated in the third month, at first unsteadily, but more steadily by the fourth month;

(2) two qualitatively different sounds can be differentiated 'on the spot' in the second month, two tones an octave apart in the third month, and finer discriminations of 5·5 tones are possible in the fourth and at the beginning of the fifth month;

(3) two smells can be differentiated at the end of the second month or during the third, and several smells in the fourth month;

(4) tactile stimuli, when placed a considerable distance apart, can be differentiated in the third month;

(5) several taste differentiations can be made in the second half of the second month, and the basic taste substances can be differentiated fairly exactly in the third month.

Kasatkin, in a monograph on early conditioned reflexes, writes:

. . . it may be regarded as proved that, immediately after positive conditioned reflexes have been formed, an analysis of external stimuli also begins and the environment is broken down into 'units'. The facts thus discovered enable the infant to make an advance in which discriminations are formed. In the second month of life practically all the analysers can differentiate fairly dissimilar stimuli. In some cases capacities for differentiating appear on the spot, in others a certain time is required. As a rule, capacities for differentiation in the second month of life are still very unstable. In the third month the analysing function becomes more complete, while all receptors develop the capacity for differentiation. By this age, just as in the fourth month, it is possible to produce more stable and exact differentiations [26: 182].

Similar investigations into the process of inhibition (extinctive, conditioned and delayed) justify the conclusion that, even in the first half year, almost every variety of inhibition can occur; extinction of conditioned reflexes formed in the second month of the child's life occurred very readily; conditioned inhibition can occur at the age of four months, and inhibition of delay has also been produced in children of this age, though with great difficulty.

This virtually exhausts the data we have on higher nervous activity in children during the first year of life. A host of problems still await investigation. Research into the development of analyser functions has only begun. Then there is the completely neglected question of the dynamic processes of inhibition and excitation, and their inter-action in the cerebral cortex; this is extremely important, both theoretically and for the practice of medicine and education. Moreover, investigations have been concerned chiefly with the first year of life, and especially the first six months. It is extremely important to clarify how the child's cortex functions at the end of the first year and during the second and third years of life, for new specific traits form at these periods which characterize this activity. In order to understand why research has stopped short at the first six months to begin again at pre-school age, so that these extremely important questions have not been tackled, a critical survey may be made of the work done.

Practically all investigators of conditioned-reflex activity in infants at the breast have relied on food and defence unconditioned reflexes. As effector elements in these unconditioned reflexes they took sucking movements in feeding, or defensive movements (blinking) when a jet of air or a bright light struck the eye. On this basis various temporary connections were formed, i.e. conditioned reflexes. This method, however, is only justified when the most *general* laws of children's nervous activity are being established, laws which are not fundamentally different from those governing the behaviour of animals; in other words, only while it is a question of discovering when the cortex is functionally ready for the basic process of conditioned-reflex formation. When the task is to investigate the *development* of this basic function, this method must be supplemented.

It should be remembered that the development of the coupling function of the cortex consists, primarily, in a change in the *basis* on which the formation of temporary connections takes place; then in the character of the signals connected with this new basis; and, finally, in the way that temporary connections are established between the new basis and the new signals.

Although food and defence unconditioned reflexes have been primarily used in research, it does not follow that these reflexes, in fact, govern the emergence of new forms of behaviour. Observation of child development during the first year of life shows that the role of food-behaviour gradually decreases. This decrease in the importance of unconditioned reflexes to food in the acquisition of new forms of behaviour may be connected with the fact that adults ensure satisfaction of this need. In animals, owing to the struggle for existence, the connections between food and the agents signalizing it play a decisive role, but in children food behaviour develops less than other forms. A child of 7 to 8 months, for example, sits down independently, or may even try to stand up; he gets toys for himself by crawling after them; he waves a rattle, throws it down and changes it from one hand to the other; he taps one object against another, and so on. Yet his food movements, even if he has been trained to eat from a spoon, amount to reaching towards the spoon with open mouth as soon as he sees it lifted up and taking the food with his lips.

On what basis, then, does the child's brain develop and form the more complex mechanisms which link the endless flow of new temporary connections?

Attention must first be drawn to the great importance of the adult, not only as organizer of the child's whole life, but also as the object of his first needs. Describing an infant's development between the first and third months, Figurin and Denisova [8: 26] draw attention to a new and important quality that forms at this period—the so-called complex of animation.

The complex of animation begins with a smile at the talking face. Smiling at a talking face can be taken as the sign that the second period has started and as a boundary between the first period and the third. It usually appears in the fifth week, but often earlier (in the third or fourth week) or later (in the sixth or seventh week). At first it is difficult to evoke the smile; one has to chatter with the child for a long time and make him concentrate on one's face, and then, at last, a feebly expressed smile will flit quickly across his face, twice. After that, smiling at a talking face can be evoked more easily and made to last longer. The smile at first appears only to this one stimulus and to no other. This and many other reactions *appear primarily to the human face and voice*. Only experimental examination can decide whether this is to be explained by the

54

frequency of the stimulus or by its specific nature (my italics— D. B. E.).

This experimental examination unfortunately is still wanting. Yet it is through intercourse with adults that a number of specifically human forms of behaviour develop, among them speech. The first problem requiring attention may, then, be briefly formulated as follows: what is the role played by intercourse with adults, as a basic condition of existence, in the development of higher nervous activity in the infant?

Secondly, there has been insufficient research into the orienting-investigatory reflex in young children. Pavlov attached exceptional importance to this unconditioned reflex.

Each minute, every new stimulus that strikes us evokes a corresponding movement on our part to find out more about this stimulus. We look at an appearing form, listen to a sound that arises, strain to inhale a smell, and, if there is a new object near us, we try to touch it; in general we endeavour to encompass or grasp every new phenomenon or object, using the corresponding receptor surface, the appropriate sense organ [48: 308].

Figurin and Denisova, in their careful study of the first year of life, point out that the mechanism of the orienting-food reflex is ready from the moment of birth; the orienting reflex to labyrinthine stimuli is also inborn. The orienting reflex to sound and sight stimuli emerges somewhat later, the aural orienting reflex at the second week (the authors call it 'aural concentration') and the visual orienting reflex at between three and five weeks.

It is scarcely rated highly enough—this reflex that one might call the investigatory reflex, or, as I call it, the 'What-is-it?' reflex; this is . . . one of the fundamental reflexes. Both we and the animals, at the slightest environmental variation, dispose the appropriate receptor apparatus in the direction of the agent of the variation. The biological significance of this reflex is enormous. If an animal lacked this reflex, then its life would every moment hang by a thread. And for us this reflex goes a very long way indeed, appearing finally in the form of that curiosity which creates science and gives and promises us supreme, unlimited orientation in the surrounding world.[1]

It is on the basis of orienting reflexes—which subsequently take the form of an active investigatory reflex in relation to every new

[1] Pavlov-Anrep, 12.

thing—that the child becomes acquainted with the activity around him and forms his first images of the objects of reality. On the basis of orienting reflexes, which at first have the character of passive orientation, there arises the conditioned-reflex way of active search of the object in one of its forms (turning the head to a voice at six months); grasping movements develop on the basis of this, and from these all possible manipulative hand-movements with the object. It is also, presumably, on the basis of the orienting reflex that the child develops connections between those different properties of one and the same object which underlie the formation of the image, and between the properties of an object and the means of action with it.

Since there has been practically no research into this question, it is only possible to make assumptions about certain features. We may suppose that the connections between the separate properties of the objects with which the child has to deal are not the same as connections between the essential and inessential properties of food; the process of formation of connections between them, however, is very similar to the formation of early natural conditioned reflexes; to judge from observations, they form almost 'on the spot'. One remarkable property of the orienting reflex is that it possesses its own natural 'self-reinforcement'; that is, each new position of an object reinforces by its novelty the orienting-investigatory reflex underlying the parallel activity, and simultaneously reinforces the connections between the stimulus and action with the object. This is probably the reason why the child of 7 to 8 months can occupy itself for so long with the same object, provided this has enough possibilities of 'novelty'. Yet the orienting reflex extinguishes rather rapidly; according to Denisova and Figurin [9], extinction occurs after 15 to 25 minutes of play with an object, when a 'new' object turns into an 'old' one.

Finally, attention should be paid to the important part played by the orienting reflex in the formation of new types of temporary connections of exceptional significance to the child's development; for example, imitation, which originates with the development of the orienting reflex.

Ivanov-Smolensky has drawn attention to the exceptional importance of study of the motor conditioned reflexes, and of the orienting reflex which underlies their formation, and has worked out a special method of forming motor conditioned reflexes with an orienting reinforcement [16]. This method has been successfully applied in research conducted with children of pre-school and school age, but there have been no investigations with children of one to three years. This is chiefly due to the difficulties of experimental work with children of this age, but not all the possibilities have been tried. There is every reason to suppose that, if the orienting reinforcement through 'novelty' were properly used, improved methods could be found for experimenting with younger children. This is particularly important because it is at the age of from one to three years that the processes peculiar to the child's higher nervous activity are formed.

Ivanov-Smolensky's collaborators have succeeded in forming temporary connections without prolonged training. Their investigations indicate that, apart from the classical mechanism whereby new connections are formed as a result of coincidence in time, there are several other mechanisms: (a) by irradiation, (b) by means of cross-coupling, (c) with the support of verbal instruction, (d) selective irradiation between direct and symbolic projections, (e) by the method of trial and error, (f) on the basis of imitation—direct, successive or generalized.[1]

Thus the student of early childhood is faced with many unsolved problems. The most important of these are: (1) How does the orienting-investigatory reflex arise and develop in early childhood? (2) What connections can be formed on the basis of the orienting reflex, and how are they formed? (3) How do the connections of early childhood, which require few repetitions, arise and what is their mechanism?

II

The Specific Features and Age Characteristics of Higher Nervous Activity in Children

What are the specific properties of children's higher nervous activity? In early researches, investigators only succeeded in establishing a certain quantitative distinction in the formation of temporary connections and in the course of excitation and inhibition. Mention should be made here of Krasnogorsky's research into conditioned reflexes in children. The most important characteristics he found may be summarized in his own words [33: 16].

It is obvious that the mechanism whereby temporary connections arise is the same in children as it is in animals. Nevertheless conditioned reflexes in children have certain features which distinguish them from those in animals. One of their basic characteristics is the speed of formation. In normal children it is sufficient for a stimulus to be combined from 2 to 10 times with an unconditioned reflex in order to turn a previously indifferent stimulus into a conditioned one which begins to evoke the motor act. The character-istic features of conditioned reflexes in children are high stability

---

[1] Investigations by Narodnitskaya, Khozak, Kotliarevsky, Faddeeva, Pen, referred to below.

and rapid extinction. A newly-formed conditioned reflex lasts a long time in a normal child, but may at any moment be quickly extinguished and re-established.

Krasnogorsky attaches particular significance to stability as an important distinguishing quality of conditioned-reflex connections in children:

> Conditioned-reflex connections are often cited as a mechanism of temporary connection. This statement must be made more precise. The study of conditioned-reflex activity in children has shown that their conditioned reflexes are characterized by high stability and are preserved for several years. The cortical cells of the child's brain possess an enormous capacity for prolonged fixation and retention of the contacts that have been established, and this capacity is one of the most important factors determining the quality of the work of the cerebral hemispheres [33: 180].

When studying trace conditioned reflexes in children, Krasnogorsky established that the mechanism of their formation provided a particularly clear example of the difference between cortical activity in man and in the animals.

> In the dog, for example, trace reflexes are formed with great difficulty, and extinguish rapidly—if, for example, they are left once without reinforcement. Trace reflexes form just as quickly in children as ordinary conditioned reflexes. In normal children it is sufficient to combine the action of traces from some stimulus with the unconditioned motor reflex from 20 to 30 times for these traces to begin to evoke a conditioned reflex. Extinction of trace reflexes in children is also quite different from that in animals. Trace reflexes in children extinguish just as do simple conditioned reflexes. Thus high specificity, speed of formation, high stability in relation to time, and gradual extinction are the characteristics of this group of reflexes in children [33: 18].

Elsewhere, following up the same idea, Krasnogorsky points out:

> Trace reactions in children, as opposed to animals, are highly delicate, subtle and specific reactions. Their trace periods, that is, the intervals of time between the end of the conditioned stimulus and the moment of reinforcement, may be very prolonged (half-an-hour, or even hours). Thus the trace reaction enables us to make

a strictly physiological study of cortical functions during the protracted 'waiting' [33: 89].

Krasnogorsky's data showed that the mechanism of the trace reflex develops during the second year of the child's life. He found analogous distinctions when external stimuli were differentiated and in various aspects of internal inhibition. He points out that only at the suckling stage does differentiation show the same phases as in animals.[1] 'The formation of conditioned-reflex innervation occurs far more quickly in children than in animals. . . . In normal children the first two phases are not sharply pronounced, and differentiation rapidly passes into the phase of absolute differentiation' [33: 23].

Specific features of one of the aspects of internal inhibition, so-called conditioned inhibition, were discovered in the course of special investigations: 'The formation of conditioned inhibition occurs more quickly in children than in animals. . . . Rapidity of formation, the solo inhibitory effect, rapid extinction and high stability in time, are characteristic features of conditioned inhibition in the normal child' [33: 24].

Krasnogorsky's data show that the development of the mechanism of conditioned inhibition begins at the end of the first year of life. He points out that: 'Intra-cortical inhibition is more inert during the first year than at a later age. It becomes more and more mobile as the cortex develops, and reaches functional completeness when the child is three or four' [33: 24].

Such, briefly, are the chief characteristics of the basic mechanisms of higher nervous activity in children, as shown by the researches of Krasnogorsky and his colleagues. They have demonstrated that the higher nervous system of children obeys all the basic laws discovered by Pavlov, but has at the same time certain specific traits—in particular, the speed and dynamic nature of the nervous processes. These features are presumably connected with the special conditions in which children—indeed human beings in general—live. As Ivanov-Smolensky points out, the first signal system in man is by no means completely identical with the cortical activity of the higher animals. 'In the first signal system, as in the second, man reflects his social milieu, and the activity of the first system is just as socially determined as is that of the second' [17: 65].

[Here the author turns aside to consider some questions of

---

[1] These are, first, extinction of a conditioned reflex in an inactive cortical area evokes the same extinction of the reflex in an active area; second, a stimulus in an inactive area still evokes the reflex, but its extinction does not make the reflex disappear from an active area; third, stimulation of the inactive area does not evoke the reflex, and stimulation of the active area gives a positive effect.

methodology, which arise in comparing Krasnogorsky's results with those of other investigators. The formation of trace reflexes is taken as an example. Z. G. Lavrova [37], a colleague of Ivanov-Smolensky, studying orienting trace reflexes in children of pre-school and school age, found—in opposition to Krasnogorsky—that these were very difficult and slow to form, marked by great instability, and quickly extinguished. In both cases it was a question of motor-conditioned reflexes, but the methods used differed. With Krasnogorsky's method, reinforcement did not depend on the motor reaction evoked; whereas with Ivanov-Smolensky's method, reinforcement depended on an active movement made by the subject. Therefore, both the nature of the temporary connections concerned and the process of their formation were different. In fact, the second method required the formation of two temporary connections. This presumably explains why extinction occurred after 3 to 10 non-reinforcements of the conditioned reflex according to Krasnogorsky's data, but only after 10 to 26 non-reinforcements according to the data arrived at by Ivanov-Smolensky's method. This illustrates that a detailed analysis of the objective conditions in which the connection was established is necessary before data can be adequately interpreted.]

In comparing the formation of conditioned reflexes and the processes of excitation and inhibition in man with those of animals, purely quantitative criteria (e.g. speed of formation) cannot help to explain the specific features of the neurodynamics of the cortex in the child, particularly when different methods are used. A quantitative description is only adequate at the first stages, to prove that the cortical activity of man in general, and of the child in particular, obeys all the basic laws of the higher nervous system discovered by Pavlov. But today such a description is insufficient. Bykov, criticizing some earlier attempts to interpret data about man in this way, concluded: 'The creation of artificial experimental conditions, or experiment only on animals, cannot reflect all the variety of higher forms whereby functions are regulated and developed in the natural conditions of human life.' [1]

Consequently, to discover the specific features of the higher functioning of a child's cortex, experimental methods must be devised which reflect the features of the child's development in his natural conditions of life and activity. Above all, it must not be thought that the formation of new connections in man occurs only in the conditions applied by Pavlov, i.e. when the signal stimulus coincides frequently with the unconditioned stimulus. The peculiar characteristic of man's cortical processes is to be found in the method whereby new connections are formed. This is why the experiments of Ivanov-

[1] *Scientific Session*, 60-1.

Smolensky and his collaborators merit special attention: they illustrate the different ways in which conditioned connections form in the child's cortex. Some of the conclusions reached may be given.

Narodnitskaya [45] studied whether new conditioned connections could be formed in children without prolonged practice. Her conclusions were:

(1) The formation of new conditioned connections in the child is possible even without preliminary practice—at once, 'on the spot', suddenly.

(2) The development of a new conditioned connection without preliminary practice occurs through generalization (static irradiation) on the basis of past experience.

(3) Generalization (static irradiation) is observed in both receptor and effector, that is, this generalization relates not only to the conditioned stimulus (visual or aural) and to the form of instrument (various forms of bulb), but also to the form of conditioned-motor reactions (in connection with the change of form and position of the instrument).

(4) The proportion of children able to form new conditioned connections without preliminary practice increases with age: at 5 to 6 years 28% give correct solutions, at 7 to 8 years 40%, and at 10 to 12 years 80%.

This investigation did not, however, throw sufficient light on the neurodynamic connections underlying the use of past experience. This question was specially studied by L. E. Khozak [27], who devised particular experimental conditions for its investigation. His conclusions were that, when two conditioned connections are produced, they may interact and give rise to a new conditioned connection qualitatively different both as concerns the stimulus evoking it and the form of its effect. This formation of new conditioned connections occurs as the result of interaction between two fields of static irradiation from the first preliminary conditioned connections; this interaction leads to fresh linking.

Two further investigations also show how conditioned connections arise without preliminary practice, and how the new temporary connections link on the basis of past experience. Kotliarevsky [30] studied the mechanism of 'suddenness' in the setting up of a connection, and Faddeeva [12] studied the way connections are formed by means of the orienting-testing reaction. Both found selective animation of conditioned connections, formed in the children's previous individual experience, with certain differences in the mechanism whereby the previous experience was 'brought to life'.

These investigations were united by a common aim: to discover the mechanism whereby new conditioned connections are formed without previous elaboration. The data show that new temporary connections may appear in children both suddenly and through orienting-testing reactions, and that a stable conditioned reflex is obtained in both cases. This research has established a new type of formation of temporary connections and thrown light on the physiological mechanism underlying it. But much that has been said about the latter is still insufficiently clear and has the air of interpretation rather than proof; further investigation of this physiological mechanism is necessary.

The way in which new conditioned connections are formed by imitation has been the subject of some interesting research by Pen [52]. He produced a positive and inhibitory conditioned reflex in one of his subjects (the 'imitated' one), and, after reinforcing it, introduced the other subject, who observed the work of the first before submitting himself to the test. The nature of imitation varied: direct, successive and generalized imitation were each tried. New connections were formed in each case. Interestingly enough 'in many cases, where a conditioned connection could not be produced in the child in the usual way (by timing a signal just before or at the same time as reinforcement) it sprang up easily by imitation'.

All these experiments showed that new connections can be formed in children, not only by the classical method of forming conditioned reflexes, but also suddenly, by cross-linking, through orienting-testing reactions and, finally, by imitation. These conclusions are of particular interest for child psychology because they state, more exactly than before, what is specific in the functioning of the child's cortex. They give grounds for supposing that the qualitative peculiarity of the mechanisms of the human brain lies in the possibilities for forming connections in different ways. Further investigations will probably discover yet other mechanisms whereby temporary connections are formed in the child.

Certain important tasks remain. First, it is of vital importance to child psychology to investigate how these new mechanisms arise and at what age they develop; to establish this is particularly important for education, since it would enable teachers to rely at each age on the most productive mechanisms. Second, there are certain points that still require clarification: e.g. the way in which the special new connections operate, how they are extinguished, how they are influenced by external inhibition, how they provide a basis for differentiation, whether static irradiation occurs in their formation, what is the degree of their stability and mobility. We can only suppose that the quality of temporary connections and the dynamics of the nervous processes concerned may differ in some degree from those of classical conditioned-reflex formation. The investigations cited show, for example, that a connection becomes stable immediately after linking, that is, a stable conditioned reflex is obtained; whereas in the classical method of forming connections a whole series of reinforcements was necessary between the origin of a connection and its consolidation. Third, the great potentialities of the child's cortex are not, presumably, exhausted by the types of formation of new temporary connections already described. It is of fundamental importance to analyse the many-sidedness of the process whereby the child acquires experience during the course of his life and activity, and to create experimental models capable of revealing the physiological mechanism of all these varied forms. This will not only show the special potentialities of the cortex in man's ontogenesis; it will also deepen our understanding of the dependence of cortical activity on the external conditions of life, which, by their very complexity, require new methods of forming temporary connections.

This is the general position of research into the specific nature of conditioned-reflex formation in the child. An allied question, one that is at present neglected, is the specific way these connections form at each age; this problem has not yet been solved.

[Here the author refers briefly to three investigations into the age characteristics of different kinds of internal inhibition in children, and summarizes the conclusions. These and many other researches contribute to an understanding of higher nervous activity in children, but since their data are derived from different methods, age characteristics appear to vary according to the nature of the reinforcement, the type of motor reflex, the conditioned stimulus used, and so on.]

Systematic research into the characteristics of higher nervous activity at different ages is, therefore, required. Presumably the aim should be to clarify the *optimal* conditions at each age for the development of temporary connections and for the occurrence of inhibition and excitation. On what basis can temporary connections be created most quickly and easily at each age? Under what conditions is inhibition most stable and intensive at each age? The answers to these and similar questions are important because they will influence educational practice, guard against the possibility of aggravating weak sides of cortical activity, and show what are the strong sides of cortical activity at each age, and the mechanisms for exercising them. Research has shown that inhibitory processes are highly responsive to practice, and this may also be true of all other processes. To find out to what extent the basic mechanisms can be trained is particularly important. It would be wrong to understand development merely as the accumulation of an increasing number of new connections. It is also the birth of new ways of forming connections, a process that

63

continually grows in complexity, constituting the dynamics of the cortex. That is why investigation of the problems outlined is vital to child psychology.

III

The Development of Interaction between the First and Second Signal Systems in Children

In 1917 Ivanov-Smolensky, studying the qualitative differences between cortical connections in man, noted the possibility of setting up temporary connections between a conditioned stimulus and a motor reaction on the basis of verbal reinforcement. He correctly saw this as a qualitative difference in human conditioned-reflex formation, and connected it with the particular nature of the dynamics of the nervous processes in the human brain. These temporary connections arise independently of any unconditioned reflex, the effector relations establishing the movement itself being acquired during individual life. Experiments in forming conditioned reflexes using verbal reinforcement showed that such connections obeyed all the basic laws of higher nervous activity. At this stage of research, speech appeared to be a stimulus which could act as a substitute for unconditioned-reflex reinforcement; it seemed to have been drawn into the circle of the usual agents of the external world capable of functionally replacing unconditioned reinforcement.

Krasnogorsky and his colleagues took the next step and applied the conditioned-reflex method to the study of the speech functions themselves. It was shown that

every verbal stimulus can be made conditioned and begins to evoke the appropriate positive or inhibitory activity, if it is synchronized with that activity several times. From the physiological point of view every simple sound in any language is a conditioned acoustic stimulus, every word is a conditioned-reflex complex and every phrase is a conditioned system . . . [33: 97].

It was then shown that the basic laws of conditioned-reflex activity preserve their validity both for complex stimuli and for systems of such stimuli, and that conditioned verbal reactions can be accelerated, differentiated, abandoned and inhibited, in just the same way as simple conditioned reflexes.

This trend of research, therefore, was concerned to draw language into the general system of conditioned stimuli, and to show that language also was capable of changing from a neutral to a conditioned stimulus. But no essential difference was discerned between a word and a complex acoustic stimulus. This trend resulted from ignoring the special function of language and words in human society and in the life of every individual; the investigations not only failed to discover the differences in the quality of cortical activity owing to the use of words, but even obliterated this special quality, reducing words to the level of simple physical agents, on the same level as other physical stimuli such as sound, light, touch and so on.

When Pavlov encountered the problem of speech signalization, he at once put it on a completely new level and advanced the idea of a special 'second signal system'. In his very first statement on this question, he said:

For man, the word is just as real a conditioned stimulus as any other that he has in common with the animals, but at the same time the comprehensiveness of words is such that they cannot be compared either quantitatively or qualitatively with the conditioned stimuli of animals. As a result of an adult man's previous life experience, words are connected with all external and internal stimuli that reach the cerebral hemispheres; words signalize and stand for all these, and can therefore evoke all the actions and reactions in the organism that the stimuli themselves produce.[1]

This statement constitutes a criticism of every attempt to put words on the same plane as other conditioned stimuli. Pavlov perceived in words a universal means of signalization, capable of taking the place of all other possible stimuli and therefore not on a level with these, but standing above them. This could naturally not fail to have an effect on subsequent investigations.

Ivanov-Smolensky's research was concerned to clarify the interrelations between the first and second signal systems, or, to use his terms, between direct and symbolic productions. The first investigation published was by Kapustnik [23], who produced a conditioned reflex in children to the sound of a bell and then replaced the conditioned stimulus by its spoken symbol, the word 'bell'. It was then discovered that a conditioned connection to the word 'bell' formed immediately, evoking the same reaction as the sound of the bell. Again, in the formation of a conditioned reflex to the word 'bell' the conditioned action also appeared to the direct stimulus denoted by the word, that is, to the sound of the bell. These experiments showed that, when a conditioned reflex is formed to an external stimulus, the associated word-stimulus is also involved; and, conversely, that when a conditioned reflex is formed to a word the direct stimulus it denotes

[1] Pavlov-Anrep, 407.

is involved. Ivanov-Smolensky called the mechanism of this phenomenon elective (or selective) generalization or irradiation. Elective
irradiation spreads in the cortex along connections created during
the whole of the child's life-experience.

But there is a clear qualitative distinction between the nervous
mechanisms underlying the two conditioned reactions. The excitation evoked in the brain by the sound of the bell connects this
stimulus with its answering reaction relatively directly. But not in
the second case, when the same reaction appears in response to the
word 'bell'. The neural excitation evoked by this stimulus first re-
animates the old association between the word 'bell' and the sound
of a bell; this association had been impressed in the cortex at some
time in past experience. Only then does the same excitation proceed
on its way, joining the cortical impression of the latter stimulus with
the given reaction, and bringing into the action the conditioned
connection produced in the experiment.

In the first case the motor reaction appears to be an almost direct
and unmediated response to the stimulus; in the second it is the
result or product of interaction between the stimulus on the one
hand and the experience impressed in the cortex by past experience
on the other. The previous experience reflected in the brain as an
old association seems to come in between the stimulus and the
reaction, yet at the same time joins the stimulus with a reaction
with which it had never previously been connected [17: 59].

Traugott [66] and Smolenskaya [62] extended the investigation to
the formation of inhibitions and differentiations, and reached the
following basic conclusions:

(1) When a conditioned inhibition is set up in children, the *word*
denoting the agent of inhibition also acquires an inhibitory effect,
and inhibition arising in the direct projection irradiates into the
verbal or symbolic projection along paths formed during ontogenesis.
(2) The nature and paths of irradiation of inhibition in the symbolic
(speech) projection is determined by the nature of these processes
in the direct projection.
(3) Inhibitory processes, arising in a direct projection, involve inhibitory processes in the speech projection.
(4) Differentiation produced to direct stimuli is transferred to verbal
symbols of the differentiated stimulus.

The basic tendency of these researches was to show the dependence
of processes taking place in the symbolic projection on processes

occurring in the direct projection. They proved Pavlov's theory that words can take the place of all external and internal stimuli, and evoke all their reactions.

Pavlov considered that the second signal system is the dominating one, and that it exerts a regulating and damping effect on the activity of the first.

In man there is added—it may be assumed in relation to the frontal lobes which no animals possess in comparable size—a second system of signals, signalizing the first; that is, speech, the basis or basal components of which are the kinaesthetic stimulations from the speech organs. Thus a new principle of nervous activity is introduced, the abstraction and generalization of the innumerable signals of the preceding system, and, again, together with this, analysis and synthesis of these new generalized signals; on this depends man's infinite capacity for orientation in the surrounding world, and, too, his highest form of adaptation—that is, science, both in the empirical form common to all mankind and in its specialized form. This second signalling system and its organ, being the last acquired in the evolutionary process, is particularly fragile and succumbs to the first diffused inhibition that develops in the cerebral hemispheres in the initial stages of hypnosis. *Then, instead of the second signalling system having precedence, as in a sound state, the activity of the first comes to the fore* (my italics— D.B.E.).[1]

Once children have mastered language, the second signal system takes a direct part in the formation of first signal system connections, and the whole cortical dynamics, and this is relevant to the speed of formation of connections, their stability, etc. There are factual grounds for this supposition. Krasnogorsky, after studying the possibility of forming conditioned reflexes in children during hypnosis, pointed out:

It is worth noticing that new conditioned reflexes could be formed in the hypnotic trance only when there was full amnesia.

[1] *Selected Works*, 537. Pavlov did not consider that the frontal lobes had a superior regulating function. 'Our facts definitely discountenance the theory of separate associative centres, and, in general, the existence of any special part of the hemispheres possessing a supreme nervous function.' But he did, in a sense, 'regard the second signal system as a higher *system* of the brain, though he always stressed the danger of separating it from the first signal system, from the direct reflection of objective reality. Therefore, we may speak only of a relative supremacy of the second signal system, which Pavlov really did consider to be an important, but not the exclusive function of the frontal lobes.' A. G. Ivanov-Smolensky, *Scientific Session*, 151 (Ed.).

Then, however, the new reactions did not enter into the general synthetic activity of the brain, but remained subconscious. Children gave intensive conditioned reactions, without in the least realizing this, whereas actions connected with reflexes formed when the brain was in a sound state were well motivated [33: 95].

However, as Krasnogorsky says, conditioned reflexes are formed quite differently in a normal state and under hypnosis. If we bear in mind Pavlov's remark that the second signal system goes out of action during hypnosis, then we may suppose that this affects the formation of conditioned reflexes during hypnosis, if only partially. We may further suppose that differences in the formation of secretory and motor reflexes may also be explained by the differing degree to which the second signal system is involved, for secretory reflexes are conditioned-extrapyramidal, while motor reflexes are conditioned-cortical. There is also much data on the role of speech reactions in the work by Kapustnik and Faddeeva on internal inhibition referred to above. These facts from various investigations show that, even in normal conditions, the first signal system operates under the regulating influence of the second signal system, with its direct participation and in interaction with it.

The interaction of the first and second signal systems is not continuous throughout childhood. There cannot, of course, be any question of the participation of the second signal system in the activity of the first until language itself has been mastered; but as a child learns words, and learns how to use them in intercourse, the second signal system grows and begins to take a part in all the dynamics of his mental activity. Such a conception of the interaction between the two signal systems corresponds to Pavlov's theory. This is the key problem in child psychology which further research must elucidate.

THE PSYCHOLOGY OF UNDERSTANDING [1]

BY

D. N. BOGOIAVLENSKY

ATTEMPTS TO GIVE a precise psychological description of the processes of understanding, and to indicate their different levels, have rarely been satisfactory. For instance, in the college text-book *Psychology*,[2] understanding is defined as 'the reflection of the connections between objects and phenomena of the real world'. Though correct, this definition is too general, since it may also be applied to thinking. It refers to what is reflected, but completely omits any description of reflection as a process. Similarly, 'levels' of under-standing are later distinguished only by the nature of what is under-stood. Again, Smirnov deals with the process of understanding in *The Psychology of Memory*. But, though a great deal of factual material underlies his observations, his formulation is diffuse and far from concrete. Soviet psychologists have failed in this way because neglect of Pavlov's teaching has deprived research of a scientific foundation. The present paper is an exposition of the scientific basis of the psycho-logy of understanding as outlined by Pavlov.

I

The temporary nervous connection is a universal physiological phenomenon in both the animal world and our own. But at the same time it is a psychic phenomenon—what psychologists call association—whether it be the combination of different actions and impressions, or of letters, words and thoughts.[3]

The universality of the mechanism of temporary connections applies to the second signal system as well as to the first. In his sum-marizing article 'The Conditioned Reflex', Pavlov wrote, 'the funda-mental laws governing the activity of the first signal system must also

---

[1] *Sovetskaya Pedagogika*, No. 12, 1951, pp. 28–40 (translated by N. Parsons).
[2] Edited by K. N. Kornilov, A. A. Smirnov and B. M. Teplov, 1948.
[3] Pavlov-Gantt ii, 171; *Selected Works*, 251.

govern the second, because this is activity of the same nervous tissue'.[1] Again, when discussing the problem of learning at a Wednesday seminar, Pavlov summed up by saying, 'All learning consists in forming connections; this is thought, thinking, knowledge' [50: 580].

Psychologists must therefore discard as unscientific the view that there are 'pure associative' connections in contrast to 'sense' connections, a view that implies the existence of connections that are not purely associative; for Pavlov shows that the mechanism by which temporary connections are formed is the same for 'sense' as for 'mechanical' connections. The study of levels of understanding must, therefore, be based on Pavlov's theory of association and on relevant elements in his discussion of the second signal system.

Pavlov provides an aid to understanding the nature of temporary connections in his discussion of the terms 'conditioned reflex' and 'association' [51 : 262].

Association is a generic conception, i.e. a combination of that which was previously separated, a joining or generalizing of two points in a functional relationship, their fusing into one association; whereas a conditioned reflex—this is a conception within a species. It is also, of course, a joining of two points which were not previously connected, but it is a particular case of joining and is of precise biological significance. In the case of a conditioned reflex, the permanent, substantial features of a certain object (food, an enemy, etc.) are replaced by temporary signals. It is a particular application of association.

Another example is when two phenomena are connected because they affect the nervous system simultaneously, that is, they are always connected in the external world. This is another aspect of association, this is the foundation of all our knowledge, the foundation of the great scientific principle—causality. The connection between signals is an aspect of association which probably has an even greater significance than the conditioned reflex.

And, finally, there is the simple case (whatever it is called—artificial, chance, inessential, unimportant) when, for example, two sounds, which have nothing in common, are connected psychologically simply because one is repeated after the other, until finally one evokes the other.

Two significant points emerge from these statements. First, Pavlov considers that 'association' has the same meaning as 'temporary connection'; the conditioned reflex being a particular case of association (a connection with an unconditioned stimulus). Second, the other two

[1] Pavlov-Gantt ii, 179; *Selected Works*, 262.

cases of association (causal connections and chance connections), which coincide exactly with the psychological division of associations into 'sense' and 'mechanical', may be divided according to the importance of their stimuli but not according to the mechanism of their formation, since in both cases this is the mechanism of conditioned-reflex formation. Thus Pavlov found a distinction between causal and chance connections in the properties of the objects concerned: some phenomena are 'always connected in the external world', so forming 'the foundation of all our knowledge'; others 'have nothing in common', and are connected by chance 'simply because one is repeated after the other'.

Like every other intellectual process, understanding consists in the formation of associations.

It must be realized that the formation of temporary connections, of 'associations' as they are usually called, *is* understanding, *is* knowledge, *is* the acquisition of new connections. When a connection, or 'association', is formed this is undoubtedly knowledge of the matter, knowledge of definite relationships existing in the external world; and when you use it the next time this is called 'understanding'; i.e. the utilization of knowledge, of acquired connections, this is *understanding* (my italics—D. B.).[1]

Thus Pavlov considers understanding in connection with the processes of cognition of reality, that is, with the so-called intellectual or thought processes. He puts the formation of temporary connections among the thinking processes, reserving the term understanding for the moment when previously formed connections are used. Pavlov stated clearly that 'thinking is association'. 'This means that every small, first association is *the moment of the birth of a thought*. . . . These associations grow and increase. Then it is said that thinking becomes more profound, more extensive . . .' (my italics—D. B.).[2]

Criticizing Köhler's idealist theory of 'insight', Pavlov explained the behaviour of the anthropoid Raphael in terms of conditioned reflexes and continued:

We see in this experiment the origin of insight: it is the result of trial and error. This is insight, understanding, the moment when the physiological fuses completely with the psychological. Thought, association, understanding, knowledge, these are what is achieved as a result of the method of trial and error. That is all there is to it. All human thought comes into being in this way. All insight involves an animal using associations that have been formed previously. . . . An animal which has not had the experience of getting

[1] *Selected Works*, 581.　　　　[2] *Ibid.*, 582, 587.

71

round an obstacle will hurl itself at the screen and apply its crude methods of breaking, biting, etc. An animal will only hit upon the roundabout way as a result of knowledge which it has acquired previously [50: 574].

Pavlov considered that temporary connections—associations— were the basis of all human thought, including scientific thought:

All habits of scientific thought consist, first, in establishing a more constant and precise connection, and, second, in rejecting chance connections. Everything can be understood from this point of view. Thinking definitely begins with association, with synthesis; then comes the combination of synthesis with analysis. Analysis is based, on the one hand, on the analysing capacities of our receptors, the peripheral endings, and, on the other, on the process of inhibition which develops in the cerebral cortex and separates that which corresponds to reality from that which does not. This is how I see the matter in the light of our material. . . . It is a fundamental point. Here psychology is covered by physiology, the subjective is understood in a purely physiological, objective way. And this represents a great gain. We begin to understand men's thinking, about which there has been so much talk, and such a lot of empty twaddle.[1]

Pavlov's views on the nature of intellectual processes, and in particular of understanding, may, then, be summed up as follows. When the nervous connections in the active region of the cortex are coupled, this marks the birth of a thought. Understanding is the correct use, next time, of previously formed connections; faulty understanding is unsuccessful use of these. Thinking develops and understanding occurs when associations grow and increase. The processes of understanding and thinking are not peculiar to man; they exist in an embryonic form in animals, particularly the anthropoid apes.

There are two other hypotheses which are very important in relation to the problem of thinking. Pavlov speaks first, of understanding as the use of previous connections, and second, of the deepening of thought as the growth and increase of associations. The reflection in the brain of the connections of reality does not necessarily constitute understanding. Understanding occurs only when a neural connection is established between fresh cortical excitation and 'old associations'. This means that the so-called creative acts of thinking cannot be understood without considering the role of previous connections; no creative thought can take place without the support of previous ex-

[1] *Selected Works*, 588, 589.

perience. This is the basic argument whereby Pavlov refuted Köhler's idealist theory of 'insight'. According to Pavlov, the role of understanding in the formation of new connections (i.e. in thinking) should be studied as part of the cognitive activity of previous experience, which is an indispensable element in every kind of thinking.

These ideas on the nature of the neural mechanisms underlying thought and understanding have been developed and upheld by the experiments in the formation of conditioned reflexes in children conducted by Ivanov-Smolensky. Summing up his work in 1934, Ivanov-Smolensky wrote that his data had enabled him to raise the question

of the influence of earlier social experience, imprinted on the cortex, on the formation of conditioned connections. It was then that we first saw, with unexpected clarity, the way ahead in investigating the dynamic cerebral processes underlying those complex activities of the brain which psychology has long studied under the heads of intellectual, affective and volitional activity [18: 16].

Later, Ivanov-Smolensky described the physiological significance of past experience:

A conditioned reaction may be evoked not only by a conditioned signal but also by various other stimuli that have become associated with it during ontogenesis. The connection develops by the mechanism of secondary excitation, which activizes past experience previously impressed on the cortex. The connection between stimulus and reaction is then effected without preliminary elaboration, and the new linkage occurs, as it were, instantaneously, the secondary excitation moving from stimulus to reaction in one or more intervening stages which involve the cortical impressions of past experience [19: 57].

In the light of this, it becomes possible to explain how a given stimulus evokes a fresh reaction which is psychologically equivalent to a creative act of thinking. 'The previous experience, reflected in the brain in the form of an old association, intervenes, as it were, between the stimulus and the reaction, yet at the same time links the stimulus with a reaction with which it has never previously been connected' [17: 59].

Thus research directed to a physiological analysis of creative acts of thinking confirms the conclusion reached by Sechenov many years ago on the basis of choice in the process of inference.

In whatever relationship the conclusion stands to the premisses, it is impossible to discover any content in it which was not contained either in the given premises or in the elements of some corresponding old experience. . . . What is really new in such cases is either that objects are joined which have never been joined before, or that new sides of them have been joined which have only been discovered in the last analysis, or which have previously simply escaped attention [58: 173–4].

The concepts of 'previous experience' and 'old associations', which make possible a materialist explanation of the processes of thinking and understanding, are becoming key concepts in physiological research. Pavlov's views are also relevant to a consideration of levels of thinking and understanding in man. 'Previous experience' means connections or systems of connections impressed upon the brain as a result of earlier social activity. There can obviously be differences in the number and variety of connections between new and old experience, and also in the range of previous experience. The very first association emerging between separate elements of new and old experience marks the 'birth of a thought'. This connection is, from the outset, 'knowledge of definite relationships existing in the external world'; but the latter may be chance, superficial, external, and may not reflect any frequently recurring material features. In the course of further activity, connections between new and old associations 'grow and increase', and their reflection becomes more full and exact. Not only do isolated associations appear, but also 'a chain of associations, linking one association with another'.[1] Then 'it is said that thinking becomes more profound, more extensive'.

In other words, from a physiological point of view, levels of understanding and thinking are distinguished by the number and variety of the cortical connections, or systems of connections, which develop in the brain and which activize increasing numbers of nerve-cells, reviving old 'traces' or creating new centres of excitation. These propositions provide a scientific foundation for the analysis of thinking and understanding. But the chief problem remains, that is *verbal* thinking, a specifically human characteristic based on the second signal system.

II

Pavlov's teaching on the interaction of the second signal system with the first lays the scientific foundation for a Marxist understanding of the direct connection between language and the thought pro-

[1] *Selected Works*, 586.

cesses, and makes possible an elucidation of the physiological function and role of language in thinking.

Language, which arises and develops in society, constitutes a new system of stimuli unknown in the animal world. A word, as an element of speech, constitutes a 'signal of signals' when it ceases to be merely an aural stimulus and acquires meaning. This occurs as a result of man's generalized and mediated reflection of reality, a process beginning with the action of external stimuli on the analyser receptors. The intimate connection between word and perceptual stimulus is of central importance. It illustrates that the second signal system grows out of the first, is based upon it, and interacts with it.

The key importance of the second signal system is that it strengthens man's conceptual advances. Although a word rests ultimately on direct sensations and perceptions, it acquires properties as a stimulus which cannot be found in the sensory stimuli of the first signal system; this is because of the word's 'generalization and abstraction' from reality, to use Pavlov's description.

> For man, the word is just as real a conditioned stimulus as any other that he has in common with the animals, but at the same time the comprehensiveness of words is such that they cannot be compared either quantitatively or qualitatively with the conditioned stimuli of animals. As a result of an adult man's previous life experience, words are connected with all external and internal stimuli that reach the cerebral hemispheres; words signalize and stand for all these, and can therefore evoke all the actions and reactions in the organism that the stimuli themselves produce.[1]

Here Pavlov, as a consistent determinist, seeks the origin of the particular functioning of the second signal system in the character of the internal and external influences which act upon the higher nervous system—in this case, in the characteristics of words as stimuli. He sees the comprehensiveness of words as the peculiarity of the second signal system.

Since words can reactivize so many of the most varied connections established during previous experience, they 'cannot be compared either quantitatively or qualitatively with the conditioned stimuli of animals'; such a comparison is also impossible because a word comprehends not only individual experience but also the conceptual advances of all mankind. This property provides the basis for a materialist explanation of the development of thought. Pavlov, speaking of the comprehensiveness of words, has good reason to stress the dependence of this quality on the 'adult man's previous life-experience'.

[1] Pavlov-Anrep, 407.

Psychological studies of children's speech have shown that the concept for which a word stands grows in range and content as the child's experience increases. Initially, a child's words are word-names which denote, or serve as, mere impressions of concrete objects. Such word-names have as their physiological basis a neural connection between the centres of excitation corresponding to perception of an object and its verbal designation. As is well known, the transition from word-names to the more abstract word-concepts is prepared for by increasing the number of times the child 'meets' the given object in different forms; as a result the given aural complex is related to the external world on the basis of more complicated connections. The word then acquires a greater degree of generalization, its meaning becomes conceptualized.

During the emergence of speech 'it became possible to abstract from reality, complementing sensation with words. This led further to generalizations, in which a word takes the place of a mass of sensations, and, finally, to the formation of general concepts—matter, time, space, etc.' [49: 238].

The broader, the more abstract, a concept, the greater the experience needed for its formation. On the basis of generalizations of direct experience arise the data of mediated experience, a kind of 'generalization of generalizations'; but, no matter how far the meaning of *concept* is extended, beneath this broadening comprehensiveness of words lies a quantitative increase of neural connections, in whole systems and in the most varied combinations. The resulting new quality in human thinking is usually called *conceptual thinking*.

Sechenov has some interesting comments on this question, for, though he did not postulate a second signal system, his approach is strictly materialist. He points out that, although a child and a parrot produce speech sounds in the same way, the child's speech shows intelligence in contrast to the parrot's mechanical conversations. This property of intelligence 'depends principally on the association of aural impressions with visual-tactile ones; and the richer, the more varied, the forms of this association, the more pronounced it becomes'. Here Sechenov anticipates Pavlov's view of the comprehensiveness of words as stimuli, and directly connects the intelligence of human speech with an increased number of associations joining aural impressions (words) with other sensations. He concludes, 'All knowledge of present objects is really nothing but an infinitely vast conception of each of them, i.e. the sum of all possible sensations evoked in us by these objects in all conceivable circumstances' [57: 83].

It is well known in psychology and education that the level of understanding depends upon the varying 'capacity' of words. This implies that an identical word-sign has different meanings for different people, a divergence which appears most clearly when children learn formal rules and definitions. If children use each word in the definition, but only as a sign without meaning or with a meaning different from the true one, we say that the definition has been learned mechanically, without understanding the sense, that is, without any support from previous experience. This may occur because such experience is lacking; or it may occur because the projection in the cortex of the stimulus of the new concept has not become linked with the corresponding 'traces' of previous associations. The opposite case is the fully mastered concept secured by a word. This must obviously be preceded both by the formation of temporary connections for the main features of the object, and of interconnections with other concepts. One may then speak of deep understanding and exhaustive knowledge of the object.

Between these two extremes there are all possible shades of understanding, each distinguished, it must be supposed, by numerous connections secured in the brain as a result of meeting with the given phenomenon in previous experience. Each 'meeting' (the essential condition of which is an active state of the cortex) not only strengthens the 'traces' from previous 'meetings', but also may lead to further differentiation of the distinguishing elements of the concept. This involves isolation of the essential and most frequently recurring signs from the secondary ones (those not always found in the particular kind of object); then follows their generalization and so on.

It follows that words, as stimuli of the second signal system, are not constant in their effect on the higher part of the central nervous system. The influence of a word increases as it comes to comprise the accumulation of past experience. This comprehensiveness of words is based on the universal principle of temporary connections, though the action of a word acquires qualities which are in no way comparable to the conditioned stimuli of animals. On the other hand, 'levels of understanding' which, as a human form of thought, are inseparably connected with speech, depend in the second signal system on the quantity and quality of temporary connections; i.e. on the same principle that obtains in the first signal system. This is why Pavlov could say that the development of thinking has followed a single biological line, from elementary 'animal thinking' to verbal human thinking.

III

The 'comprehensiveness' of words does not, however, exhaust the characteristics of the second signal system. The work of Pavlov and his pupils, in particular of Ivanov-Smolensky, points to another feature—the specific character of the coupling of neural connections.

Owing to abstraction, that specific property of words which has brought about greater generalization, we infer our relation to reality in the general forms of time, space and causality. We make direct use of these generalizations, which are ready to hand, in orienting ourselves in the surrounding world, and rarely analyse the facts on which the general concept is constructed [51: 320].

Pavlov's remark that we make direct use of concepts 'ready to hand', is not a chance one; this is clear when we recall his statement that understanding is the use of old associations. This was based on experiments with anthropoid apes, but Pavlov considered that it was only applicable to man with his capacity for verbal thinking. Accordingly, another feature of the second signal system seems to be the possibility of using our previous experience at once, without a retracing of paths, provided that this experience has been given verbal expression.

The work of Ivanov-Smolensky and his collaborators [1] on the second signal system in children has confirmed Pavlov's thesis experimentally. Running through this work like a red thread is the idea of the special action of words-as-stimuli, which Ivanov-Smolensky calls the 'sudden coupling of connections'. In 1936, he wrote of the action of the second signal system that 'the connection between stimulus and reaction occurs without preliminary elaboration; the new coupling seems to take place suddenly'. He once more stressed this feature in an article summarizing years of research. In the formation of more or less complicated dynamic stereotypes in the first or second signal systems it was shown that

owing to the strength of elective irradiation of excitatory and inhibitory processes in the neural paths previously linked during ontogenesis, it is possible to obtain, without previous elaboration *as if by a sudden coupling*, a complete and exact reflection of this stereotype, its complete and exact transference to the other system (my italics—D.B.).

Again, referring to the dynamic transfer of a new verbal connection, Ivanov-Smolensky notes that there arises in the first signal system 'straight away, without preliminary elaboration as if by a sudden

[1] O. P. Kapustnik, L. I. Kotliarevsky, V. K. Faddeeva, G. D. Narodnitskaya and others.

coupling, a new connection between the direct stimulus and the direct reaction, as if reflecting the verbal connection or association formed with the aid of instruction' [20: 575].

Here we have a picture of the physiological effect on the central nervous system of a word as a stimulus.

Postponing discussion of elective irradiation, we may now consider what happens when the paths between a word and the corresponding reactions become linked during ontogenesis (i.e. when a word is understood). The key is to be found in the term 'suddenly'—that is, at one stroke previous experience is included *in* the activity and excluded *from* it according to the 'extent' of the connections which have been formed in the brain and which furnish the meaning of the word.

This peculiarity of the word as a stimulus, the fact that it does not require disclosure of all the connections built up during the course of life, may be compared with the 'insight' referred to by Pavlov. But this 'insight' in man, since it is connected with verbal thinking, has a fundamentally different character to that in animals. When we use language, 'insight' accompanies every perception or expression of a word (assuming, of course, that we understand its meaning) so that we make no effort to include our previous connections. This is what we have in mind when we refer to the 'automatization' of speech. Here it must be recalled that a word, as an agent which links connections, begins to act as soon as experience has endowed it with meaning; but its sphere of action, the extent of the field it includes or excludes, depends entirely on the extent of this experience. A word which lacks a 'biography' is unable to carry out the function of coupling connections and must be regarded essentially as a simple aural stimulus. This shows clearly that the 'sudden' action of a word is caused by its other property, that of concentrating connections.

Pavlov also points to another functional property of words, their constancy. 'Human speech, once man has learned it, lasts. This means that conditioned reflexes are not the same as our words; here is a different process' [49: 240]. Pavlov did not develop this idea, but it may be supposed that he had in mind a property opposite to the extinction of conditioned reflexes, a sort of 'inextinguishability' of words without which the process of generalization would be impossible.

This constancy of the functioning of temporary connections which are activized by a word does not contradict the fact of their quantitative growth, since Pavlov relates this constancy to a defined level of speech and does not touch upon the question of its development. But it may be supposed that, while speech is becoming established, the unity of constancy and development is ensured by the dual aspect of words: their constancy of form and their changing meaning in relation to the individual's experience.

IV

According to Pavlov, the second signal system is constantly subordinating or damping down the first signal system, and exercises a powerful regulating influence upon it; in the normal man, the second signal system is the supreme regulator of conduct. This influence can be discerned in the fact that second signal system stimuli include or exclude a given system of temporary connections established in previous experience, so making it possible 'to distinguish that which corresponds to reality from that which does not'; and the second signal system also regulates the sequence in which the 'chain of traces' of the first signal system is linked.

Pavlov reached his conclusion on the regulating role of the second signal system on the basis of observations of pathological cases. Reporting on a case of progressive paralysis he noted that the patient's condition was

exactly the same as that of someone in the first phase of sleep or hypnosis, either going to sleep or waking up. The constant negative induction from the second signal system becomes weaker, so that the traces of the first signal system attain the strength of direct impressions. The patient has combinations of impressions that have never existed in reality because the activity of the second signal system, which orders his general concepts of time, space, causality, etc., and on the basis of these regulates the chain of traces of the first signal system, is lacking. These traces are reactivized on the basis of their relative strength, freshness, etc. That is why the linking and connections may take place in direct opposition to the laws of reality [51: 321].

The weakening of the second signal system means a lack of regulation of the linking of traces; it is, then, clear, according to Pavlov, that when the brain is in a sound state the regulation of traces is a normal function of the nervous system. Thus the second signal system regulates associative traces not only by activizing or inhibiting them, but also by ordering and systematizing them on the basis of general concepts.

To designate the regulating activity of the second signal system, brought to light during his work with children, Ivanov-Smolensky advanced the concept of *elective irradiation*. Many children, when the word 'bell' was spoken or shown to them in writing, responded with the same conditioned reaction as had been produced earlier to the sound of a bell; but the reaction was inhibited to any other words, such as 'window'. Ivanov-Smolensky points out that three specific stimuli are selectively generalized, that is the sound of the bell and the spoken or written word 'bell'

and the points corresponding to these are in different regions of the cerebral cortex. We called this phenomenon *elective generalization* or *elective irradiation*. The experiments showed that the dynamic irradiation of inhibitory processes may bear an elective character by extinguishing one of the selectively generalized stimuli [19: 52].

The term elective generalization covers, therefore, the familiar fact that a child understands a word, irrespective of whether it is spoken or written, and that a word so understood 'stands for' the corresponding direct stimulus (to use Pavlov's words). This may be explained physiologically by the supposition that stable temporary connections have been formed between the three different points of the cortex in the child's past experience. Ivanov-Smolensky writes elsewhere of the formation of such a system of connections: 'A connection, or association, had been acquired and linked in previous life-experience in every one of our subjects' [20: 574].

In his later work (1951) Ivanov-Smolensky draws an analogy between elective irradiation and the psychological concept of 'semantic connection'. But this material shows that the problem posed by Pavlov, the regulation of traces of previous stimulations on the basis of general concepts, is not solved by enunciating the principle of elective irradiation; it is only named. The main question remains unsolved, namely, why and in what way do new physiological foundations for the linking of semantic connections appear? Proof that there is irradiation of nervous processes from the second signal system to the first on the basis of past experience does not constitute an explanation of the actual moment of electivity; though it provides experimental evidence of the general Pavlovian principle that the second signal system regulates the linking of traces in the first.

The experiments referred to show the regulating role of concepts of concrete objects such as 'bell' and 'red light'; or of words which denote a simple physical action, such as the word 'squeeze' in the verbal instruction 'squeeze the bulb for a red light'. Other investigations of verbal associations, conducted by Krasnogorsky, show the influence on the first signal system of more general generic concepts connected with direct stimuli through corresponding specific concepts.[1]

[1] Research of A. Fedorov.

In one experiment, the names of birds were taken as object concepts: dove, turkey, hawk, owl, hen, swallow. A particular conditioned reaction was connected to each of these when presented separately, whereas the names of other birds did not evoke this reaction. It was then found that the conditioned reaction was also evoked 'on the spot' by the word 'bird'. Krasnogorsky notes: 'This shows clearly that there are in the speech system integrating symbols of a higher order, in this case of the second order, which connect the group of differentiated primary symbols (of the first order) and have a direct conditioned-reflex connection with each of them.'

In other words, here was a case of the logical subordination of specific concepts to more inclusive generic ones not directly connected with real stimuli. Thus the child's conditioned-reflex activity is regulated and directed selectively by a general concept. This shows that Pavlov's view about symbols of the second order was correct; and, clearly, a similar regulating role may be discovered with reference to the more abstract concepts of space, time and causality. Krasnogorsky generalizes these facts when he writes: 'Integrating symbols may be connected in the most varied chains, and this raises the cortical chain-processes to an exceptionally high level, providing a physiological basis for the most complex verbal functions of the brain' [34: 144–5].

There are, therefore, numerous experimental facts testifying to the presence of a special principle of selectivity in the second signal system, whereby connections formed in past experience are linked in a particular order and sequence. This order of formation of temporary connections differs from the usual order of formation of conditioned reflexes in animals (simultaneity of stimuli, freshness of traces, etc.). Thanks to this peculiarity, man is able, in any situation, to use not only his personal experience but also the experience of all mankind comprised in language. Physiological data show that semantic connections formed in the second signal system are based on corresponding connections fixed in the first signal system. But the physiological significance of electivity still remains, to a considerable extent, obscure.

These are some of the special characteristics of the second signal system in relation to which we have definite physiological data. They do not by any means provide an exhaustive description. Further investigations will probably reveal a whole series of new features which will permit of a more profound understanding of the full complexity of the human psyche.

To sum up, it must be stressed that a scientific explanation of the process of understanding is possible only on the firm foundation of Pavlov's theory of higher nervous activity. This raises a corner of the veil covering the laws of man's thought processes, and opens the way to a genuine understanding of the whole complex and ordered work of the human brain in its objective reflection of reality. The scientific material on the physiology of higher nervous activity given above throws light on certain features of the process of understanding which could in no other way become the property of scientific psychological research. Of outstanding importance to the psychology of understanding are all the characteristics of the second signal system: the comprehensiveness of words, sudden coupling, the regulation of traces, selectivity. All these data describe the formation of temporary connections at one level or another, and it is on this very characteristic that the process of learning depends.

INVOLUNTARY AND VOLUNTARY ATTENTION [1]

BY

E. A. MILERIAN

THIS PAPER OPENS with a critical examination of definitions of attention advanced by various Soviet psychologists. Some treat attention as a special psychic process, others as an aspect of all psychic processes; it is regarded by some as a peculiarity of consciousness, by others as a property of psychic activity. Many definitions are merely descriptive or rely on analogy, and fail to reveal the specific characteristics of attention as a psychic phenomenon. The physiological mechanisms underlying attention are then outlined in an attempt to clarify theoretical treatment of this problem; reference being made to the work of Pavlov, Ukhtomsky and Bekhterev. Their findings give grounds for defining attention as a form of organization of psychic activity, manifested particularly in the orienting reflexes. The properties of attention are then discussed in the light of this definition, the essential constituents emerging as concentration, 'set' [2] and relative stability (steadiness). Attention, then, is *that form of psychic activity in animals and man which manifests concentration, 'set' and relative stability*. This definition is only provisional, but is comprehensive insofar as it covers the essential properties peculiar to the given phenomenon; the exclusion of any one of these would lead to the disappearance of what is known as attention. By contrast, all the other properties attributed to attention are derivative; e.g. switching of attention is a change of its direction and therefore a derivative of 'set'; distribution of attention appears as a derivative of concentration since it is included in simultaneous concentration on two or more objects; fluctuations of attention are also closely connected with relative stability, since particular fluctuations are changes in the degree of steadiness. Finally investigations into the 'span of attention' have shown that 'span' cannot be considered as a fundamental property of attention. These investigations are rather concerned with perception; what is called 'span of attention' is nothing but the qualitative aspect

[1] *Sovetskaya Pedagogika*, No. 2, 1954, pp. 55–67 (translated by J. and M. Ellis).
[2] *Napravlennost.*

of the content of short-duration perception. The final section of the paper, given below, is concerned with involuntary and voluntary attention.]

I

Contemporary psychology recognizes two forms of attention, involuntary and voluntary; some psychologists also postulate the existence of post-voluntary attention. But there is as yet no scientific foundation for this classification, since the subject has not yet been treated in the light of the physiology of higher nervous activity. If attention is considered as a form of organization of the reflectory activity of an organism, and study is based on Pavlov's findings about the phylogenetic stages of development of this activity, it is possible to construct an adequate foundation for the classification of forms of attention.

Defining the fundamental levels, or stages, in the development of higher nervous activity, Pavlov wrote:

> In the higher animals, up to and including man, the first stage of the complex relations of the organism with the external environment is represented by the sub-cortex adjacent to the cerebral hemispheres, with its more complex unconditioned reflexes. . . . These reflexes are evoked by relatively few external agents which are unconditioned, i.e. which operate from birth. Hence the limited orientation to the external environment.[1]

Thus Pavlov connects the first stage of complex relations of the organism with the environment with the function of the mechanism in the subcortical centres. If we suppose that reflectory activity, at this first stage, has its own special form of organization, it is possible to regard this as the original, most primitive, form of attention. This may be termed *unconditioned-reflex involuntary attention*.

This, the most elementary form of organization of the reflectory activity of living beings, is expressed in certain kinds of unconditioned reflexes which Pavlov called orienting-investigatory reflexes. These have a vital significance for the organism. Every sufficiently strong stimulus, acting upon an animal, initially evokes a reflex state of the corresponding receptors, and this process gives rise to an adaptation allowing for the most effective perception. In other words, the influence of each new stimulus evokes an adaptive organization of the receptor apparatus of the organism.

The orienting reflexes represent a peculiar form of organization of

[1] Pavlov-Gantt ii, 113; *Selected Works*, 536.

reflectory activity, one which arises on the basis of activization of those unconditioned connections which are brought under the influence of stimuli from the environment. According to Pavlov, the principal characteristics of this form of organization are corresponding movements of the receptors in the direction of the action of the stimulus: '. . . the eyelids, eyes, ears and nostrils of the animal . . . are turned and oriented this way or that'. That property of attention which is called 'set' is expressed in these necessary components of the orienting reflex. Another property of attention, relative steadiness, is expressed in the fact that an animal 'adopts a definite posture' for a certain time. Concentration also appears in the disposal 'of the corresponding perceptive surfaces in such a way as to allow for the best impression of the external stimulation'; Pavlov emphasizes that this process arises naturally as a result of the activity of one or another part of the central nervous system.[1] Thus all the fundamental properties of attention appear distinctly, in their most elementary form, in the shape of orienting reflexes.

Experiments involving the removal of the cortex of the cerebral hemispheres in animals have shown that the physiological mechanisms of these reflexes are localized in the subcortical centres. This indicates that these mechanisms represent phylogenetically early forms of organization of the reflectory activity of living organisms. There are grounds for supposing that the predecessor of the orienting reflex is a still more elementary form of organization of psychic activity, one which Pavlov called 'reflex natural awareness'. Characterizing the role of this latter reflex in the life activity of human beings, Pavlov pointed out its continuous connection with the orienting reflex. This more primitive form of organization of psychic activity is expressed in the inhibition of the whole organism that takes place every time there is a sufficiently intensive fluctuation of the environment; one of the proofs of the phylogenetically earlier origin of 'reflex natural awareness' is its presence in lower animals. In sum, unconditioned-reflex involuntary attention, as a form of organization of the reflectory activity of the organism based on the functioning of the subcortical mechanisms, is expressed in such interconnected forms of unconditioned reflexes as the reflex of natural awareness and the orienting reflex.

The orienting reflex plays a specific role in the life activity of the organism; it is one of the necessary conditions for the formation of new connections. Pavlov's researches showed that the cortex exercises an essential regulatory influence on the orienting reflexes, inhibiting reflexes to stimuli which have no biological significance for the organism.

[1] Pavlov-Gantt i, 134.

Therefore, though the physiological mechanisms of the orienting reflex are localized in the subcortical centres, its normal functioning depends on the interaction of the cortex and sub-cortex. Without the intervention of the cortex, the orienting reflex loses its quality of plasticity or variability, and becomes a permanent stereotyped response to all sufficiently powerful stimulations, irrespective of their significance for the organism.

II

Together with the orienting reflex there exist other, more developed, forms of organization of psychic activity. These may best be defined after consideration of the succeeding, higher level, that of higher nervous activity.

The second stage consists in the cerebral hemispheres, excluding the frontal lobes. Here, with the help of the conditioned connection, or association, arises a new principle of activity: the signalling of a limited number of unconditioned, external agents by a countless mass of other agents, which are, at the same time, constantly analysed and synthesized, so making possible very extensive orientation. This constitutes the sole signalling system of the animal organism and the first signalling system in man.[1]

A new principle of nervous activity arises on the level of the first signalling system. At this level reflection is realized on the basis of conditioned connections, giving rise to a new, more developed, form of reflectory activity. This implies a more developed organization of psychic activity by comparison with unconditioned-reflex involuntary attention, namely *conditioned-reflex involuntary attention*. This is based on the functioning of the cortical mechanisms of the first signal system, and is most markedly shown in what are called conditioned orienting reactions. These, which are connected with orienting reflexes of unconditioned origin, arise in the process of formation of conditioned reflexes, and have been studied in detail by Ivanov-Smolensky.

The essential aspect of conditioned orienting reactions is revealed when, after an indifferent stimulus has been repeatedly associated with the presentation of food, an animal first reacts to the conditioned stimulus, and then to the place where the food has been found; that is, the animal changes the 'setting' of its analysers in relation first to one and then to another stimulus in a definite sequence determined by the functioning of conditioned connections. This represents a new, peculiar form of reflection of objective reality in response to stimuli

[1] Pavlov-Gantt ii, 113; *Selected Works*, 536-7.

of the external world; the reflectory activity of the organism is immediately re-formed and organized according to the conditioned signal. This form of organization completely determines the sequence and relation of the influences of the environment; it is here that the external stereotype sets its stamp upon the organization of reflectory activity.

When the signalling principle is thus realized in the organization of reflectory activity, the organism can, in good time, according to a definite signal, turn its attention to this or that stimulus of essential importance for itself. Thus the presence of a smell serves as a signal for a dog to search; here the smell acts as a permissive stimulus which activizes, directs and organizes the behaviour of the animal.

Consideration of the structure of reflectory activity in the formation of conditioned connections shows the unbreakable connection of unconditioned-reflex and conditioned-reflex attention. This is expressed in the fact that each new stimulus gives rise to a reaction in the form of an unconditioned orienting reflex. But if the action of the stimulus is reinforced, the formation of a connection between the operative stimuli brings into being a new, more developed, form of reflection of objective reality in the shape of a conditioned orienting reflex.

This may be illustrated by quoting Ivanov-Smolensky's description of the formation of a given reflex in man.

A bell was rung. An orienting-visual reinforcement was associated with the third to fifth seconds of its ringing. This took the form of the flashing of a lamp and the slipping of a tachistoscopic slide across the opening of the apparatus. After several repetitions of this combined stimulation, the head turning in the direction of the source of light . . . began to appear sooner than the flash, in response to the sounding of the bell. That is, a conditioned orienting reflex was formed [16: 39].

Ivanov-Smolensky's special investigations of conditioned orienting reflexes discovered the formation of a more developed organization of psychic activity, which arises on the basis of simpler forms: conditioned-reflex involuntary attention.

III

Describing the third and highest stage of higher nervous activity, Pavlov wrote:

In man there is added . . . a second system of signals, signalizing the first; that is, speech, . . . Thus a new principle of nervous activity is introduced, the abstraction and generalization of the innumerable signals of the preceding system, and, together with this, analysis and synthesis of these new generalized signals; on this depends man's infinite capacity for orientation in the surrounding world, and, too, his highest form of adaptation—that is, science, both in the empirical form common to all mankind and in its specialized form.[1]

The organization of higher nervous activity at this level has a qualitatively new character, its principal feature being the systematic, expedient, word-directed, voluntary action of man in the process of reflection of objective reality. It is at this stage when words, as the signal of signals, become an organizing agent of human psychic activity, that *voluntary attention* arises. The part played by speech in voluntary attention may be considered in the light of the dialectical materialist principle of the unity of language and consciousness. Marx and Engels wrote: 'Language is as old as consciousness, language is practical consciousness, as it exists for other men, and for that reason is really beginning to exist for me personally as well.'[2] This thesis was developed by Stalin when he showed that language is a tool of communication between people and at the same time a means of struggle and development of society. Language is connected both with man's productive activity and with every other human activity. Man has no thoughts free from 'the natural material' of language; thoughts always come into being on the basis of linguistic terms and phrases.[3] Pavlov's theory of the two signal systems is in harmony with these Marxist propositions. Voluntary attention, as a specifically human form of organization of reflectory activity, is indissolubly connected with the functioning of the second signal system in its interaction with the first.

Man, when regulating and controlling the exchange of objects between himself and nature in the labour process, 'not only effects a change of form in the material on which he works, but . . . also realizes a purpose of his own that gives a law to his modus operandi, and to which he must subordinate his will'.[4]

Man's actions in labour are always subordinated to the aim of labour which he recognizes and which is, consequently, reflected in words. It is the presence of a conscious aim that gives human activity a systematic and voluntary character. In the labour process man confronts the reality surrounding him as an organizing force of nature,

[1] Pavlov-Gantt ii, 113–14; *Selected Works*, 537.
[2] *The German Ideology*, ed. R. Pascal (London, 1940), 19.
[3] *Marxism and Linguistics* (London, 1950), 29.
[4] K. Marx, *Capital*, ed. F. Engels (1889) (London, 1945 ed.), 157.

acts upon nature and changes it in accordance with his aims. It is precisely such activity that gives rise to voluntary attention. Speech, called into life by man's need to communicate in the labour process, also produces a new specifically human form of organization of reflectory activity—voluntary attention.

Attention, as a reflectory activity of the brain, appears in close connection with man's needs and with the labour which is directed to their satisfaction. Voluntary attention arises at that stage of human evolution when man begins to distinguish the objects of the external world, when it is necessary to the satisfaction of his needs to give them names, to classify and master them. The selective activity of attention has therefore, as its foundation, the conditioned connections formed as a result of the influence both of objects and of words, those new 'signals of signals'. At this higher level of reflectory activity, when men begin to distinguish external objects by using words and abstract thought to generalize, to classify, and so on, psychic activity can arise, in the absence of a given object, with the help of the word which signals it. Voluntary attention is conditioned in the same way.

Voluntary attention, like all other voluntary actions, is determined. This proposition was first advanced by Sechenov and was experimentally upheld by the work of Pavlov and his school. Studying the physiological mechanism of voluntary actions, Pavlov concluded that 'every *mechanism of movement of the will* is a *conditioned associated process* subordinated to all the laws of higher nervous activity described'. Voluntary actions are causally conditioned; their apparent 'spontaneity' is the outcome of complex determining influences both from the immediate and the more remote aims of life. In his analysis of man's voluntary actions Pavlov showed that this complex conditioning was the essence of willed activity, and that there is no absolute difference between voluntary and involuntary behaviour.

A voluntary action has its first foundation in a first signal system conditioned reflex. With the rise of the second signal system, when words begin to act as conditioned stimuli involving abstraction and generalization, there is no limit to the development of voluntary activity; the conditions are created for the rise of voluntary attention, a qualitatively new form of organization of reflectory activity. Voluntary attention always has a mediated character; it is indissolubly connected with the generalized, mediated reflection of objective reality, expressed in the form of words. This feature greatly extends the influence of voluntary attention on the formation and functioning of temporary connections.

This organizing and regulating influence of words is particularly clearly indicated in the investigations, directed by Ivanov-Smolensky, which showed that by using speech as reinforcement it is possible to form complex temporary connections. The data obtained concerning the stages of development of the second signal system in its interaction with the first illuminate the problem of the stages of development of attention during ontogenesis, the transition from one form to another. They also clear up the problem of so-called post-voluntary attention, indicating that this may be considered to be one of the varieties of voluntary attention which arises in the following circumstances: when the foci of optimal excitability are connected with a steady dynamic stereotype, and their functioning is uninterruptedly strengthened by the influences of the environment and supports the dynamic stereotype, new conditioned connections are formed on the basis of this stereotype; as a result a particularly steady form of attention arises which requires no effort of will for its maintenance, and which leads to more productive and highly developed forms of activity.

Other problems concerning attention may be illuminated in the same way. In particular, there is the pressing problem of the development of attention in schoolchildren, and of its maintenance during teaching.

HIGHER NERVOUS ACTIVITY AND THE PROBLEM OF PERCEPTION [1]

BY

E. N. SOKOLOV

T HE MOST IMPORTANT TASK in the study of perception is to supersede the subjective method which is restricted to a description of observed phenomena. Pavlov's theory makes possible a materialist analysis of the process of perception as a reflectory activity of the brain.

Perception of a stimulus, being a condition of adequate reaction by the organism, is itself a reflex process. In this process, the orienting reflex is of primary significance; it participates in regulating the receptor system and ensures optimal conditions for perceiving the external stimulus.

The inhibitory influence of the orienting reflex on conditioned reflexes arising under the action of outside stimuli (external, inductive inhibition) has been studied in detail. But little attention had been paid to the role of the orienting reflex in the perception of stimuli. The investigation here described was concerned with the part played by the orienting reflex in the perception of indifferent (non-signal) and conditioned (signal) stimuli affecting the human organism.

Method

Experiments were conducted with normal adults, aged from 20 to 40 years. A record was kept of a number of components of the orienting reaction. Besides the general organic, vascular and skin-galvanic [2] reactions, we studied physiological changes arising in the optical analysing system such as eye movements, changes in electrical activity of the occipital region of the cerebral cortex, and fluctuations in the light sensitivity level. When studying the role of the orienting reaction

[1] Communication to the Fourteenth International Congress of Psychology, 1954; published in *Voprosy Psikhologii*, No. 1, 1955, pp. 58–66 (translated in the U.S.S.R.).

[2] *Kozhno-galvanicheski*.

in a conditioned motor reflex, a record was made of the electrical changes in the muscles of the hand. The light sensitivity level of the eye was recorded automatically on an adaptograph, using a method of continuous registration of the threshold devised in our laboratory.

The photofilter which changes the brightness of the test-field was operated by the subject; its movements were registered electrically, on a self-recording voltmeter, in the form of an adaptogram reflecting fluctuations of the threshold. The skin-galvanic reflex was registered as fluctuations in the resistance of the skin of palm and head to the direct current of the self-recording electronic potentiometer, after Féré. A self-recording oscillograph was used for registering the skin-galvanic reflex according to Tarkhanov's method, together with an electroencephalogram of the occipital region, and electrograms of the eye movements, and of the finger flexor muscles. Changes in the blood pressure in the vessels of the fingers and the brain were recorded by means of a special apparatus, namely a photo-plethysmograph.

Auditory, visual, tactile, thermal, proprioceptive and pain stimuli of varying intensity, duration and quality were made use of in the experiments. These stimuli were strictly apportioned, and were produced by means of a low frequency generator and monochromator.

Results and Discussion of the Experiments

(a) *The role of the orienting reflex in the perception of indifferent (non-signal) stimuli*

An orienting reflex, arising as a result of a novel stimulus, affects the entire organism. Thus a sound stimulus causes not only functional changes in the auditory analysing system, but also reflex changes in the condition of other analysing systems, specifically in the optical system. It influences the direction of the visual axis and the frequency and amplitude of the electrical activity of the occipital region, affects the threshold for light sensitivity, and also causes general organic reactions: i.e. it alters the functional condition of the skin, changes the condition of the vascular system and inhibits the general motor activity of the organism.

There are two forms of the orienting reflex: (1) changes which swiftly give place to a return to the initial level (the phasic orienting reflex), and (2) a lasting increase of excitability (the tonic orienting reflex).

The reactions mentioned above, arising in response to indifferent stimuli, can become extinguished while the stimuli are being presented, and this is usually regarded as proof of their orienting nature. But this criterion is inadequate, since other special reflexes, such as food reflexes, can also be extinguished. The essential proof of the orienting nature of these reactions is the fact that they arise in response to every change in the environment: whether the stimulus is switched on or off, increased or decreased, or qualitatively changed.

Our experiments have shown that eye movements, changes in the electrical activity of the brain, changes in sensitivity to light, vascular and skin-galvanic reactions may be components of the orienting reaction arising in response to every change in the presented stimulus. The biological significance of such a complex orienting reaction, affecting the whole organism, consists in the increased reactivity of the analysing system necessary for better perception of the stimulus. This is obvious as regards increased sensitivity to light and the movement of the eye. But the vascular reaction and the related skin-galvanic reaction also participate in ensuring optimum conditions for stimulus perception: a simultaneous contraction of the peripheral vessels and dilation of the brain vessels takes place, so creating more favourable conditions for the work of the cortical cells. The skin-galvanic reaction arises in the same way: when a new stimulus acts on the organism, the resistance of the skin of the palm falls, while the resistance of the skin of the head rises. Opposite signs characterize the skin potentials of the palm and the head.

During the presentation of an indifferent stimulus the orienting reflex is extinguished, both in its afferent and efferent activity.

Irradiation of inhibition, caused by the use of an indifferent agent, leads to afferent inhibition of the orienting reflex in the case of a whole group of stimuli. The special character of the inhibition which spreads during the extinction of the orienting reflex finds its expression in the skin analysing system, and is a process exactly similar to the inhibition of conditioned reflexes. Thus the extinction of the skin-galvanic component of the orienting reflex, shown by changes in the resistance of the skin produced by tactile stimulation of the centre of the hand, causes inhibition of all reactions of the surface of the hand. But the inhibition developed in one part of the skin analysing system spreads only partly to adjacent sections. Therefore the effect of tactile irritation of the forearm and the shoulder is the greater, the farther the tested spot is from the place where the orienting reaction was extinguished.

Similar phenomena develop in the auditory analysing system: the extinction of the orienting reaction to one frequency often leads to the extinction of these reactions to a whole band of frequencies. The effect of the reaction is the greater, the more difference there is between the new frequency and the frequency used in extinguishing the orienting reaction.

Simultaneously with the extinction of orienting reactions to one group of stimuli, induction and restoration of orienting reactions occur to stimuli other than those previously applied. Thus after the application of uniform tactile stimuli, the reaction to a sound stimulus, previously extinguished, is restored; again, after the application of uniform sound stimuli, extinguished reactions to tactile stimulation are restored. Owing to the systematic extinction of reactions to the stimuli used, positive induction of orienting reactions takes place to stimuli which have not yet been applied; the effect of this is to ensure maximum efficiency of reaction to a new stimulus. Owing to irradiation of excitation, a new stimulus causing a strong orienting reflex can, after one or two repetitions, restore the orienting reactions extinguished by the repeated use of the stimulus previously applied. This restoration of extinguished orienting reactions after an interval is a particular case of the dynamic interrelation of the processes of excitation and inhibition manifested when the orienting reactions are functioning.

The efferent part of the orienting reflex is inhibited during the continued application of an indifferent stimulus. This inhibition takes the form of a non-simultaneous extinction of separate components of the orienting reaction; the disappearance of several components does not, therefore, imply its full inhibition.

The inhibition of orienting reactions to stimuli which affect a particular analysing system causes a decrease in its reactivity to these stimuli. Thus, after repeated short exposures of a dark-adapted eye in conditions where the orienting reaction is extinguished, a peculiar adaptation to exposure arises, so that the light which previously caused a reduction in the sensitivity of the eye no longer influences it. The restoration of orienting reactions to certain stimuli is accompanied by an increase in the reactivity of the analysing system to these stimuli. Thus when the eye no longer reacts to exposure to light, a sudden reduction in the intensity of the exposure, which causes an orienting reaction to the change of the stimulus, results in the restoration of the reaction in the form of a reduction of light sensitivity to the weakened light. Thus the development of an orienting reaction increases the reactivity of the analysing system to the group of stimuli which causes this reaction.

(b) The role of the orienting reflex in the perception of conditioned (signal) stimuli

An orienting reflex that has been extinguished in relation to a certain stimulus is restored as soon as that stimulus is used as a signal in the formation of a conditioned reflex.

Verbal stimuli play a primary part in the formation of conditioned reflexes in man, and verbal instructions or verbal reinforcement can give a stimulus the meaning of a signal.

The restoration of orienting reactions during the formation of a conditioned reflex is of a generalized character. This is explained by the process of irradiation of excitation over the cortical part of the analysing system. Thus the formation of a conditioned reflex to one stimulus results in the restoration of orienting reactions to a whole group of stimuli.

Orienting reflexes in the structure of the conditioned reflex also follow the laws of reciprocal induction. Simultaneously with restoration of reactions to one group of stimuli we observe their inhibition to other stimuli which are more distant from the conditioned stimulus. An enduring selective reactivity to specific stimuli arises, its mechanism being a dominant focus of excitation in the cerebral cortex which causes the intensification of some stimuli and the inhibition of others. This selectivity is expressed, for example, in the way a verbal instruction to count light signals produces a strong orienting reaction to light alone, while a verbal instruction to count sound signals causes a reaction only to sound stimuli. During the formation of a conditioned reflex to a sound stimulus, we observe selectivity only with reference to a group of sound signals: orienting reactions arise only in response to stimuli which are close to the conditioned stimulus. For this reason, strong stimuli which have no signal function sometimes cease to cause orienting reactions, while weak signal stimuli may produce them. Thus weak audiometer tones during threshold measurements cause considerable vascular reactions, while strong, regularly repeated thuds do not evoke them. Just as in the case of indifferent stimuli, orienting reactions within the structure of the conditioned reflex arise in response to every change of the signal stimulus as well as to stimuli akin to the signal stimuli. These reactions, too, are gradually extinguished with the stabilization of the conditioned reflex, but the process of inhibition proceeds more slowly than is the case when indifferent stimuli are used.

Some efferent components of the orienting reaction are not extinguished simultaneously in the process of elaboration of a conditioned reflex. Those components of the orienting reaction which are the precondition for the perception of the signal stimulus are more persistent. Thus during the action of a light stimulus, the skin-galvanic reaction is the first to be extinguished, and only later is the electrical activity of the occipital region extinguished, this region being the cortical part of the optical analysing system, directly participating in the perception of the light signal. The gradual inhibition of the orienting reflex leads to the inhibition of some components as a result of the spreading of the process of inhibition. At the same time this leads to a concentration of excitation and so to a limitation of the orienting reaction to those systems specifically connected with the perception of the stimulus.

These facts show that orienting reactions remain within the conditioned reflex as a requisite for the adequate perception of the signal stimulus.

The role and place of the orienting reaction in the structure of the conditioned reflex depends on the nature of the signal stimulus and on the way it is reinforced. An orienting reaction, largely extinguished in the course of applying a single stimulus, is restored when the stimulus is changed.

In cases where differentiation is difficult the extinction of orienting reactions is particularly slow. The development of orienting reactions both to a positive and to an inhibitory stimulus is added proof of their orienting nature, since these reactions, as a condition of correct differentiation, are equally necessary for the perception both of positive and negative stimuli.

A particular case of the intensification of orienting reactions where differentiation is difficult is the development of especially strong and lasting orienting reactions to stimuli which are close to the absolute threshold. While the stimuli are in the region of average intensity, orienting reactions follow the law of force, they are intensified as the threshold is approached, and become particularly strong and lasting at the threshold; specific threshold reactions to light, sound and tactile stimuli were observed.

The intensification of orienting reactions to particular stimuli results in increased reactivity of the analysing system. Thus the adaptation of the eye (in complete darkness) to slight exposure of light is destroyed by the instruction to differentiate between exposures according to their duration.

Similar results were obtained in recording the electrical activity of the occipital region. After repeated slight exposures of the dark-adapted eye, light stimuli no longer caused changes in the electrical activity of the occipital region. But the influence of light on that activity was restored as soon as the subject was instructed to differentiate the exposures according to their intensity.

The orienting reaction influences the assimilation of the rhythm of the light stimuli by the cortex. Thus when a flashing light is passively fixed by the eye, the occipital region barely assimilates the given rhythm after a number of presentations. The instruction to differentiate between the light stimuli, according to their frequency, brings about a clearly manifested assimilation of the rhythm of the light stimulus by the cortex. Under these conditions, the skin-galvanic reaction is restored simultaneously, proving the

97

importance of the intensification of the orienting reaction in this phenomenon.

The intensification of the orienting reaction in the structure of a conditioned reflex, which takes place when a difficult differentiation has to be made, influences the process of conditioning itself. Thus when the subject is instructed to clench his fist only in response to sound of a frequency similar to that of the conditioned stimulus, this causes not only a restoration but a considerable intensification of the orienting reaction as shown by changes in the skin-galvanic reflex, changes in the electrical activity of the occipital region, and eye movements, all of which were extinguished in the process of reinforcing the conditioned reflex. A prolongation of the latency period of motor reaction is also observed, this being evidence of a temporary inhibition of the motor system. The strong orienting reaction, which arises when differentiation is introduced, begins immediately after the production of the sound, before the motor response, inhibiting the latter. The same strong orienting reaction arises in response to a negative stimulus when there is no motor reaction to it.

The significance of the intensification of the orienting reaction and of the accompanying inhibition of motor reaction under difficult conditions of stimulus perception, is that the special activity of the organism is postponed until the properties of the new stimulus are ascertained; this is accomplished by the system of orienting reactions.

Conclusions

(1) The vascular reaction, the skin-galvanic reflex, eye movements, changes in the electrical activity of the occipital region and fluctuations in sensitivity to light may appear as components of a complex orienting reaction, which ensures perception of a stimulus.

(2) The presentation of indifferent stimuli causes a generalized extinction of orienting reactions to some stimuli and positive induction of orienting reactions to other stimuli.

(3) The inhibition of orienting reactions to stimuli which affect a specific analysing system is associated with a decrease in the reactivity of the system to the given stimuli. The restoration of orienting reactions is characterized by increased reactivity of the analysing system to the given stimuli.

(4) Orienting reactions, which are extinguished in relation to indifferent stimuli, are restored in a generalized form if at least one of the indifferent stimuli becomes a conditioned stimulus, resulting in response activity on the part of the organism. In this case, the response activity of the organism intensifies the excitation of the analysing system which is perceiving the signal stimulus.

(5) In the process of formation of a conditioned reflex, some components of the orienting reaction become extinguished; those which remain are those which are involved in the systems directly participating in the perception of the signal stimulus.

(6) Orienting reactions in the structure of a conditioned reflex become intensified when difficult differentiations are introduced; a particular case is the intensification of orienting reactions in the discrimination of two similar stimuli near the (human) threshold.

(7) The intensification of orienting reactions, where difficult differentiations have to be made, is connected with an increase in the reactivity of the given analysing system to the applied stimuli.

(8) The intensification of orienting reactions, in cases of difficult differentiation, prolongs the latency period of conditioned motor reaction; this reaction is postponed until the properties of the operating stimulus are ascertained.

RAISING THE SENSITIVITY OF THE
VISUAL ANALYSER [1]

BY

L. A. SHVARTS

OUR KNOWLEDGE of the surrounding world is obtained through the analysers. It is, therefore, extremely important to find means of raising their sensitivity. We understand by sensitivity the value which is in inverse proportion to that of the threshold of sensation. It defines the level of adjustment of the analysers to the perception of given stimuli. According to Pavlov, changes in the sensitivity of the analysers are linked with changes in the dynamics of the cortical processes.

Investigators who have worked on the problem of raising analyser sensitivity have used a variety of methods. The effectiveness of these methods has depended ultimately on their effect on the functional condition of the cerebral cortex, although this has not always been pointed out. The investigation here described [2] set out to trace how the level of visual sensitivity changes under the influence of different reception through a shifting balance of excitation and inhibition in the higher nervous centres. To this end various methods were applied to reinforce the subjects' verbal reactions to visual stimuli. By the subject's verbal reactions we understand the naming by the subject of the stimulus presented to him on a particular occasion.

For a stimulus to be adequately perceived under threshold conditions, the corresponding centres in the cerebral cortex must reach a certain level of excitation. This process of excitation, evoked by signals of the first signal system, must be sufficiently intensive to reach the second signal system and give rise to a verbal reaction in the subject—that is, as a verbal account of the stimulus.

The method of the experiment was as follows: subjects were placed in darkness and allowed a 50-minute period of dark adaptation.

---

[1] *Speeches at the Conference on Psychological Questions, July 1953* (Moscow, 1954), pp. 217–28 (translated by N. Parsons).

[2] Carried out in B. M. Teplov's laboratory.

100

Thresholds for recognizing shapes were then determined with a Kravkov adaptometer.[1] The object to be recognized was mounted on a rotating disc; it was an optician's test-sign resembling, according to the position of the disc, the letters **ш**, **т**, **з** or **E** (Figure I).[2]

FIGURE I

The illumination of the stimuli could be varied by means of a diaphragm, from a point at which the letter stood out clearly, to a point when not even a white patch was visible to the untrained eye. A value, inversely proportional to the amount of light admitted by the diaphragm, was taken as a comparative measure of the sensitivity of peripheral vision. Thresholds for recognition of the shapes were defined by the minimal illumination at which the subject could distinguish the letter presented in a given instance.

To fix the threshold, the subject had to identify correctly five times in succession. We took as 100% the index of the level of sensitivity at the beginning of Series I, and all subsequent calculations were carried out in relation to this initial level of sensitivity (the base).

In each experiment there were 40 stimuli. The order in which they were presented was changed from one experiment to another. The investigator noted the correctness or otherwise of the subject's answers, and the time elapsing between stimulus presentation and response.

Before the experiments, subjects received the following instruction: 'When the letter is presented you must name it correctly and as quickly as possible. The illumination of the letter will be progressively reduced. You will have to learn to recognize the letter presented when the light is very dim indeed.' Four series of experiments were carried out with the first group of subjects.

The task in Series I was to discover how, after this instruction, the level of shape-recognition was influenced by repeated presentation of visual stimuli without knowledge of results. The stimuli shown were

---

[1] See p. 93 for an explanation of this method.
[2] **т** and **ш** are the Russian characters for T and Sh. **E** is similar to the English E. **з** was referred to as if it was the Russian character э (E). (Ed.)

presented 400 times in the course of the 10 experiments in this first series.

The results of the experiments showed that subjects' sensitivity increased on an average 40%, from 100% 'base' to 140%. As stated above, the subjects in this series of experiments did not know whether or not they had correctly recognized the stimuli presented to them. Consequently, the conditioned connection between the stimuli and the corresponding response was not reinforced, and the increase in sensitivity was insignificant.

The purpose of Series II was to see what effect verbal reinforcement of right and wrong responses would have on the threshold for shape-recognition. In all other respects the conditions of the second experiment remained the same as in the first; the essential difference was that the subject's responses to stimuli were verbally reinforced.

The results of the second series of experiments showed that visual sensitivity rose, on an average, a further 170%, from 140% to 310%.

In contrast to Series I, the rise of sensitivity was not only much quicker, but also continued longer, up to 230–250 stimulus presentations; in Series I the maximum had been attained very quickly, after a mere 25–30 presentations. The subject's knowledge of the quality of his answering responses to visual stimuli considerably assisted the further growth of visual sensitivity.

The explanation of the great rise in sensitivity in Series II is probably that the subject's responses were reinforced. Every time the subject made a correct response, this was positively reinforced by the investigator, and positive impulses went from the second signal system to corresponding points of the cortex. Consequently, there was a strengthening of the conditioned connection between the given stimulus and the subject's response. Every time the subject made an incorrect response this was negatively reinforced, and inhibitory impulses presumably travelled from the second signal system to the corresponding point of the cerebral termination of the receptor; as a result there was a weakening of the conditioned connection between the stimulus presented and the subject's incorrect response to it, evoked by inexact perception of this stimulus.

It may be supposed that, as the threshold of stimulus illumination is lowered, there is a change in the signs by which the stimulus is recognized; that is, the mastery of a new threshold of visual sensitivity presupposes the formation of new differentiations, the inclusion in the reflex act of new conditioned connections. There are, probably, 'zones' of sensitivity, connected with the perception of particular features of the stimulus. Some confirmation of this hypothesis is provided by observations made during these experiments. Sometimes a subject reached a new threshold of sensitivity with great difficulty, but when illumination was decreased still further began to recognize the letters more correctly and quickly.

The basic features by which a letter change is recognized with the lowering of the level of stimulus illumination, may be judged by the comments of one of the subjects (protocol No. 167), typical of others.

When working with an aperture of 30–35 divisions, the subject stated: 'I can get the letters straight away.' On proceeding to the 45th division he said, 'At first I see a white spot, which seems to "gather itself" into a letter. Usually I distinguish by the spaces between the forks of the "letter".' During work at the 60th division, which admits 10 times less light than the 30th, the subject made the following statement: 'At first I see a faint light, then a spot, which immediately becomes either broad or narrow. A broad spot is the letter ⊓ or ⊔, a narrow spot is the letter E or Ǝ. I distinguish between ⊓ and ⊔ by size: ⊓ appears smaller and lower, and is more distinct than ⊔, while ⊔ is dimmer. Ǝ is shifted to the left, and E to the right. The spaces are scarcely visible now, which makes recognition difficult.'

In the process of training, the guess was usually replaced by direct vision. Necessity made subjects use new features of which they were not always conscious. Frequent successful use of the new features enabled them to attain a new threshold of visual sensitivity and include new conditioned connections in the conditioned-reflex act.

The purpose of Series III was to examine how the threshold of shape-recognition was influenced by negative reinforcement of incorrect responses with a weak electric shock. All conditions remained as before, except that, instead of negative verbal reinforcement, a weak electric shock was applied as a punishment, while for correct responses there was none. By introducing a rheostat into the circuit and conducting preliminary experiments, it was possible to establish for each subject the strength of current which would cause a certain unpleasant prickling without positively painful sensations.

The results of Series III show further growth in subjects' sensitivity —less marked, however, than in Series II, averaging 160%, from 310% to 470%. In contrast to Series II, when a rise in sensitivity continued up to 230–240 stimulus presentations, Series III showed a maximum rise after 55–65 presentations. In this series of experiments there were typical sudden drops in sensitivity with following rises. Individual differences were reported. How are the results in this series to be explained?

Reinforcement by shock has a dual character. On the one hand it is a signal to the subject of the correctness or otherwise of his responses, and thereby causes corresponding impulses from the second signal system to defined points of the cortex; this helps to maintain the necessary balance between excitation and inhibition. On the other hand, negative reinforcement by shock may cause excessive subcortical inhibition, which may in these cases lead to negative induction of defined points of the cortex and destroy the necessary balance of excitation and inhibition. Such is the negative side of this method of reinforcement (the falls in sensitivity observed in the experiments were exactly typical of such an inhibitory condition).

The aim of Series IV was to see how the further growth of visual sensitivity was affected by a new method of reinforcement—by giving the subject 'instructions' which set him a concrete task. Apart from this, all the conditions of the experiment remained the same as in Series II, i.e. the experimenter applied a verbal reinforcement to the subject's responses.

Before the beginning of Series IV the subject was given the following instructions:

> You will have to learn to recognize the letter presented with still less light. When we started our experiments, you distinguished letters at aperture p (each subject is given his figure), but now you can distinguish them at aperture q (again the figure is given). Your task is to recognize the letters quickly and correctly even when the aperture is moved several divisions further forward (figure given). When you succeed I shall move the diaphragm one division further. We have only ten experimental days at our disposal.

Series IV resulted in a significant rise in sensitivity. All subjects not only achieved their targets, but exceeded them. Their visual sensitivity increased by an average of 375%, from 470% to 845%.

Visual sensitivity in this series of experiments went on growing for a longer time than in any preceding series. It only reached its final level after an average of 300 stimulus presentations. All the subjects showed great activity, were interested in the results of their work, and tried to attain their goals as quickly as possible. Before the beginning of the experiments they usually asked at which division they were working that day. Of all the methods we employed to raise sensitivity, this proved to be the most effective.

In the experimental investigations by Leontiev, Zaporozhets and their colleagues into the recovery of arm functions following a wound, it was established that a subject with limited shoulder mobility could move his arm considerably higher when he was shown to what point on a graduated screen he was to raise his arm, than when he was told in a general way to raise his arm as high as possible [39: 12].

Experience continually demonstrates that a clear aim and a concrete perspective assist the carrying through of a task. Thus the Stakhanovite, having received a fixed production norm for each day and knowing the work-plan for the year, mobilizes all his powers to over-fulfil these norms, making good use of every minute of working time. Athletes achieve better times when they are told to run a fixed distance in a fixed time, than when they are told in a general way to run as fast as they can. It is, therefore, in accordance with expectation that the methods used in Series IV produced the highest rise in sensitivity, an increase which continued progressively for a considerable time.

How are these results to be explained?

The following hypothesis may be advanced. The task set in the whole series of experiments, and in the separate experiments serving as stages, caused close interaction between the first and second signal systems, because of the subjects' concrete conceptions of the dimensions of the task and of their progress towards its completion. The instructions (which required subjects to increase their visual sensitivity to a defined extent in a fixed space of time) caused, at corresponding points at the cortical end of the analyser, a sufficient level of excitation which was *continuously* maintained by positive impulses from both signal systems. The maintenance of this functional state of the cortex was also partly due, of course, to the powerful impulses reaching the cortex from the sub-cortex; these were indicated by the heightened sensitivity observed in subjects in this series. All this led to the strengthening of the conditioned connection between poorly discriminated stimuli and an adequate response, and led to a heightening of sensitivity. However, this interpretation of our results requires to be confirmed and made more precise.

In order to establish whether the increase in visual sensitivity was permanent and stable, the experiments were suspended for five months, and a second measure was then taken of the subjects' threshold of sensitivity when shown the stimuli ⋂, Ш, Э and E. In spite of the considerable interval, subjects showed a high level of sensitivity, almost the same as before the break (an average rise of 830% in relation to the original level or base).

Further experiments were then carried out to find if the rise in sensitivity was maintained in the recognition of other perceptually similar objects. After the subjects' sensitivity in recognizing the 'letters' ⋂, Ш, Э and E had been recorded, measurement was also made of their sensitivity in recognizing the letters H and П,[1] which they had not formerly seen. The level of sensitivity in recognizing these letters was found to have risen by almost three times relative to the 'basic' level.

---

[1] The Russian characters for N and P (Ed.).

Thus the considerable increase in visual sensitivity in recognizing letter-shapes is, as it were, a generic acquisition for the subject; owing to the strength of the conditioned connections formed in the experiments, it is maintained for a long period of time and appears in the recognition of any new objects that are perceptually similar.

It was considered essential to investigate further the complex situation revealed by Series IV, in order to find out which factor was causing the increase. Since the first problem was to estimate how much of the increase was due to the training carried out in the preceding series, a second group of subjects was used. Initially, the first series of experiments was carried out, that is, simple repetition of stimulus presentation; this produced only a small increase in sensitivity (from 100% 'base' to 150%). The subjects then immediately embarked on experiments identical with those of Series IV; that is, each was given concrete instructions requiring him to increase his sensitivity to a given level in a fixed time.

The results showed that subjects' visual sensitivity rose on an average from 150% to 1200% relative to a 'base' taken as 100%. This rise in sensitivity continued on an average up to 570 stimulus presentations, i.e. it went on growing for a longer time than in any preceding series. These results convinced us that preparatory training, applying other means of reinforcement, had had no influence on the success in Series IV, and provided further evidence of the effectiveness of the Series IV method of raising sensitivity.

The next point to decide was how far the success of the last series depended upon the subjects' degree of mobilization and intensity in their work, since the concrete task which the subjects were given in this series was of considerable extent. Experiments were therefore initiated with a third group of subjects. After these subjects had been given Series I (with simple repetition of stimulus presentation), and had shown a slight rise in sensitivity (averaging from 100% 'base' to 150%), a new Series II was instituted.

As a preliminary, a concrete task was set which required no intensive effort; i.e. it required four times less discrimination than the task given to the first group of subjects in Series IV and to the second group in Series II. This definite but easy task was found to produce an average rise in sensitivity from 150% to 330% relative to the 'base', since it did not give rise to sufficient tonus in the higher nervous centres.

The instructions were then changed and subjects were given a task as extensive as that set in the initial Series IV, one which could not be carried out without intensive effort.

It was discovered that the new, more mobilizing task produced a rise in sensitivity averaging 920%, from 330% to 1250% relative to the initial level. The rise was, therefore, not only a product of the concrete nature of the task, but also of its extent and the intensity of the effort it required from the subject.

Thus all our experiments showed that the magnitude of the rise in visual sensitivity in each separate series depended upon the methods employed to achieve that rise. The rise achieved averaged more than 1000% relative to the initial level. This is evidence of the enormous, apparently limitless potentialities of man.

Conclusions

(1) It may be assumed that, as the illumination of the visual stimuli falls, there is a change in the differentiating features by which these stimuli are recognized. This means that the mastery of a new threshold presupposes the incorporation of new conditioned connections in the reflex act.

(2) The visual stimuli presented in the experiments became physically weaker and weaker as their illumination diminished. Consequently, in order to raise sensitivity in recognizing the form of the stimulus under conditions of threshold perception, it is necessary to raise the level of activity of the cerebral cortex.

(3) After the formation of a 'plateau', the application of new methods of raising sensitivity, which raised the level of cortical activity, always produced a new rise in visual sensitivity.

(4) Of all the methods used in the experiments for raising sensitivity, the most effective is that which, besides applying verbal reinforcement of the separate responses of subjects, set them specific tasks requiring a considerable increase in visual sensitivity within a given time. Such a task presumably favours the close interaction of both signal systems, and creates a permanent level of excitation in certain cerebral centres which is supported by impulses coming from the sub-cortex. Consequently, conditioned connections are easily formed between the visual stimulus and its adequate response, and visual sensitivity is raised.

(5) The strength of the conditioned connections established in these experiments is such that the rise in visual sensitivity achieved is maintained for a long time, and appears in the recognition of other similar objects.

THE DEVELOPMENT OF VOLUNTARY
MOVEMENTS [1]

BY

A. V. ZAPOROZHETS

HUMAN VOLUNTARY MOVEMENTS may best be studied by investigation of their development in children. Such an investigation should not start from the standpoint that voluntary movements are the opposite of motor habits. As Sechenov demonstrated, and as many subsequent experiments have shown, voluntary movements are *learned* movements. Pavlov gave a definite physiological meaning to this conception by establishing that such movements are, physiologically speaking, conditioned motor reflexes. The development of voluntary movements represents the formation of complex systems of conditioned reflexes, which together constitute motor skills and habits. Research, therefore, should be directed primarily towards study of the process whereby a child masters certain types of movement. What is the nature and role of the psychic activity that takes place during the formation and use of motor habits; and what forms does this activity take at different stages of the child's development? In an attempt to answer these questions, research was undertaken into the process of formation and use of motor habits in children from 2 to 7 years.[2]

I

In one series of experiments, children had to master a system of movements, to press reaction keys in a definite sequence according to the order in which light and sound signals were presented; in another series, maze habits were formed; in a third, children had to learn an

[1] Communication to the Fourteenth International Congress of Psychology, 1954; published in *Voprosy Psikhologii*, No. 1, 1955, pp. 42–9 (translated in the U.S.S.R.).

[2] At the Institute of Psychology, Academy of Educational Sciences, and the Department of Psychology, Moscow University.

elementary system of gymnastic movements. These motor habits were formed in different ways; by means of undirected trials, by imitation, and, lastly, with the aid of verbal instruction.

In the course of the investigation, components of a different nature were observed in the behaviour of a child mastering definite motor habits. First, the child performs a number of executive movements which help directly to achieve the final result required. Thus he presses a certain key which switches off a corresponding lamp; he pushes a toy car along a path in the maze towards a set destination, etc. Second, the child performs a number of actions which, by their nature and the part they play in behaviour, differ essentially from executive movements. For example, he touches the reaction keys or feels the paths in the maze; he turns his head towards sound and light signals, his eyes follow the lamps as they light up in succession and the movements of the investigator, or turn to the objects named, etc. In accordance with Pavlov's conception of orienting reflexes, we designate such actions as orienting-investigatory activity.

This activity, while not leading to the accomplishment of the required results directly, enables the child to orientate himself more precisely in the situation and ensures the performance of executive movements conforming to the conditions of the task. For example, when the habit was formed of pressing a number of keys in succession, according to a system of light signals, it was observed that children who initially actively investigated the situation (touched the reaction keys, followed the light signals, watched the investigator's actions) learned more quickly and made fewer mistakes than those who exhibited a less active orienting reaction to the conditions of the task. The degree of intensity and the distinctive features of this orienting-investigatory activity influence, not only the speed of habit formation, but also the nature of the motor behaviour.

In one experiment, which involved teaching children to push a toy car along the paths of a maze with their eyes closed, we suggested that, before starting, the children should familiarize themselves with the maze as a whole by touch, that is, they should feel the path they would have to follow with their fingers. In a second experiment, the children had to fulfil the same task without this preliminary orientation practice. The motor habits were formed much more rapidly in the first case than in the second. The totals of both orienting and executive movements necessary to form the habit in the first experiment were, on average, much less than the movements made by the children in the second experiment (without orientation) (Table I).

The executive movements of the subjects, formed on the basis of preliminary orientation, acquired distinctive features. The children pushed the car in the required direction with confidence and without

TABLE 1

Number of exercises necessary to form a motor habit with or without preliminary orientation [1]

Age of children	Experiment 1			Experiment 2
	With preliminary orientation			With preliminary orientation
	Number of preliminary orientation exercises	Number of motor exercises (executive movements)	Total	Number of motor exercises (executive movements)
4 years	15	9	24	28
5 years	10	3	13	31
6 years	10	4	14	32
7 years	5	1·5	6·5	22

error from the outset; they could say in advance where they had to go and mentioned the *cul-de-sacs* to be avoided. By comparison, the motor behaviour of the children in the second experiment was of an extremely chaotic character and for long did not match the requirements of the task; mistakes were only corrected slowly and often wrong movements were repeated. It is interesting to note that, in this case, the children consistently tried to disobey the instructions; leaving the car, they would investigate the situation by touching the walls of the maze, following the paths with their fingers, etc. Thus here, too, orienting-investigatory activity took place, but owing to unfavourable conditions it could not develop and this reflected negatively on the organization of motor behaviour.

Other experiments also demonstrated that the nature of orienting-investigatory activity not only influences the formation of motor habits but also their subsequent functioning. During the development of a system of motor reactions in response to light signals, it was observed that habits formed on the basis of a thorough investigation of the environment by hand and eye prove to be more flexible, more readily adaptable when the order of the stimuli is changed, than habits formed without any preliminary acquaintance with the environment in which the task is to proceed.

Proof of the importance of orienting activity in the formation of motor habits has been obtained by Luria in his investigation of feeble-minded children. The orienting reactions of such children are

[1] Research of O. V. Ovchinnikova.

usually very primitive and weakly manifested so that the formation of habits proceeds slowly and with great difficulty, but when, with the help of special devices, orienting-investigatory activity is stimulated, an improvement in the efficiency of learning can be observed.

There is, therefore, a considerable amount of data testifying to the important part played by orienting-investigatory activity in the formation and subsequent use of motor habits. Its principal significance is that it indicates the existence of early forms of psychic regulation of behaviour in cases where both the executive movements and the orienting-investigatory activity preceding them bear the character of an external activity performed in relation to available objects.

As a result of orienting-investigatory activity, the child forms new temporary connections; while, of the old connections, those conforming to the conditions of the given task become active. The child begins to form an idea of the situation and is guided by this in his subsequent behaviour. The origin of this idea is indicated objectively by a specific change in the orienting-investigatory activity, observed in the course of experiments. When the child is just beginning to acquaint himself with the conditions of the experiment, his orientation is not yet systematized, and every separate stimulus provokes a separate orienting reaction. For example, searching for the path in the maze, the child initially performs haphazard touching movements, which are scarcely connected with each other, and correspond inadequately to the features of the object. But later, a system of touching movements is gradually built up corresponding to the configuration of the object examined; at this stage, one section of the path signalizes the next section, and the child stretches his hand in this direction in anticipation.

It must be stressed that this is still not the motor habit itself; this will only take shape later. What we have here is a system of orienting, touching movements of the hand, elaborated in conformity with the conditions of the task. As a result of the formation of such a system, the child gets an initial idea of the conditions of the task and of the actions that should be performed under these conditions. The formation of the motor habit then takes place more rapidly and acquires a more purposeful character. Wrong movements are inhibited at the very beginning of their performance, as movements which do not correspond to the idea formed, before they actually receive a negative reinforcement.

II

After observing the important part played by orienting-investigatory activity in the development of motor behaviour, it was necessary

A. V. ZAPOROZHETS

to examine its development and the changes it undergoes at different ages. To this end, a special series of experiments was conducted which showed the decisive importance of motor-touch orientation at the early stages.

Though younger children follow the presented stimuli, the investigator's actions, etc., with their eyes, they cannot yet form a correct idea of the situation only by means of visual acquaintance of this kind. It seems that, because of insufficient experience, visual impressions do not yet produce the necessary associations, so that the meaning of different signals is not clear. Only a more or less prolonged investigation of the conditions of the task, with the help of the hand, can give younger children the knowledge required to determine the nature of their subsequent motor behaviour.

The eye, which at first follows the hand, later assimilates the experience accumulated by the hand, and can perform the orienting reaction independently. Sometimes it is sufficient for older children to see the manner in which the investigator presses the reaction keys, or to follow with their eyes the path their hand must travel in the maze, to be able to perform the required movements correctly (Table 2).

TABLE 2

Number of exercises necessary to form a motor habit with preliminary motor-touch orientation (A) or preliminary visual orientation (B) [1]

Age of children	A			B		
	Number of preliminary orientation exercises	Number of motor exercises	Total	Number of preliminary orientation exercises	Number of motor exercises	Total
4 years	15	9	24	13	13	26
5 years	10	3	13	5	6	11
6 years	10	4	14	2	4·5	6·5
7 years	5	1·5	6·5	2	1·8	3·8

In the process of child development, speech (i.e. the second signal system) acquires increasing importance in the regulation of movements. A comparison of the formation of motor habits, by means of visual demonstration and by means of verbal instruction, has also been made. It appeared that younger children are better taught by visual demonstration, but that, with increasing age, the efficiency of verbal instruction increases both absolutely and relatively (Table 3).

[1] Research of O. V. Ovchinnikova.

112

TABLE 3

Number of children who perform gymnastic movements after visual
demonstration or verbal instruction [1] (every age group consists of ten
children)

Age of children	Visual demonstration	Verbal instruction
3–4 years	0	0
4–5 years	2	0
5–6 years	9	3
6–7 years	10	9

It has also been demonstrated that verbal regulation of the child's
motor behaviour can only be accomplished with the help of his own
orienting-investigatory activity. For most of the youngest children,
and some of the older children, the investigator's verbal instructions
alone do not produce the essential orienting reactions to the presented
objects; consequently, they cannot carry out the instructions. But, if
the child's orienting-investigatory activity is specifically organized
(e.g. by suggesting that he look at or touch the objects presented),
the efficiency of teaching by verbal instruction is greatly increased for
children of all ages (Table 4).

TABLE 4

Number of exercises necessary to form a motor habit after verbal
instruction [2]

Age of children	With verbal instructions alone	With specially organized orienting-investigatory activity
3 years	11·0	4·7
4 years	6·4	1·8
5 years	4·9	1·5
6 years	3·5	0·4

Initially, the instructions give rise to orientation only in the conditions of the given situation. At this stage the child obeys the verbal
instruction only if, while listening, he simultaneously perceives the
conditions in which he has to act. At later stages, as has already been

[1] Research of I. G. Dimanstein.   [2] Research of G. A. Kisliuk.

noted, the child gradually forms specific systems of orienting reactions which conform to the features of the various objects and the tasks that he has to perform with them. These systems become associated with verbal instruction and undergo abbreviation and schematization in their subsequent development, while their effector part is inhibited; traces of movements of the eye or hand, corresponding to the imagined object, can only occasionally be discerned.

At this stage, verbal instruction can produce an idea of the conditions of the task and the actions necessary, in the absence of a direct perception of the situation. Thus, in further experiments, older children, after hearing the verbal instructions but without having seen the experimental device, could imagine this clearly and were able to designate the location of its parts in space, to demonstrate the actions they must perform, etc. Correspondingly, with increasing age, there is an improvement in the efficiency of movements performed in accordance with verbal instructions when these are given without visual demonstration of the conditions of the action.

To summarize briefly, the formation of voluntary psychically regulated movements in children proceeds as follows: at an early age motor behaviour is regulated by means of external orienting-investigatory activity. Initially, this activity has the character of motor-touch investigation of the situation; this serves as a foundation for the subsequent formation of visual orientation, which is more economical, does not require direct contact with the object, and provides the basis for more distant foresight of motor activities. Gradually, as stable systems of adequate orienting reactions are developed, the requisite conditions are created for a transition to the higher forms of regulation of movements. These systems become connected with words, and can be evoked by means of words, without the child directly perceiving the situation. At this point, the words of the instruction, or the child's own words, produce mental orientation in the situation and foresight of subsequent movements.

THE ROLE OF LANGUAGE IN THE
FORMATION OF TEMPORARY CONNECTIONS [1]

BY

A. R. LURIA

THE THEORY of the formation of temporary connections in man has developed in close connection with investigation of the part played in this process by the second signal system. A complete examination of the role of language, as a stimulus in the analytic-synthetic activity of the brain, is the prerequisite for significant advances in the theory of higher nervous activity, and in study of the mechanisms of psychic activity.

I

At the outset of this work, which was initiated by N. I. Krasnogorsky and A. G. Ivanov-Smolensky, two points were brought out which have since occupied a central place in investigations. First, it was shown experimentally that language as a special signal can successfully replace unconditioned reinforcement, and so lead to the formation of new, specifically human, cortical connections. This proposition underlay the method suggested by Ivanov-Smolensky for developing motor reflexes on the basis of speech reinforcement. Second, it was experimentally established that language can also take the place of a conditioned (direct) signal. This finding, first described by O. P. Kapustnik [23], led to a large number of experiments which showed that if a direct conditioned stimulus is replaced by a word, this not only gives rise to all the reactions formerly produced by direct signals, but in certain cases is even more effective, occasioning reactions of noticeably greater intensity. These results were thoroughly investigated by Krasnogorsky and K. M. Bykov [5], and underlie many propositions now firmly established in clinical practice.

It is undeniable that the word, 'which is just as real a conditioned

[1] *Voprosy Psikhologii*, No. 1, 1955, pp. 73–87 (translated by H. Milne).

stimulus as any other', but at the same time much more comprehensive than other stimuli,[1] can replace not only an unconditioned reinforcement, but also conditioned signals. But this by no means exhausts the role of language in the analytic-synthetic work of the human brain, in the formation of temporary connections in man. When Pavlov introduced his conception of two signal systems (now regarded as one of the central ideas in his later work), he insisted that, with language, 'a new principle of nervous activity is introduced, the abstraction and generalization of innumerable signals', and that it is precisely this 'new principle which enables the second signal system to become 'the highest regulator of human behaviour'.[2] Modern psychology appreciates the importance of this abstracting and generalizing function of language in the formation of new experience, but it has not been fully taken into account in experimental investigations concerned with the development of temporary connections. There is no doubt that this function of language is especially important and must become a main object of study.

Attention was first directed to this question in the 1920's.[3] Study of the way a pre-school child solves practical problems (modelling in plasticine, tracing a drawing, and so on) led to the conclusion that a child only performs his actions in silence until he meets with some difficulty. As soon as he is presented with such a difficulty (e.g. by hiding his pencil or a piece of plasticine, or by taking out the drawing-pin used to fasten a sheet of tracing paper, his activity at once begins to be accompanied by speech. Speech appears to play an important role in the child's subsequent activity. By fixing the new situation it mobilizes the systematized connections built up during past experience, gives the child direction among the possible ways out of the impasse, and makes possible the choice of methods enabling him to solve his problem. Speech, therefore, is one of the essential means whereby the child finds his bearings in the external world; it activizes the generalized connections formed in past experience, which play a substantial part in the mediated, specifically human, form of regulation of action.

In the early stages of child development, speech is only a means of communication with adults and other children, whereby the child masters in a generalized form the experience of other people. Subsequently it becomes also a means whereby he organizes his own experience and regulates his own actions. So the child's activity is mediated through words. The full significance of this fact can only be appreciated in the light of Pavlov's teaching on the interaction of the two signal systems, characteristic of human beings.

[1] Pavlov-Anrep, 407.　　　　[2] Pavlov-Gantt ii, 114; *Selected Works*, 537.
[3] By L. S. Vigotsky and his collaborators.

Observations have also disclosed that the child's speech, which directs his solution of a problem, is at first unabbreviated and full; but that later, as he masters his actions, it becomes increasingly abbreviated and contracted. First, the child ceases to say everything aloud and in full; his speech sinks to a whisper, its grammatical structure becomes contracted and broken, he begins to utter only separate words indicating necessary objects or actions at critical points; after a certain time his speech ceases, and he begins to perform his task in silence. Occasionally, when children utter stray remarks, the fact that speech has not disappeared, but has only taken new concealed forms, is revealed. Full, overt speech, therefore, gradually becomes transformed into contracted, internal speech. This internal speech, however, continues to fulfil the same function, that of mobilizing the systematized connections of past experience, which may be useful for orientation in the new conditions and for the regulation of future actions. The child's speech, in this contracted form, is indissolubly linked with his thinking, and continues to share in those forms of activity which the child now performs in silence.[1]

Later investigations, which confirmed these findings, traced the part played by innervation of the speech organs in the solution of intellectual problems.[2] It was found that speech impulses (registered electromiographically) gradually contracted as a problem was progressively mastered, until they became hardly perceptible. As a result of this work, the direct share of speech in the formation of new connections, or, to use Pavlov's words, the real function of the 'kinaesthetic stimulations which proceed from the speech organs to the cortex', and their subsequent fate, are becoming increasingly clear.

All this justifies a deduction of great significance for future investigations. To begin with, the child's speech, by replacing a directly perceptible stimulus and direct reinforcement, serves as a means of obtaining a fuller reflection of reality; but, as it develops, it increasingly becomes a means of systematizing past experience, and so a means whereby the child orientates himself in the directly perceived real world, and regulates his actions. This proposition compels us to formulate more precisely many current conceptions about the formation of new temporary connections in man.

It would be wrong to imagine that language only replaces an unconditioned reinforcement or a conditioned signal; that the closing of new connections takes place initially in direct experience (in the first signal system), and that these connections are only later reflected in language and 'handed over' to the second signal system. Such a

[1] These observations by Vigotsky were reported at the Ninth International Congress of Psychology.
[2] A. N. Sokolov [63], L. A. Novikova and others.

situation arises only in certain cases which will be discussed below. As a rule, if a series of direct signals (one of which is reinforced positively, the others negatively) is presented to a child of $5\frac{1}{2}$ to 6 years of age, it is at once subjected to verbal analysis and fitted into certain cortical systems formed with the help of speech; these enable the child to make use of his past experience (already generalized in a verbal system) in developing new connections, and to re-orientate himself in the new situation with the aid of language.

This is clearly shown by this fundamental fact. In a normal child aged from $5\frac{1}{2}$ upwards, and still more in an adult, the formation of new connections takes place with the closest possible participation of the verbal system, that is, it takes place in both signal systems simultaneously. Indeed, the formation of connections in the verbal system, which plays a basic systematizing role, not infrequently takes place even before the formation of a 'direct' motor reaction. Therefore, if we are to speak of the 'handing-over' of connections from one system to another (a phrase which only has a conditional, relative meaning), we ought rather to recognize that in the case of the normal pupil or adult, it frequently happens that connections, built up with the participation of a verbal system, are realized in motor acts. It is this regulation by the verbal system of direct actions that comprises the real basis of conscious behaviour.

Experiments have shown that the verbal system does not play a leading role in the formation of new connections at all ages.[1] Investigation of the development of motor reactions in pre-school children by the method of speech reinforcement, has shown clearly the gradual way in which language comes into play in this process. Under laboratory conditions, speech may not play a leading role in the development of direct connections in a three-year-old child; it is itself subordinate to the influence of a diffuse, weakly irradiating neurodynamic process; frequently it does not run ahead of, but only follows, connections which are established directly. However, the child's direct reactions are very soon complicated by the participation of speech. He begins to speak to the adult, and this speech, in turn, is replaced by the participation of a full, and then a contracted, verbal system in the analysis and systematization of the proferred signals.

The participation of a verbal system in the formation of new connections can be significantly accelerated by training. One has only to question a child about the exact occasions when he reacted appropriately, for this form of verbal communication with an adult to cause substantial changes in behaviour even of a child of three years. When the signals are constantly mediated through speech in this way, children easily begin to find their bearings even among complicated

[1] Research of N. P. Paramonova [47] under my direction.

systems of signals. It is characteristic that when relatively simple differentiations have to be made, the verbal system is contracted in form, but when complex differentiations are being worked out, requiring a preliminary verbal analysis of the stimuli and a separation of the significant elements of the signals with the aid of language, speech continues for a long time to flow in full, uncontracted form.

By the junior school age (9 to 11 years) speech employed in the elaboration of new connections finally becomes contracted and internal, and most of the differentiations are attained without pronouncing words aloud. But this does not mean that such differentiations are worked out without the participation of the verbal system, as has been proved during experiments. When a child subject is questioned he formulates clearly in words the rule he must follow in reacting to stimuli, and separate remarks are also made by subjects when motor reactions are developed by the method of speech reinforcement (e.g. 'Now it's clear; at a long signal—I must press; at a short one—I don't press!').

Investigations have shown that the most varied forms of child activity develop in the same way.[1] Orientation in the surrounding real world, effected at first in the form of unabbreviated practical action, gradually begins to be effected with the aid of speech; this initially follows the activity and is unabbreviated, but gradually assumes a leading role, becomes contracted, and is included as the main mechanism whereby the child performs a 'mental action'. This method of forming complex types of human activity must be taken into account when the formation of new temporary connections in man is examined.

II

The normal child of $5\frac{1}{2}$ years and upwards forms new connections in these conditions largely by using a verbal system, which enables him to abstract and generalize the significant elements in the signals and to find his bearings among them. This indicates important new characteristics in the development of temporary connections, which clearly distinguish this process from that observed in laboratory experiments with animals.

This can be demonstrated by the simplest experiments dealing with the formation of motor reactions by the method of speech reinforcement. When Ivanov-Smolensky [17: 20] first suggested this method, his main purpose was to demonstrate that man's voluntary motor reactions develop in accordance with the same laws of nervous activity as do temporary connections in animals, and that, consequently,

[1] A. V. Zaporozhets [69], P. Ya. Galperin, cf. p. 213.

even man's higher processes are open to physiological analysis. There followed a careful study of the hypothesis that a connection, arising through closure of the nervous circuit, is 'transferred' by virtue of 'elective irradiation' to the second signal system, and that closed connections can be directly reflected in various ways in the verbal report of the subject in various normal and pathological conditions. The investigations established these fundamental facts.

But it would be quite wrong to limit ourselves to this proposition, and fail to see that, even when new temporary connections are formed without the perceptible participation of speech, the process differs substantially from that discovered as a result of experimental study of animals.

In the case of animals, under laboratory conditions, the development of new connections, and especially of differentiation, always takes place with a certain gradualness, requires many repetitions, and sometimes difficult and prolonged work. Also, as a rule, the process follows a series of strictly consecutive stages, beginning with generalization of the stimulus, and only thereafter proceeding to concentration and the gradual development of inhibition of inappropriate reactions. Finally, the developed system of connections, consisting of positive reactions and differentiations, remains unstable for a certain time and is easily disrupted if complicating factors (e.g. an external inhibitory factor) are introduced; only if it is 'learned by rote' for a more or less lengthy period, does it become so firmly stabilized that it ceases to be influenced by complicating and irrelevant conditions.

New systems of connections in man do not always necessarily follow all the consecutive phases of this gradual process. This may be the typical course of development for certain difficult sensory and motor differentiations, but it occurs only rarely in the formation of those systems of connections and differentiations which can rest on verbal systematization of the material.

For example, experiments in the formation of new systems of connections in a normal subject (schoolchild or adult) show that speech enters into the process of forming conditioned motor reactions from the first. The subjects in whom new motor reactions are being developed by the method of speech reinforcement either ask the experimenter, 'Must I press now?' or themselves attempt to analyse verbally the system of signals presented to them, and its connection with corresponding reinforcements. In other words, faced with a certain *problem*, they always find their bearings by using the abstracting and generalizing, analysing and synthesizing power of language. It is important to note that this is so even when the experiment is concerned with relatively simple, perceptible connections; when speech does not

120

replace the signals presented and is not mentioned in the subject's verbal report after the experiment.

Former connections, systematized in speech under more complex conditions, can be brought into play to help the subject orientate himself in the conditions of the experiment; but this may not happen immediately. This speech orientation may often bear a prolonged and uncontracted character, and sometimes passes through a phase or generalization before leading to more precise definition. If simpler problems are set, the stage of generalization can be by-passed and bear a contracted character; the temporary connection can then be established 'on the spot'. But even here, language invariably plays its systematizing role in the formation of connections; it is this participation of a verbal system, one gradually built up in ontogenesis, that adds substantially new features to the process of forming a new connection. This process, involving an integral use of language, loses its direct and gradual character and becomes transformed into the act of including the given signal in a system already formed with the help of language. A subject who has already used speech to formulate the rule, 'Press for a short signal, do not press for a long one' (that is, who has already formed a certain system of connections on a verbal background), has no need gradually 'to work out' the connection between a motor reaction and a direct stimulus. This new connection is included in an already existing system of connections and is established at once. The whole basic process is changed, from the gradual establishment and consolidation of visuo-motor connections into the formation of a speech system. The motor reactions only put into effect what has already been prepared by this basically verbal orientation. A new connection formed in this way does not require all the stages in the process usual in a laboratory experiment with animals (initial generalization and subsequent gradual concentration), nor is a long 'learning by rote' necessary. The connection at once acquires the necessary stability thanks to its inclusion in the corresponding system.

When a new system of connections has been developed in an animal it usually needs constant reinforcement. If this is withheld for a certain time the connection begins to fade. Only those connections which are systematically reinforced over a long period of time show any great stability.

Connections formed with the aid of a verbal system are not, however, subject to this rule. The experimenter, working with a normal subject, can safely cease giving continual speech reinforcement (either direct, of the type 'press' or 'don't press', or assenting, of the type 'good', 'correct'). If the connection has been developed with the participation of a verbal system, and the subject reacts to signals by mediating them through words (i.e. through a formulated rule), constant external reinforcement appears unnecessary to him, and the connection formed does not fade until cancelled by some other connection. This does not imply that there is no reinforcement whatever in these cases. A verbal formulation of a system of connections (in the shape of a rule which specifies each reaction) itself acts as a constantly operating reinforcement, sufficient to preserve the stability of a connection. This fact, experimentally established, underlines the validity of Pavlov's proposition,[1] 'man is, of course, a system . . . but . . . a system which, within the present scope of our scientific vision, is unique in that it possesses very great powers of self-regulation'.

Any alteration in a system of connections, developed under laboratory conditions, involves considerable nervous energy on the part of an animal; in some it requires a considerable time and in others produces a state of collapse. A system of connections formed with the aid of language is, on the other hand, extraordinarily mobile, and, unless very complex, is easily replaced by a new one. The new, verbally formulated system of connections, as it were, 'cancels' the old connection, and the subject's reaction is immediately included in this new system. Only in certain special cases, indicated later, does a broad, verbally generalized, system of connections hinder the development of new connections relating to another system of generalizations. Therefore the alteration of connections mediated through speech also bears a special character. By altering only one link in this complex verbal system, it is possible to obtain, 'on the spot' and without any reinforcement, the alteration of all its remaining links. This points yet again to the special role of verbal generalization.

Lastly, we may notice a fact of great significance concerning the peculiarities of the process of forming new connections in man. The development of new temporary connections in an animal under laboratory conditions depends largely on the 'perceptibility' of the proferred signals. Where the significant element in the signal is not directly perceptible, it takes many months to develop a system of connections, and sometimes proves impossible. Moreover, even if it is developed, the connection is easily broken if the manner of presenting the signals is changed. A good example is the development of a system of reactions to the order in which identical signals are presented (e.g. to every third and fourth signal). This presents a difficult problem to an animal, which must traverse a long road to solve it.

But experiments show that this crossing of the limits of the directly perceptible does not present any particular difficulty to man. On the contrary, typically human behaviour is oriented, not only to easily perceptible signs, but also to abstract principles which are assimilated

[1] Pavlov-Gantt ii, 144; *Selected Works*, 446–7.

with the aid of speech. Pavlov often commented on the ease with which man develops a system of reactions to a certain order of signals, because 'man in solving this problem makes use of his own abstract thought' and because 'he possesses the idea of number' [50: 56, 246].

All these data [1] show that the introduction of speech—which analyses and synthesizes the given signals, and transforms the process of developing new connections into a process, mediated through words, of forming generalized systems of connections—changes certain important rules governing the development, preservation and remoulding of connections; it gives to this process the character of conscious activity.

The facts outlined explain the cases, often mentioned in psychological literature, when a new temporary connection is formed by a leap, sometimes 'on the spot'; and also those paradoxical instances when a temporary connection (with speech reinforcement) sometimes takes a long time before it is closed, and appears not to be fully developed. Such cases can be understood in the light of the mediating role of the verbal system. The apparent impossibility of developing connections in these cases is explained by the influence of the verbal formula—'react only to a direct order, and do not react to the preceding signal'—which is, naturally, formulated by certain subjects accustomed to perform a task accurately. This means that the signal stimulus preceding the command, 'press', does not become a conditioned stimulus for these subjects, and so does not produce the required reaction.

Substantial differences in the process of formation of temporary connections, depending on the nature of the verbal generalizations, have also been brought to light. [2] A sharp acceleration of the process of forming a new connection has been secured, when this was developed on the basis of an earlier generalized system (e.g. when, on the foundation of a developed system of reactions 'through one signal' another system of reactions was developed—'through two signals to a third'). A sharp slowing down of the same process (sometimes even a complete stoppage) resulted when an attempt was made to form a connection in the same subject in response to a sign which did not enter into an existing verbally generalized system (e.g. when, in the context of an established system of reactions to an *alteration* of stimuli, the *duration* of a stimulus was made the significant element in the signal). In the latter case a stable, verbally generalized connection 'to react to some sequence or other in the signals', directed the

[1] From the experimental investigations of Paramonova [47], Meshcheriakov [44], Lubovsky [40] and others.

[2] Investigations carried out in our laboratory by Meshcheriakov [44] and M. S. Shekhter.

subjects' search, and therefore the duration of the stimuli, which did not enter into this generalized system, did not become a significant element for a long time. The development of a new connection under these conditions required, on average, 15 to 17 times more repetitions than in the first case.

All this shows that it is unscientific to attempt to study the mechanism of the development of new temporary connections in man while ignoring the crucial role of language. Only by attentively studying the part played by the verbal system in the development of even simple 'direct' connections, only by taking into account the 'new principle of nervous activity' which the second signal system, with its abstracting and generalizing functions, contributes to the flow of nervous processes, can we improve on a mere description of the most general laws of nervous processes which belong to the animals as well as to men, and provide new, concrete material characterizing the unique features of the formation of connections in man.

III

When a child develops normally, the closest interaction between the two signal systems is established as early as the age of 5 or 6, and, under laboratory conditions, the abstracting and generalizing function of language begins to play a decisive role in the development of new connections. At the same time pathological changes in the normal working of the cortex, and abnormal development, lead to profound changes in the joint working of the two signal systems, to disturbance of the abstracting and generalizing functions of language, and sometimes to its exclusion from a share in forming new connections. This is one of the principal features of pathological changes in man's higher nervous activity.

Numerous investigations [17: 20] show that, when the working of the brain is upset (in cases of poisoning, mental disease, comatose conditions, and so on), a certain dissociation of the two signal systems ensues, and elective irradiation, which enables language to replace a direct signal, breaks down; the connection developed in these cases ceases to be transferred to the second signal system and is not adequately reflected in the verbal report.

But these are not the only results of the profound change in the interaction of the two signal systems which takes place in such cases. Another scarcely less important change observed, both in cases of shock to the brain and in cases of abnormal development, is that language often ceases to play any part in the formation of temporary connections, and no longer fulfils the function that it successfully fulfils in the normal person.

LANGUAGE IN FORMATION OF TEMPORARY CONNECTIONS

In normal activity, previously acquired verbal connections play an active orienting role in the formation of new connections; in this process, language abstracts the essential significant elements, systematizes past experience, and, in certain cases, can, as it were, run ahead and establish new systems of connections before these have been formed in action. But in cases of pathological and abnormal development, which we subjected to a special study, language had lost this role, could not fulfil its orienting function, began to lag behind the development of direct connections, and only fixed connections which had already been developed, and then not always completely.

The evidence for this conclusion was obtained in studies of many cases of organic localized diseases of the brain,[1] and in experimental investigation of the peculiar features of the development of new connections in cases of mental retardation.[2]

The starting point of these investigations was the established fact that verbal connections, formed with the help of a preliminary instruction, which in normal subjects firmly regulate the stream of motor reactions, lose their regulating power in certain cases where the hemispheres, and in particular, the frontal lobes, have received widespread damage. Such patients can successfully retain verbal instructions, and reproduce them after considerable intervals of time; but the weakness of the nerve cells of the motor analyser in the injured cortical areas, and the inertness of nervous processes characteristic of a pathologically altered cortex, are so great that they are unable to produce motor reactions in response. The conditioned significance attached to the stimuli with the aid of the verbal instruction (e.g. 'when there is a knock raise your hand') easily fades, and the connection of the signal with the movement is lost. Often the pathological inertness of the excitatory or inhibitory processes is so great, that the necessary responses are completely inhibited; they are replaced by an inert repetition of one and the same motor stereotype, which finally loses its connection with the verbal instruction. A similar phenomenon is observed in certain cases of abnormal development where severe lesions in the brain have caused great mental retardation.

In such cases the working of the specifically human areas of the cortex is disturbed, and well-established speech connections are excluded from the task of regulating action. This change in the role of the verbal system is revealed even more clearly in experiments on the

[1] N. A. Filippycheva [13], B. G. Spirin [64], A. I. Meshcheriakov [44], M. P. Ivanova [21], E. K. Andreeva [2], N. M. Kostomarova [29] and others.
[2] V. I. Lubovsky [40], E. N. Martsinovskaya, A. I. Meshcheriakov [44], N. Nepomniashchaya, E. N. Vinarskaya, O. K. Tikhomirova and E. D. Khomskaya.

development of new connections by the method of speech reinforcement. These showed that children suffering from a brain injury, and children with severe mental retardation resulting from early organic disease of the brain, could form sufficiently stable systems of connections by the method of speech reinforcement;[1] the process by which these connections were formed, however, differed considerably from that in normal subjects.

In experiments dealing with the development of the simplest differentiations (e.g. when a red signal has a positive meaning, and a blue signal a negative one) a system of connections was usually developed quite easily by the method of speech reinforcement; but as soon as the use of speech was made necessary, the position changed radically. This happened, for example, when differentiated reactions to signals identical in colour but of different duration were being developed (when each short flash of a green lamp was reinforced positively, and each long flash negatively). In such cases the subject had to abstract the element of duration of the signal from its repeated and directly perceived quality (colour); a long duration of signal, added to this basic element (colour), had to serve as a conditioned inhibition, as it were, for the motor reaction. Analogous conditions obtain in the development of a system of differentiated reactions to a sequence (ordinal number) in which identical signals are presented.

A normal subject, with the aid of speech, isolates the significant element in the signals, quickly includes his reactions in the necessary system, and easily develops new systems of connections in more complex conditions. But this is frequently an impossible task for a subject suffering from widespread injury to the great hemispheres, or with gross retardation of cerebral activity.

The main common characteristic of these subjects [2] is the failure of speech to play its full orienting and systematizing role in the development of such connections. In some cases language does not lead to the abstraction and isolation of the supplementary significant factor in the signal (duration of the signal or place in the series) from its directly perceived quality (colour). In other cases it ceases to play a part in the analysis and synthesis of the signals presented, and in the formation of the connection between these and the corresponding reinforcement. In such cases it is impossible to regard the development of new temporary connections as mediated by speech; the pro-

[1] Continual positive speech reinforcement of some, and inhibitory reinforcement of other signals led to a far greater concentration of nervous processes than a preliminary spoken instruction could lead to; this explains the possibility of developing a stable system of connections with the help of this method. This question has been treated in detail in Paramonova's work cited above.

[2] The peculiarities which distinguish each of the groups indicated are the subject of a special investigation.

cess acquires characteristics which do not occur in the case of normal people.

The crucial point is that, even after the connection between signals and reactions is established after a long series of repetitions, the subject remains unconscious of it for a long time, and unable to express it verbally. Though he gives a clear positive reaction to a short signal, and a negative one to a long signal (or a positive reaction to every first and second, and a negative one to every third of a series of identical signals), the subject cannot say in his report to which signals he reacted and to which he did not. This fact, surprising at first glance, which shows that the orienting function of speech does not play its due part in developing the new connection, has been carefully investigated.[1] It has been shown that the report of a subject, in whom the necessary direct connection has already been developed in practice, quite often continues to reflect some old, long cancelled reaction. Although he correctly presses the key in response to a short signal, and refrains from pressing in response to a long one, the subject continues for a long time to assert that he is pressing when a red light appears, and not pressing when a blue light appears, despite the fact that the red and blue lights have long since ceased to be presented.

The pathological inertness characteristic of cortical disturbance, particularly notable in the verbal system, not only makes it impossible for speech to run ahead and to play its active, orienting role in the development of new connections, but also changes verbal reactions into a stereotype which inertly reproduces earlier connections. Only after a long process of consolidation of the new system of connections (and moreover, under specially arranged conditions) can the verbal system reflect the new system of direct connections which has been strengthened in practice.

A similar retardation of the system of verbal connections was observed in other experiments.[2] The subjects were asked to replace their motor reactions, already stabilized, with speech reactions, by responding to each positive signal with the words 'I must' (or 'I must press'), and to each negative signal with the words 'I must not' (or 'I must not press'). Subjects suffering from the most severe form of mental retardation, who had already in practice developed the appropriate system of motor reactions, were often not only unable to give a correct, generalized, verbal account of the connections they had developed, but could not even replace the motor reactions which had

---

[1] It has been described in patho-physiological literature by the collaborators of Ivanov-Smolensky [17], and studied in detail in my laboratory by Meshcheriakov [44], Ivanova [21], Lubovsky [40] and Martsinovskaya.
[2] Conducted by Khomskaya and Martsinovskaya.

been stabilized in the experiment with the corresponding verbal responses. Their responses rapidly became an inert stereotype, and subjects, who had just been giving well differentiated motor reactions, began to respond to the changing signals always with the same words ('I must—I must—I must'), or with just as monotonous an alternation of formulae ('I must'—'I must not', 'I must'—'I must not'), completely failing to reflect the significant element in the stimuli offered to them. Naturally enough, with such a degree of pathological inertness of nervous processes (which produces an inert speech stereotype in place of adequate speech evaluations of signals), there is no way of making speech acquire its orientating and regulating function. Only in subjects suffering from less severe injury to the brain was the transfer made from a system of motor reactions to one of spoken responses without transformation of the latter into a stereotype. But, even in these cases, the replacement of motor by verbal reactions by no means universally led to the necessary conscious awareness of the connection which had been previously developed in practice.

Naturally, this breakdown of the verbal system means that the process of formation of new connections is very different from that in a normal person. If language does not participate in the development of new connections and differentiations, this process loses the organized character previously described. While in a normal person signals are usually included in ready-made systems of connections, in abnormal cases this process is replaced by the gradual development of separate direct connections, and this development passes through the phases, first of generalization, then of concentration of the stimulatory and inhibitory processes. Sometimes speech plays a part in the formation of crude, insufficiently differentiated, and inert generalizations, which, far from helping the development of the necessary connection, actually hinder it.

Further experiments have shown that the development of systems of connections in cases of severe mental retardation can take up many sittings, and sometimes requires hundreds of repetitions.[1] This is because the process takes place without the participation of a verbal system, and so frequently requires long, continuous reinforcement, and for a long time does not begin to acquire the necessary signs of 'self-regulation', which only arises when a generalization has been formulated in words. If, therefore, the continuous speech reinforcement (of the type 'press' and 'you must not press', or even of the type 'correct') is removed, the connection may lose its stability and gradually fade. This dependence of a formed connection on continual speech reinforcement is characteristic of connections developed without the participation of verbal system.

¹ Conducted by Lubovsky [40] and Martsinovskaya.

A connection developed without the participation of speech can for long remain very inert, and can be remodelled only with great labour and very gradually. Sometimes it is impossible to cancel by words a 'rote-learned' connection. Sometimes a slight pause, or the action of some complicating factor (an external inhibition, a change of regimen), is sufficient to cause the remodelled connection to disappear, and the old inert connection to reappear. Therefore, the remodelling of connections, once they have been assimilated, involves no less (and it may be considerably more) nervous energy than the first development of a new connection.

Finally—and this is not unexpected—a connection formed without the due participation of a verbal system is wholly dependent on the concrete conditions in which the stimuli are presented. It has been demonstrated experimentally that when, in the case of abnormal subjects, a complex system of connections has been successfully developed, it is an inert stereotype, rather than a dynamic system based on the isolation of an abstract distinguishing factor and changing with a change in certain conditions of the experiment. Thus, even if a system of reactions to an alternation of identical signals (e.g. reaction to every third signal) is successfully developed in a seriously retarded child, it is sufficient to change the way of presenting the signals (e.g. by speeding them up or slowing them down), to realize that the system of reactions has not been mediated in any way by the verbal report, but is a 'rote-learned', rhythmical stereotype which is easily destroyed with each change in the concrete form of presentation of the signal.

The breakdown of the basic mechanism—the participation of the verbal system in the development of new connections—leads, therefore, to profound changes in this process, and deprives it of the very high degree of mobility and self-regulation which it attains, with the aid of language, in a normal person. It is precisely because of this qualitative difference in the development of new connections in cases of abnormal development of the cortex or of pathological conditions of the cortex, that new laws are being discovered which are not revealed in normal cases, and which provide a key to the explanation of many phenomena of the pathology of the higher nervous activity of man.

PART III

THE BASIS OF SPATIAL DISCRIMINATION [1]

BY

B. G. ANANIEV

I

EVERY FORM OF MATTER in motion acting on the organs of sense is reflected in the brain as a sensation which corresponds to this form of movement of matter.

The different forms of motion of matter (mechanical movement of bodies, molecular oscillations in the form of heat, electrical or magnetic current, chemical dissolution and combination, organisms), acting on different sense organs phylogenetically adapted to specific forms of matter in motion, are reflected as different sensations: cutaneous, visual, auditory, olfactory, gustatory, and so on. The concept of sensations is, therefore, inextricably bound up with the concept of matter which evokes sensations and is reflected in them. As Lenin has said: 'Matter is a philosophical category designating the objective reality which is conveyed to man by his sensations, and which is copied, photographed and reflected by our sensations, while existing independently of them.' Lenin further formulated the proposition: 'Sensation is an image of matter in motion. Save through sensations, we can know nothing either of the forms of substance or of the forms of motion; sensations are evoked by the action of matter in motion upon our sense organs.' [2]

The number and variety of sensations—sensory images of the external world—are determined by the variety of phenomena of the

---

[1] This constitutes the opening chapter of a book published at the close of 1955 under the title, *Spatial Discrimination* (translated by H. Milne).

[2] *Selected Works*, xi, 192, 355.

external world acting on man's sense organs and brain. But a sense organ is only part of a more complex nervous mechanism, the analyser, which consists of the sense organ, the sensory (afferent) nerves, and the cerebral terminals of the analyser. The whole analyser is brought into activity when energy from the external world is transformed into a nervous process arising in the sense organ. The human brain—the material organ of consciousness—is linked with the external world through the sense organs. Therefore sensations, which are produced by the activity of the sense organs and of the analyser as a whole, are the most elementary elements of consciousness, directly reflecting the external world in images.

Sight, hearing, touch, smell, and the other sensory operations of the brain produce a countless multitude of sensations through which we cognize the external world. As Lenin said,

> For every scientist who has not been led astray by professional philosophy, as well as for every materialist, sensation is . . . the direct connection between consciousness and the external world; it is the transformation of the energy of an external stimulation into a state of consciousness. Every human being observes this transformation literally at every step, and has observed it millions of times.[1]

A calculation made by Sechenov illustrates this proposition. If the maximum duration of each new phase of perception is taken to be five seconds, in the course of twelve hours a man experiences no less than 8000 separate visual sensations and approximately the same number of aural sensations, especially if the part played by the ear in oral communication between people is taken into account. The number of motor sensations which produce a fractional analysis of body movement (working movements and actions, walking, articulatory movements of the speech apparatus) is even greater. To these must be added many thousands of olfactory and gustatory sensations, and also sensations from the internal organs of the body. But, in fact, a man is awake for more than twelve hours a day; moreover, in light sleep the sense organs continue to work, though at a reduced tempo. Thus, during twenty-four hours the number of sensations runs into several tens of thousands. The accumulation of this enormous quantity of sensations, and of their traces and endless associations with each other, comprises the sensory basis of thinking. The association, the combination and recombination of sensations, forms more complex images of reality—perceptions and ideas. Sensations and perceptions together make up the living representation which a man

[1] *Selected Works*, xi, 118.

forms of objective reality, his sensory knowledge of the external world. But cognition is a complex, contradictory process, in which the living representation, abstract thought and practice are dialectically interconnected.

Without sensations, which give a relatively faithful snapshot of the external world, animals and men could not live and act normally. It is through his sensations that a man is able to find his bearings amid the phenomena and objects of the external world which create the various conditions of his existence. No abstract thought, no mental (generalized and mediated) reflection of existence can arise without, and apart from, sensations. But sensations do not give complete knowledge of the phenomena of the external world; this is only formed in unity with thought, on the basis of language. The factor of decisive importance for the whole process of cognition, from sensation onwards, is practice. It is through practice that we test the accuracy of our images, and separate the true from the false. The classics of Marxism-Leninism provide detailed proofs of the proposition that, in practical activity, we use things in conformity with their real properties.

The accuracy and truth of images cannot always be tested by the personal experience of a single man, but it is perpetually tested by the social practice of men; and it is social practice which conditions the individual's personal experience. Psychology has accumulated scientific data showing the leading role of activity in the dynamics of sensations, and this proposition has a physiological basis. Sechenov, guided by the hypothesis of the reflex activity of the brain, proved that sensation and movement comprise a single reflex whole. External stimuli acting on the eye, the ear, the skin, are signals for movement, since the brain receives these signals and transforms them into impulses for the neuro-muscular apparatus. The movements which ensue, on the basis of these external signals, themselves cause the so-called muscular-skeletal sensations which inform the brain of the correctness or incorrectness of the movements, in relation to the external conditions which gave rise to the given activity.

Sensations, which are inseparable from man, developed historically in the course of the development of social labour. The development of labour means a progressive extension of the frontiers of man's knowledge of the external world, and this decisively influenced the qualitative transformation of human analysers and sensations. As man discovered more and more new qualities and properties of the objects of the external world, he simultaneously acquired new possibilities of reflecting it in sensation. It is, therefore, a mistake to identify the activity of the sense organs of animals and of human beings, in spite of a similarity in structure and functions. Human sensations depend on the conditions of life of human beings; that is, on changes effected in nature by social labour. The activity of the human analysers is determined by the social character of human life, and by the relation of social labour to nature. The historical development of man has led to qualitative changes not only in the conditions governing the activity of his analysers (of their terminal apparatus—the sense organs) but also in the form of activity of all the analysers.

Particularly important changes are found in the kinaesthetic (motor) analyser, since the division of functions between the extremities developed as a result of labour. The hands are not only the product but also the natural organ of labour; in their actions and movements during work, delicate sensations are experienced in the muscles and joints which send signals concerning the process of work. Again, man's straight gait and upright carriage have become an important source of his sensations; Sechenov considered walking to be a fractionalizing analyser of space and time.

Every sensation, since it is a product of the activity of an analyser as a sensory system of the brain, breaks up and separates out the external world into the smallest units. An individual sensation isolates a definite property of a given external object which acts on a given sense organ. A visual sensation isolates optical (light) properties in an object and its environment: degree of brightness, colour. Cutaneous sensations reflect the surface quality of an object (smoothness, roughness) and its temperature. A combination of cutaneous and kinaesthetic sensations makes it possible to ascertain the density and resilience of a body. Aural sensations reflect the sound waves and sound properties which arise as bodies interact with each other, and so on. Consequently, each sensation reflects a definite property of an individual object, that is, a single phenomenon of the external world.

A sensation, however, is not only an image of the individual properties of an object; it fixes the *general* property of *various* objects of the external world (e.g. the degree of brightness and colour of things which differ in their form, density and sound properties). It can be said that each definite kind of sensation (visual, aural, etc.) reflects external reality through a single general property of a given form of movement of matter.

Experimental investigations have shown that in the first moments of a visual sensation the subject is aware primarily of what is acting upon him at that instant; not sound, nor smell, but *light*, that is, the most general element in optical stimuli. Then he becomes aware of the intensity of the light or the colour of the surface of the body acting upon him. When a conditioned reflex to a light stimulus (e.g. a red light) is being developed, the analyser at first reacts to any light stimulus (though not generally to any other external influence); that is, the process of stimulation is diffused. Only as differentiation develops (between reinforced and non-reinforced stimuli) does the reaction operate only in response to a red light. Consequently, every individual sensation reflects both the general properties of the given form of movement of matter, and the particular manifestations of this property in a single object of the external world. But the combination of the general and the particular in a concrete sensation takes place on the basis of the single object which is acting upon the sense organ at a given moment.

Matter in motion, the objects and phenomena of the external world, always exist in definite spatial and temporal conditions. Therefore the properties of things are reflected in sensations, not outside time and space, but in concrete space-time conditions. Thus, the visual image of an object reflects not only its optical qualities (brightness, colour) but also its extension, size, shape, its position in space relative to other things, and so on. An aural image reproduces not only the pitch, duration, and strength of a sound, but also the position of its source. In cutaneous sensations, not only the texture of the surface of the object touching the skin is reflected, but also its extension. Consequently general features, such as the spatial features and relations of things, are also reflected in sensations. It is also known that all the analysers reflect temporary conditions affecting the existence of the reflected objects and their interconnections. It follows that the sensory activity of the brain is the source of our knowledge, not only of objects and phenomena of the external world, but also of space and time as forms of existence of matter in motion.

The material basis of sensations of all types (visual, aural, olfactory, etc.) is the activity of the analyser, that is, the sensory system of the brain. Every sensation is a function of one corresponding analyser (light, sound, smell, and so on). The analysers are one of the basic nervous mechanisms; another is the mechanism of temporary connections or conditioned reflexes, on which depends the level of activity of an analyser and so the speed and accuracy of sensations. The latter mechanism is of great importance in developing the activity of the analysers, and raising their sensitivity to specific material stimuli.

The conditioned-reflex nature of the work of the analysers is most clearly shown in their discrimination, or discriminatory sensitivity. An analyser is acted upon simultaneously or consecutively by several stimuli or a multitude of stimuli. These stimuli are objectively connected in respect of their material nature, spatial position, and the time of their action upon the receptor. But they are more distinct from each other in their quality, intensity, and spatial-temporal features and relations. The reflection of the difference between stimuli of the same kind is the process of discrimination. In this process, individual (simultaneous or consecutive) sensations are linked with each other and become the source of a complex intellectual process, namely comparison. The process of discrimination, like the process of sensation, is characterized by definite thresholds (thresholds of difference or thresholds of discrimination). An individual's differentiating or discriminatory sensitivity is determined by these thresholds.

The material basis of the process of discrimination is the discriminatory (differentiating) activity of the cerebral cortex. One of the most important characteristics of higher nervous activity is the differentiation of closely similar signals acting on the same analyser. The specialization of a conditioned stimulus, that is, the transformation of an undifferentiated stimulus into a conditioned one, is linked with this process. Pavlov and his collaborators showed that a signal repeated a thousand times and reinforced by an unconditioned stimulus does not lead to the specialization of the conditioned stimulus. In this situation the animal continues to respond to all similar signals with the salivary reaction; for example, if a metronome ticking at the rate of 120 per minute is taken as the conditioned stimulus, the salivary reaction will take place also in response to a tick of 150 or 70 per minute. But a single trial, using one of the similar signals without reinforcement and accompanying the chosen signal with reinforcement, results in specialization of the conditioned stimulus; the salivary reaction will now take place only in response to the conditioned stimulus.

It must not be supposed that, in the case of a generalized reflex, there is absolutely no discrimination between the intensity and quality of similar signals. But such discrimination is limited to a mere ascertainment or affirmation that a difference exists, depending on the difference of the oscillations in the process of stimulation. The external expression of change in the stimulatory process takes the form of tentative reaction to the replacement of one stimulus by another. Pavlov distinguished real differentiation of stimuli from such affirmation or ascertainment, and proved that differentiation is based on the development of internal inhibition in relation to the given stimuli.

Differentiations can be worked out in this way only by means of conditioned-reflex activity. The formation of a temporary connection between a (specialized) conditioned stimulus and a certain form of activity implies not only analysis of the external stimuli, but also the establishment of a connection between them by means of joining them together (synthesis). Underlying this process of discrimination is the unity of the analytic and synthetic activity of the cerebral hemispheres.

Language plays an exceptionally important part in differentiation. The expression in words of a generalized knowledge of the objects and relations of the external world assists the development of discrimination. As his vocabulary and mastery of grammatical structure increases, man learns to make fine distinctions between external stimuli which are closely similar in nature and intensity. The sharpening of a child's discriminatory sensitivity is expressed in the development of his powers of observation, which is closely connected with the formation of the second signal system as the basis of speech and thinking. In experiments designed to study the process of differentiation, the appropriate word not only replaces the stimulus which is being differentiated but also organizes the whole process. The influence of the second signal system on the first is seen very clearly in the development of discriminatory sensitivity. Shvarts' data show that, as children grow older, their discriminatory sensitivity becomes very much sharper (in older children it is much more delicate than in younger), although absolute sensitivity increases less noticeably. The development of discriminatory sensitivity in children is inextricably bound up with improvement in their speech in the course of their education and upbringing.

[Here, Professor Ananiev defines the threshold of discrimination, as the minimum difference between two stimuli which permits of their discrimination. There must be a definite interrelation between the intensities of two stimuli for these to be discriminated in sensations. Weber found that the ratio of an additional stimulus to the original one must be of a constant value (e.g. for weight, the constant increase of intensity must be one-thirtieth of the original weight). But critical testing of this proposition has shown that it is correct only in the case of stimuli of medium intensity; as the absolute thresholds of sensation are approached, the increase ceases to be a fixed constant value. Fechner developed this proposition and formulated his law that sensations increase in arithmetical progression while stimuli increase in geometrical progression; or that a sensation increases proportionally to the logarithm of the intensity of the stimulus. Only the basic idea of this law has been accepted; namely that sensations increase, not in proportion to the increasing strength of the stimuli, but much more slowly.]

A leading Soviet biophysicist and physiologist, P. N. Lazarev, has established a more exact and many-sided relationship between the increase in intensity of stimuli and of sensations, on the basis of the physiology of higher nervous activity. The relationship is determined by the interaction of the processes of excitation and inhibition, particularly internal inhibition, in the differentiation of stimuli.

Continued practice in analytical and discriminatory exercises makes it possible to generalize a formed discriminatory habit and to transfer it to other conditions. For example, it has been proved that sensitization of one eye (open at the given moment) is reflected in the condition of the other eye which is shut at that moment: a conditioned reflex heightening of the acuity of vision of an open right eye is transferred to the left eye without additional training. Similarly, a heightening of the cutaneous sensitivity of one hand is transferred to the other which is not being directly stimulated; sensitization of the right side of the nose produces a heightening of the sensitivity of the left side, which is screened from stimulation.[1] These results are explained by the fact that sensitization of one of a pair of receptors (e.g. one of the eyes) is in reality a sensitization of the analyser as a whole. The heightening of the efficiency of the cerebral terminal of the analyser changes the functional state of the other homonymous receptor which has not been stimulated. The effect of practice is also doubled, for it spreads from one homonymous receptor to the other.

The heightening of sensitivity to one stimulus can be transferred to assist in the analysis and discrimination of other stimuli which affect the same receptor. Thus, Shvarts has shown that sensitization of the eye to one colour (e.g. red) heightens the sensitivity of the eye to another colour (e.g. yellow). In chromatic vision such phenomena are many and various. When the organ of smell is sensitized to the odour of one substance there takes place a certain heightening of sensitivity to the odours of other substances (A. I. Bronstein). Sensitization occurs in the activity of any analyser, especially in relation to those properties of material objects and phenomena which are connected with the individual's activity.

At every moment in a man's life a multitude of various material stimuli act upon him simultaneously and consecutively. His brain responds to these influences with a multitude of homonymous and heteronymous sensations, which interact owing to the formation of temporary connections between the various analysers. A typical example of interaction between homonymous sensations is the transfer of changes in sensitivity from one homonymous receptor to another. Interaction between heteronymous sensations is no less important in heightening the sensitivity of a receptor. Interaction between visual and muscular-skeletal sensations makes possible the joint operation of hand and eye in a work-act (the so-called visuo-motor coordination). Interaction between the kinaesthetic and tactile sensations of the hands produces touch as a specifically human form of perception. Interaction between the auditory and kinaesthetic sensations from

[1] Researches of E. P. Miroshina-Tonkonogaya and A. A. Rykova under my direction.

the speech organs is the prerequisite of oral communication between people.

Engels expressed a profound idea when he said that 'to our eye are joined not only other senses but also our thought'. The joining of thought to vision (and also to other human sensations) is accomplished by speech, and as a result vision not only acquires an intelligent character but also becomes more sensitized. This is also true of all other sensations. Many sensations and perceptions in general ideas are generalized through language. The presence of generalized images helps the subsequent discrimination of new stimuli. Many Soviet investigators have revealed the part played by ideas in heightening the sensitivity of various sense organs. The material basis for the influence exerted by speech and thought, and also by general ideas, on the level of sensitivity, is to be found in the influence of the second signal system on the operation of the first.

It follows that the cultivation of thought and speech is a key factor in sensitizing human sense organs. The acquisition of theoretical knowledge contributes to the 'sharpening', or heightening, of discriminatory sensitivity. This explains the important fact that in children from seven to fifteen years discriminatory sensitivity shows a proportionately far greater increase than absolute sensitivity; as compared with pre-school children of from three to seven years, school-children display an ever-increasing discriminatory sensitivity, especially in vision and hearing. The explanation is that, with the formation of temporary connections between the two signal systems, differentiation of similar objects in the surrounding world is greatly strengthened in the process of education. The analysers develop, improve, change their mode of operation all the time, in the course of education; the mechanism of this development being the system of temporary connections.

This increase in discriminatory sensitivity with age is of particular interest in view of the part played by the second signal system in the development of the first. It is well known that children between the ages of 7 and 15 amass knowledge through direct contact with the phenomena of the external world to a far lesser extent than do pre-school children. The knowledge they acquire is knowledge that is interconnected, like the foundations of the sciences, that is, generalized and mediated knowledge. During instruction, both teaching and learning take place through language in the process of the development of the pupils' oral and written speech under the direction of the teachers. Certain means of instruction, and the practical activity of pupils in studying natural phenomena (in laboratory work, excursions, etc.), are very closely bound up with language. It is language, and the second signal system depending on it, which stimulate the development of pupils' discriminatory sensitivity. Educational experience confirms Pavlov's proposition that, when real conditioned stimuli are 'replaced' by words, the differentiation of temporary connections is speeded up and the orientation of the subject in the surrounding world is improved.

II

It has already been indicated that every sensation, of whatever modality, quality, intensity and duration, has a definite spatial component; the very possibility of spatial discrimination is bound up with this component, which may now be discussed.

Dialectical materialism regards space and time as basic forms of existence of matter in motion; the smallest unit of matter in motion always operates in concrete conditions of space and time. The time factor has been carefully studied in physiology and psychology; there has been a thorough analysis of the temporal conditions governing the adaptation of the sense organs, the speed of various sense reactions has been studied, and so on. But less attention has been paid to the role of the space factor in the dynamics of sensation and discrimination, although the data of psychology and physiology clearly show its importance; i.e. the dependence of seeing on the field of vision, the importance of the angle of vision for the formation of a visual image, the discrimination of such spatial characteristics and relations as shape, size, length, breadth and height, and, especially, the depth of an object or of interacting objects in the visual field—perspective.

It may be said that any stimulus acting on an analyser possesses its own spatial properties; it occupies a place in space, it acts upon a receptor from one of the directions in space (from above or below, from the left, the right, the front, the back), it has surface area (on which depends the area of stimulation in the receptor), size, and shape (it is a structural unity, the parts of which interact within the structure). Further, the exceptional importance of the spatial relations between bodies entering into a perception should be noted; the position of one body relative to another, the proportionality or disproportionality of the interacting areas, the similarity or dissimilarity of interacting shapes, and so on. Nor must it be forgotten that a man receiving sensations is himself a material body, occupying a definite place in space and possessing certain spatial characteristics (size, shape, length, breadth, height, spatial direction of movement and so on). That a man's interaction with his environment includes his body, with its own system of spatial characteristics, is clearly evidenced by the way he finds his bearings in space; his point of reckoning depends on one or other side of the body, usually the right side.

The spatial component is, then, a general and essential feature of all sensations of whatever modality, quality, intensity, or duration. In Soviet psychology the reflection of space is treated in connection with perception, which is traditionally divided into four separate sections: (1) perception of the object, (2) perception of movement, (3) perception of time, (4) perception of space. But it is clear that perception of the object acting on an analyser is impossible without reflection of its movement and spatial-temporal circumstances, and that perception of movement is always a reflection of moving objects and phenomena. Perception of space and time is also inconceivable without reflection of the material content of the spatial-temporal relations. Referring to the traditional separation of perception of the object from perception of its movement, A. A. Ukhtomsky has justly remarked that psychology has been compelled to invent this dichotomy because it is still incapable of giving a scientific explanation of the fundamental fact that the object is reflected in its movement; in confirmation, Ukhtomsky pointed to the fact that psychologists ignore the optical-vestibular connections and the visual-motor coordinations which underlie every individual act of vision.

[Here Professor Ananiev discusses the two theories of space perception, first evolved in the nineteenth century, and the effect these have had in interpreting the results of research into the physiology of the sense organs. Historians of psychology, such as Boring and Flügel, strongly underline the differences between these two schools, nativism and geneticism. Nativism, deriving from Hering, Stumpf and James, asserts that space perception is inborn; a view based on the localization of sense-impression, that is, the fact that each sense quality is perceived in a specific part of the retina, or skin. But this theory maintains, not only that the organization of the apparatus for space perception is inborn, but also that 'ideas of space' are inborn; a frankly idealist conception, based on *a priori* reasoning. The genetic theory derives from Helmholtz and from Bain, Lotze, Wundt, Lipps and others; according to this, space perception, especially perception of depth, is the outcome of individual experience during which visual perceptions are linked with tactile and kinaesthetic sensations. It follows that there is no special equipment in the material organization of an individual receptor adapted to spatial circumstances; only interaction of the apparatus of the different senses makes spatial perception possible. It is denied that there is a spatial component in a single sensation.

[The opposition between these theories is, however, only apparent. Both are more concerned with the nature of space itself than with the

141

mechanism of spatial perception; both conceive of space as a subjective category, introduced by consciousness to bring order into the chaos of external phenomena. Both, therefore, regard the mechanism of spatial perception chiefly as a philosophical problem, one relating to the means whereby the subject 'constructs' space, whereby man's mind creates it; disputes about the nature of its mechanism remain, therefore, chiefly on the philosophic plane, and here the differences may be reduced to differences between two variants of subjective idealism which have acquired in different ways the mask of science. Both schools start from the premiss that the receptor is the direct and sole apparatus of sensations and perceptions, and both ignore the reflex activity of the cortex. The only real difference between them is, therefore, that one regards the receptor mechanisms of spatial perception as inborn, the other as acquired.

[Both nativists and geneticists have used experimental data derived from the physiology of the sense organs to uphold their subjectivist conceptions. As a result, these data have been mishandled in the service of an idealist, retrogressive theory, the 'symbol' conception of consciousness; this is inseparable from the receptor theory, which both nativists and geneticists oppose to the reflex theory. When the mechanism of spatial discrimination is discussed in the light of the receptor theory, spatial vision is explained as the interrelation of monocular systems (the retinae of both eyes) in binocular vision. The physiological facts adduced in support of this view require careful examination.

[Binocular vision is quantitatively superior to monocular vision; it is broader and fuller than the field of vision of each of the eyes and so exceeds the monocular visual field in all coordinates (to the outside or inside, upwards and downwards). Moreover the binocular visual field is not merely the sum of the fields of vision from each eye; in certain directions (e.g. to the inside and upwards) it is greater and more accurate than these combined values. Further, the absolute and discriminatory sensitivity of vision (light sensation and colour sensation) is $1\frac{1}{2}$ to 2 times greater than in monocular vision; and the superiority of binocular vision is even more clearly shown in visual sensations where the angle of vision is slight. These facts underline the biological necessity for the development of binocular vision, especially with the development of complex social life. Nevertheless, these facts were not of decisive importance in the identification of the problem of spatial discrimination with binocular vision typical of traditional physiology. They show only that binocular vision is quantitatively superior to monocular vision. With one eye a man can distinguish all the gradations of brightness in perceived objects and can discriminate light-shade relations; this is also true in the sphere of colour vision. Finally, when the angle of vision is slight, both achromatic and chromatic vision is quite normal when one eye is used. It is clear, therefore, that binocular vision is not an essential condition for the normal working of such general functions as achromatic and chromatic vision.

[It is quite a different matter, however, when we come to visual sensation of depth in space, of the bulk of the perceived body (its relief), of the relationship of foreground and background in the perceived field (perspective). A great deal of experimental data from physiological optics has shown that visual sensation of depth in space and of bulk is only possible with binocular vision; with monocular vision a distant object is not seen in three dimensions but in two dimensions only, and accurate discrimination of perspective is, in general, impossible. From this it has been deduced that binocular vision is the chief prerequisite of spatial discrimination; that the problem of video-spatial discrimination is completely identifiable with that of binocular vision. Exceptions to the established rule, namely the numerous cases of monocular sensation of depth and monocular definition of perspective, are ignored.[1]

[Physiological optics has explained the binocular character of the sensation of depth in space as follows. First, a representation is built up in the optical system of the eye itself which secures the emergence of binocular parallax, the visible intersection of parallel lines in perspective, whereby the foreground and background of the perceived field and the relief features on the surface of the perceived object are distinguished. Second, this construction of a three-dimensional representation is based on a spatial interrelationship on the retina itself; in this connection it is asserted that discrimination of depth takes place when parallel pencils of light stimulate the so-called disparate points on the retinae of both eyes, that is, points which are not in a precisely symmetrical position in each retina. Three-dimensional vision depends on a certain difference in the location of these stimulations on the retina; excessive difference causes a 'doubling' of the image, while stimulation of identical (corresponding) points of the retina produces a single image of the object, but one that is flat and not three-dimensional. Comparison of these phenomena has led to the conviction that moderate disparateness is the mechanism that controls spatial vision.

[These two points make up the explanation given by physiological optics of video-spatial discrimination; an explanation accepted by many psychologists. There is an analogous theory of hearing, and spatial discrimination has been similarly established and explained in other branches of the physiology of the sense organs and of psychology; i.e. olfactory-spatial discrimination, the spatial thresholds of

[1] These cases are discussed later in Professor Ananiev's book (Ed.).

touch and so on. Moreover, in investigation of such muscular-skeletal sensations as movements of the hands during work, great insistence is laid on the fact that it is only in the receptors themselves that the mechanism of spatial-motor orientation is situated, that is, actual orientation in space as parts of the body are moved. Again, sensations important for spatial orientation, such as sensations of equilibrium and acceleration (static sensations), have been explained, and for the most part are still explained, by reference to the structure and functions of the vestibular apparatus of the inner ear. No attempt has been made to find the central mechanisms of these sensory components of spatial orientation, beyond denoting the function of the cerebellum in regulating movements and the general position of the body in space.

[What deductions can be made from this brief comparative review? First, it is clear that the facts cited actually describe the *special features* of spatial discrimination, its great complexity in comparison with other forms of discrimination, and its close connection with the operation of twin receptors. Second, the only explanation of these facts is one based on the receptor theory, which confines spatial discrimination to the structure and function of the appropriate twin receptors. But the receptor theory is inseparable from subjective physiological idealism, which treats sensations as conventional signs, symbols or hieroglyphs; receptor conceptions of spatial discrimination do not, therefore, explain, but distort, the important facts about the *qualitative* uniqueness of spatial discrimination. All the receptor theories of binocular vision, binaural hearing and so on, can be reduced to the assertion that spatial discrimination is effected without the reflex activity of the brain; whereas it has been established that it is precisely in the reflex activity of the brain that reflection of the external world takes place.

[These receptor conceptions must be superseded if a scientific, materialist theory of spatial discrimination is to be constructed. Such a theory must take as its starting point the proposition that space and time are basic forms of existence of matter, reflected (and not constructed) by the activity of the brain. The accumulated facts relating to spatial discrimination, together with those newly discovered, must be explained on the basis of the reflex theory of Sechenov and Pavlov, and of the materialist theory of reflection. It is necessary, therefore, to examine these facts in the light of the reflex theory.]

III

The facts relating to the twin operation of a receptor, and the moderate disparateness of stimulations of the cells of these homonymous receptors, have already been referred to. It is evident that, as the organism interacts with its environment, the receptors are the first to experience stimulation directly from external stimuli. It is in the receptors that these stimulations are transformed into a nervous process, initially into a stimulatory process (excitation). The facts concerning spatial discrimination derived from the physiology of the receptors only show that elements of the receptors are affected not only by the physico-chemical properties of objects but also by their spatial features and relations. When the physico-chemical properties act on the receptors, they are characterized, not only by quality and intensity, but also by *direction* of movement. When analysing the stimuli acting on sense organs, we must not lose sight of the vector definition of these stimuli. With the biological evolution of the central nervous system and the organs of sense, as Pavlov emphasized, permanent (non-conditioned reflex) connections are replaced by temporary (conditioned-reflex) connections. Individual properties of individual things (including colours, smells, sounds, etc.) become *signals* acting on the cortex from a distance. The development of this signalling function is connected with the development of complex distance relations between the organism and its environment. But here, naturally enough, the *vector* factor in the action of stimuli on the cortex and its receptors grows in importance.

Since the time of Sechenov, the special importance of the *area* of stimulation of a receptor by a mass of single stimuli has been well known. An increase in the area of stimulation means an increase in the strength of stimulation and, consequently, in the number of impulses travelling along the sensory nerves to the brain. The way in which these stimulations are spatially distributed in homonymous receptors (at corresponding or disparate points, etc.) is no less important. The *material* design of the receptor, the interrelationship of its elements and parts, have a *spatial* character. The movement of a nervous process arising in the receptors is also spatial.

An elementary analysis of space, namely an analysis of the spatial features of stimuli from the external world, takes place in the receptor. This elementary analysis plays a certain role in projecting the image of the object again into the space of the external world, but this role is not at all an independent one, nor is it definitive in spatial discrimination, for the latter is a product of higher analysis and synthesis which is a function of the hemispheres. The projection of the image is the result of higher analysis and synthesis. The functional condition of the receptors (their excitability and adaptation) is determined by the interaction of the nervous processes in the cortex. This proposition is still more applicable to the spatial-discriminatory work of twin receptors. It is easy to see that the connection of the receptors with the cortical terminals of the corresponding analysers guarantees the varied and differentiated unity of receptors and cortex.

From anatomy we know that a mass of fibres of the optical nerve, divided into three main bunches, goes from each eye to the cortex. Thus, from the outer (temporal) half of the retina of each eye a bunch of fibres passes to the homonymous hemisphere of the cortex; from the inner (nasal) half of the retina another bunch of fibres passes to the hemisphere which is on the opposite side of the head to the eye; and from the central area of the retina (the area of the macula) comes a third bunch of fibres which divides and goes to both hemispheres.

In the structure of the photo-analyser as a whole a special place is occupied by the so-called chiasma, where this partial crossing of the visual paths takes place. A partial crossing also occurs in the passage of the auditory and olfactory nerves from their own homonymous receptors to the cerebral terminals of the analysers. If one is to understand the *wholeness* of an analyser, and its place in the reflex arc, it is important to take account of the connection of *each* of the homonymous receptors with *both* hemispheres.

The muscular-skeletal receptors are no exception (e.g. receptors of the muscles and sinews of the hands). At present the majority of investigators hold that each hand is connected only with the opposite hemisphere, by virtue of a complete crossing of the nerve paths; this opinion is founded on the belief that the so-called motor area of the cortex differs radically from all the other areas which fulfil the function of 'centres' of feeling or perception. But Pavlov proved conclusively that the so-called motor area of the cortex does not constitute an exception to the general *analysing* nature of the cerebral hemispheres, since this area is also, in fact, the area of the motor analyser. In it is situated the nucleus of the cerebral terminal of the motor analyser, which is connected with the whole system of muscular-skeletal receptors and sensory nerves. According to Pavlov, the leading role in the analyser is played by the cerebral terminal which is made up of a system of nuclear cell bodies and dispersed cells. The muscular-skeletal receptors of the hand are connected with both cerebral hemispheres, and not only with one of them (the opposite one). The grounds for this proposition are the fact that there is commissural connection between both sides of the motor analyser.

On the basis of a series of investigations, we have conjectured that the twin nature of homonymous receptors is paralleled by the conjoint operation of the cerebral hemispheres. The cerebral terminal of the analyser (photo, visual, olfactory, etc.) consists of nuclear cell bodies and their processes symmetrically arranged in both hemispheres. The sole exception is the speech-motor zone of the cortex (the so-called Broca's convolution) which is located in the left hemisphere. However, it may be supposed that at least the dispersed elements of the cerebral terminal of the speech-motor analyser are situated also in the right hemisphere. In every other case a relative symmetry is to be observed in the disposition of 'centres' in both hemispheres of the cortex. The nature of the cerebral terminals and their leading role in the unitary activity of the analysers can only be understood in the light of the theory of higher nervous activity. On this basis it is possible to explain facts which before seemed paradoxical, namely functional asymmetry in the operation of symmetrically arranged parts (in both hemispheres) of one and the same cerebral terminal. We have in mind the hitherto inexplicable phenomenon of a *leading* side with functional inequality in the spheres of vision (a leading eye), of hearing (a leading ear), of kinaesthesia (a leading hand) and so on.

Pavlov's teaching regarding the unity of the mechanisms of the analyser and of temporary connections, in the undivided reflex activity of the brain, makes it possible to explain the astonishing facts of the *reorganization* of the interrelations between homonymous receptors (both eyes, both ears, etc.) as the spatial circumstances of the existence of the organism change. The explanation of these facts is also linked with Pavlov's treatment of the interaction of the two cerebral hemispheres. The primary importance of their conjoint work is that it makes possible the transfer of conditioned reflexes from one side of the body to the other, without any supplementary training. It is this transfer of temporary connections that constitutes the basic mechanism for the transfer, not only of motor skills, but also of the so-called sensory skills, especially the skill of discrimination; by means of this mechanism the developed action is, as it were, 'doubled' and generalized in the shape of a unitary action of the whole organism, and not as an isolated act of one half of the body.

[Here, Professor Ananiev discusses the experiments, conducted in Pavlov's laboratories in 1923 and later, bearing on this subject. Introducing the results, Pavlov wrote 'How is the simultaneous activity of the hemispheres to be understood and explained? What sort of compensating action is there here, and what advantage or superfluity is involved in the constant united activity of both hemispheres?' [1] He went on to note that a certain division of activity between the two had been established; but that it was also known from extirpation experiments on animals that the absence of one hemisphere can be compensated for, after a time, either partly or fully, by the activity of the remaining one. The relevant experiments were undertaken by N. I. Krasnogorsky, G. V. Anrep and K. M. Bykov. Krasnogorsky

[1] Pavlov-Gantt i, 326.

found that positive and negative conditioned reflexes, which have been elaborated on the skin surface of one half of the body, are obtainable to exactly the same degree, in the absence of any elaboration, when there is stimulation of corresponding symmetrical points on the other half of the body. Anrep found that if a conditioned reflex is elaborated as a result of mechanical stimulation of a certain point of the skin at one end of the body, then on the first tests of mechanical stimulation of other parts of the skin there is a conditioned effect, the strength of which is proportional to its distance from the point at which the conditioned reflex was developed. Exactly the same relations hold for the symmetrical points of the other side of the body, though they have not before been experimented with. Pavlov considered that this finding defined more precisely the transfer of conditioned reflexes from one side to the other. This takes place when a process of excitation begun in one hemisphere, that is, in one symmetrically disposed half of the cerebral terminal of the analyser (in Krasnogorsky's experiments, the cutaneous and motor analysers of a dog), is irradiated to the other; in general, the movement of nervous processes embraces both hemispheres in this way.

[Bykov's experiments provided remarkable supplementary data. Whereas it had been found in a number of earlier experiments that, using mechanical and thermal agents as positive and negative conditioned stimuli, the differentiation of various points of the skin on the same side of the body proceeded very easily, Bykov found it impossible to obtain the slightest differentiation between two symmetrical points on opposite sides of the body; that is, taking the two sides as A and B, when he had established a positive conditioned reflex on side A he was unable to establish a negative conditioned reflex at the symmetrical point on side B. The two sides changed together; it was impossible to differentiate them, keeping one positive and the other negative.

[Further experiments were undertaken by Bykov and A. D. Speransky involving severing of the commissural connections between the two hemispheres, in order to investigate this question [6]. After the severing of the corpus callosum, transfer of conditioned reflexes from one side of the body to the other became impossible. Each of the hemispheres then operated separately in establishing temporary connections; the dog had to adapt each half of its body separately to the signals of the external world. Under these conditions, individual experience acquired by the operation of one hemisphere did not exist, as it were, for the other; the single analyser split into two independent analysers; the processes of excitation and inhibition which arose in one hemisphere could not pass to the other as the normal movement of irradiation and concentration had been destroyed. But the spread of excitation along different points of one hemisphere took place in the normal way.

[Evidently, then, the symmetrical areas of both sides of the body are regulated by one and the same cortical mechanism; whereas different areas on the same side of the body, which are easily differentiated, are regulated by different cortical mechanisms. Bykov's and Speransky's experiment, in particular, showed the part played by the twin operation of the great hemispheres in differentiating spatial signals. The fact that the conjoint activity of the two hemispheres was necessary in differentiating the source of a sound was, in Pavlov's view, a valuable point characterizing the work of the sound analyser. Describing an experiment by Bykov, Pavlov showed how this conclusion was reached:

> The corpus callosum was severed in a dog, and after the animal had recovered from the operation the establishment of new conditioned alimentary reflexes was begun. Their formation presented no special difficulties and proceeded at the same rate as in normal animals. One of the reflexes was established to the sound of a whistle, 1500 double vibrations per second. The whistle, which was placed in a cardboard case, was supported on the wall on a level with the left ear and at a definite distance from the dog. The reflex appeared at the eighth repetition, and attained a maximum and permanent strength after 70 repetitions. The whistle was then transferred to the right side of the dog, and in this position was not reinforced by the unconditioned reflex. By repeatedly contrasting the sound from the left with that from the right a differentiation of the direction of the sound was attempted. There was, however, not the slightest sign of any differentiation, even after 115 repetitions of the non-reinforced stimulus from the right. . . .

[Pavlov concluded that for 'differentiation of the source of a sound the conjoint activity of both hemispheres is necessary';[1] and drew attention to the importance of this finding to an understanding of aural-spatial discrimination. In these same experiments, Bykov also demonstrated that dissociation of the hemispheres has an influence on the development of differentiation between the distances of signals. It proved to be impossible to develop differentiation between the directions of sounds and the distances of objects acting on the photo-analyser.]

It can be conjectured, then, that the conjoint operation of the great hemispheres is a vitally necessary condition of normal orientation in space among the higher animals and man. When I first advanced this

[1] Pavlov-Anrep, 150.

hypothesis, I did not have complete physiological proof [1]. In the physiology of higher nervous activity, there are no special systematic investigations of the differentiation of the spatial features of signals, nor of the spatial relations between signals of the external environment. In Pavlov's laboratories, plane figures were sometimes used as conditioned stimuli in experiments on dogs, but the investigators were not concerned with the ways in which spatial features of these stimuli were differentiated. Therefore, we have had to conduct a series of essentially physiological investigations into the process whereby conditioned reflexes to spatial signals are formed and differentiated. This work has been carried out on human subjects by R. A. Voronova using the method of conditioned-vascular reflexes, and by V. A. Maraev using the method of conditioned motor reflexes with speech reinforcement. These investigations have provided physiological proof of the hypothesis, and we are now engaged in testing it by various physiological and psychological-pedagogical means in a series of new experiments.

A reference to one of Pavlov's important discoveries in the province of conditioned reflexes will show the correctness of this general approach to the peculiarities of space discrimination. This consists in a special kind of conditioned reflex to the relations between external agents acting upon the brain, which was discovered when conditioned reflexes in response to time as a special stimulus were investigated in Pavlov's laboratories. Experiments on animals proved that the cerebral cortex reacts to delicate changes in the time intervals between signal and reinforcement, and to the time sequence of conditioned stimuli, within the external stereotype of the experiment, and so on.

Following the lines indicated by these experiments, which produced differentiation of conditioned reflexes in response to time as a special stimulus, we constructed a series of investigations concerned with differentiation of reflexes in response to spatial signals. These were designed to make clear some of the foundations of the sensation of space. We were convinced of the correctness of this approach by the long history of psychological study of association by contiguity; one of the forms of this being association by virtue of a consecutive (i.e. temporal) connection, and another, association by virtue of the contiguous position (i.e. spatial connection) of the perceived phenomena.

Our starting point was the hypothesis that the twin operation of the hemispheres has a special role, and we undertook a series of investigations into the process of transference of conditioned reflexes from one side of a man's body to the other. Our aim was not only to confirm transference, such as had already been established in the case of animals, but also to bring to light differences in transference from the leading (usually the right) side to the subordinate side and *vice versa*.

M. A. Guzeva, using the method of vascular conditioned reflexes, showed experimentally not only the asymmetry of the vascular conditioned reflexes of both hands, but also how the difference in the transfer of conditioned reflexes from one side of the body to the other depends on the method of interaction of the two hemispheres. A. A. Rykova has disclosed a similar picture of choice (election) in the transfer of conditioned-reflex change in cutaneous sensitivity from one hand to the other. E. P. Miroshina-Tonkonogaya has shown experimentally elective transfer of conditioned-reflex heightening of acuity of vision from the leading eye to the subordinate one and *vice versa*. The facts accumulated [1] have led to the conviction that the general foundation of spatial discrimination is a system of conditioned reflexes in response to spatial signals, closely linked with the twin work of the cerebral hemispheres in the human brain. The functional asymmetry in the activity of the human analysers in the process of space discrimination, we regard as a significant manifestation of twin duplex operation of the hemispheres.

[1] These are set out in the following chapters of the book (Ed.).

THE THEORY OF MEMORY [1]

BY

L. V. ZANKOV

[**T**HIS PAPER IS CONCERNED with a study of memory in the light of Pavlov's teaching on higher nervous activity. In the opening section the author argues that Pavlov did not deny the importance of purpose or intention in behaviour; what he did stress was the need to study the mechanism of these phenomena in a strictly scientific manner. If, in observing certain phenomena, we substitute the words 'purpose' or 'intention' for knowledge of the laws governing them, we do not advance beyond recording the facts under observation; we add nothing to our real knowledge of these processes. There is, therefore, no question of obscuring differences between the various phenomena of memory; deliberate recollection, for instance, involving intention or an effort of will, and learning by rote, are clearly two very different things. It would be a perversion of Pavlov's teaching to reduce memory to mechanical memory; but, with the aid of Pavlov's theories it is possible to make clear, from a physiological point of view, what are the real differences between the several forms of recollection or representation.]

I

The Physiological Basis of Impression and Retention

Recollection may first be considered in the light of the main laws of higher nervous activity, leaving aside for the time being the differentiation of the two signalling systems. It is evident that the phenomena of recollecting objects, words and relations between them are based on the formation of temporary connections in the cortex, but it is necessary to define the situation more exactly. If a conditioned reflex disappeared as soon as it was formed, it would be impossible to consider such a reflex as the basis of impression. But, in fact, a conditioned connection, once formed, is *retained* for a more or less

[1] *Sovetskaya Pedagogika*, No. 6, 1951, pp. 59–80 (translated in the U.S.S.R.).

lengthy period; this is clearly shown by numerous and exhaustive experiments. Pavlov explicitly indicated that 'new connections well elaborated are retained for a very long time'.[1]

If recollection is analysed from a psychological point of view, two organically interconnected forms may be distinguished; the impression of the object itself, and the retention in the memory of the connection between objects, or between object and action, etc. For example, a schoolboy studies the outline of an island hitherto unknown to him on a map, and learns its name; a connection is formed between the representation of the island and the corresponding word. If an analysis is made of these phenomena, these are some of the questions that arise: (1) In what way are the outlines of the island impressed on the boy's memory? (2) How is the name of the island impressed? (3) How is the connection between the image of the island and its name retained in the memory?

The answer to the third question is relatively simple as compared with the other two. Between the image of the island and its name there is evidently established a connection of contiguity, or, as Pavlov expressed it using psychological terminology, an association by simultaneity. It seems clear that the mechanism for forming a connection of this kind is that of the conditioned reflex. We have here the appearance of an excitatory process in the corresponding groups of nerve cells, its irradiation and also its restriction through inhibition; what happens is the formation of a road for the nerve-current and its closing-up,[2] 'when two nervous centres are connected, joined, the nervous processes move from one to the other in both directions'.[3] This explains the transition from visual perception of the island's outline to the representation of its name and, conversely, from the name to representation of the form of the island.

Why is there a lasting impression of the object (in our example, the outline of the island)? A general explanation of this phenomenon may be found in the conception of a trace remaining in the central nervous system after the action of the stimulus has ceased. The formation and retention of traces is one of the salient properties of the central nervous system. Discussing researches into the interaction of different food reflexes, Pavlov wrote:

The most striking fact in these experiments was that stimulation, by means of different kinds of food, was often accompanied by

[1] Pavlov-Gantt i, 354.
[2] It should be remembered that for a conditioned reflex to be formed, it is necessary that the excitatory process that has appeared in the cortex as a result of the action of an indifferent stimulus, shall be 'drawn' to the seat of intensive activity existing at the given moment in the central nervous system.
[3] Pavlov-Gantt ii, 142; *Selected Works*, 444.

a trace of extreme length. The physiology of conditioned reflexes has brought to light data indicating that stimulation, in the form of its *trace*, makes itself felt in the central nervous system long after the cause that produced this stimulation is removed and its visible effect has come to an end.

And further,

In Dr. Egorov's experiment the trace proves to be a very lasting one, making itself felt not only for hours, but even for days. This may be supported by certain facts from everyday life; as, for example, when some taste, particularly an unpleasant one, is remembered for a long time.[1]

It is clear that what Pavlov had in mind here is the impression of taste as such. His explanation must be taken to mean that the excitatory process in the corresponding group of nerve cells does not cease immediately with the cessation of the stimulus, but that it persists, though in a different form.

Pavlov distinguished the trace reflex as a particular kind of conditioned reflex. The formation of this kind of reflex is not brought about by a stimulus acting on the organism at a given moment, but by the trace that has remained in the nervous system after the action of some external stimulus has ceased. The type of experiment that gave rise to this conclusion may be described.

A specific sound is produced for half a minute; there follows an interval of from 1 to 3 minutes, and then the dog is either given a small quantity of food or some acid is introduced into the mouth cavity. If this procedure is repeated several times, the following results are recorded. The sound alone calls forth no reaction; neither does its disappearance; but after a definite interval a food or an acid reaction respectively takes place.[2] It is in such cases that Pavlov speaks of a trace which remains in the central nervous system after the stimulus has ceased.

Moreover, a conditioned reflex is also retained in the form of a trace. In Egorov's researches, referred to above, conditioned reflexes were formed by linking indifferent stimuli with foodstuffs. A conditioned reflex was produced when the external stimulus was reinforced by feeding sugar, and another conditioned reflex was formed when the stimulus was reinforced by giving meat powder. If, after the operation of the 'meat reflex', the 'sugar reflex' was introduced, and then, under certain conditions, the 'meat' stimulus was applied again, the reflex to the latter proved to be inhibited and no conditioned

[1] Pavlov-Gantt i, 190.   [2] Pavlov-Anrep, 39 ff.

reaction was obtained. Explaining this phenomenon, Pavlov said that the 'sugar' conditioned reflex was acting on the *trace* of the 'meat' conditioned reflex, inhibiting it.[1]

If conditioned connections are retained in the form of traces, we can understand more fully the cause of the retention of an image of an object. We can now say that a trace will only be retained if the given stimulation coincides with a state of intensive activity of any one group of nerve cells in the cortex, giving rise to the formation of a new temporary connection. If there is no such coincidence, the excitatory process that has started in the cortex as a result of the action of the object, not being 'drawn' towards the seat of intensive activity, will simply be disseminated, leaving no trace in the cortex. If a trace is to be retained in the cortex, therefore, a conditioned connection must be established with the given stimulus. This indicates that the factors treated separately in the analysis of recollection given above —recollection of an object and retention of the connection between objects—are, in fact, indissolubly linked.

We have given a general description of the mechanism underlying retention of an object. We may now turn to other aspects of the problem.

II

Impression and the Mechanism of the Analysers

The impression of an object is based upon perception of it. Objects, and their properties, are only impressed if they can be isolated, that is, separated from their surroundings by means of the analyser mechanism. 'The primary foundation of analysis is furnished by the peripheral endings (terminations) of all the afferent conducting nerves of the organism, each of which is specially adapted to transform a definite kind of energy.' [2] When an object acts upon the peripheral endings of the afferent nerves of a specific analyser, the excitatory process is conducted along these nerves to the corresponding cells constituting the nerve centre or 'brain-terminal of the analyser' as Pavlov called it. It is here, given the requisite conditions, that the trace of excitation is formed and retained.

Pavlov particularly stressed this point in his refutation of the thesis advanced by the American physiologist Lashley. From experiments in training rats to acquire habits as a result of visual excitation, Lashley drew the conclusion that the training process had no connection whatsoever with the site of the lesion in the hemispheres, whereas the mnemonic trace or engram had a specific localization. Pavlov pointed

[1] Pavlov-Gantt i, 191.   [2] Pavlov-Gantt ii, 172; *Selected Works*, 252.

out that the visual fibres do not lie only in the occipital lobe but are spread considerably beyond it, probably over the entire mass of the hemispheres. That is why these visual fibres contribute to the formation of conditioned connections outside the occipital lobe as well, though here they are influenced only by the more elementary visual stimuli. If Lashley, instead of using the elementary stimulus of an intensive light, had used a more complex stimulus (e.g. a particular object) the habit would not only have vanished after the removal of the visual lobe but could not have been formed again afterwards. In this case, Pavlov concluded, no difference would have been found between the site of the formation of the habit and that of the mnemonic trace.[1]

There is every reason to apply this statement about the site of the formation of a habit, and the site of the mnemonic trace, to all analysers. Pavlov held that the mechanism causing movement is represented in the cortex of the cerebral hemispheres primarily by the motor analyser; consequently, what was said above about the site where habit is formed is evidently an allusion to the brain-terminal of the motor analyser, and the same may be said of the other analysers. These statements about the motor analyser may be juxtaposed with corresponding statements concerning the other analysers—the auditory analyser, for example—in the case of the formation of a conditioned trace reflex. The point may be put in this way: the trace is formed and retained in the group of nerve cells constituting the brain-terminal of the corresponding analyser.

This treatment of the problems of the formation and retention of traces is organically linked with the conception of the cortex as the organ of memory. Bourgeois morphologists (Flechsig and others) affirm that there are special centres in the cerebral hemispheres which are the site of memory processes. To these they give different names, such as 'associative', 'commemorative', 'mnesic' centres. Such conceptions, in essence, separate memory processes from perception and the psychic activity of the organism as a whole. They are a convenient screen for idealist 'theories' which separate memory processes from concrete reality and present them as revelations of a purely spiritual entity.

Pavlov's statement that the function of maintaining the impressions of stimulations reaching the cortex is inherent in the whole of the cortex, and that the mnemonic trace is formed on the site to which the excitatory process is transmitted from the corresponding receptor, firmly root impression in sensation; they indicate that impression and retention are directly dependent on sensation, indeed are the result of sensation.

[1] Pavlov-Gantt ii, 137; *Selected Works*, 437-8.

This is significant not only for a materialist interpretation of the processes of impression and retention, but also from a philosophical point of view. By disclosing the physiological mechanism of impression by showing that it is rooted in sensation, Pavlov brings a scientific finding to the support of one of the major theses of the dialectical materialist theory of reflection; viz. that perception, as a peculiar stage of cognition of reality, is based on sensation, i.e. on the direct linkage of consciousness with the outer world, with objective reality.

III

Systematization of the Functioning of the Cortex

The systematization of the functioning of the cortex is of great significance in the physiological interpretation of memory. The interaction between conditioned connections assumes highly complex forms, as Pavlov conveys in the following graphic description:

Falling continuously on the cerebral hemispheres are innumerable stimulations both from the external world, and from the inner medium of the organism itself. . . . Along conducting routes, in countless varieties, positive processes make their way to the cortex where they are joined by inhibitory processes. . . . All these meet, collide and must be arranged and systematized. What we have before us is . . . a vast dynamic system. And it is through conditioned reflexes in the normal animal that we observe and study this ceaseless systematization of processes—what might be called a ceaseless impetus towards a dynamic stereotype.[1]

This systematization is of great importance in the physiological interpretation of the phenomena of recollecting material in the form of complex wholes. Such a systematization of conditioned connections takes the form of a dynamic stereotype. In animals a series of conditioned reflexes can be formed to stimuli differing both in quality and intensity, including inhibiting stimuli. Thus, a first conditioned reflex may be obtained to the strokes of a metronome, producing a reaction expressed in 11 drops of saliva; a second, to a mechanical irritation of the skin, giving 5 drops of saliva; a third, to the switching on of an electric lamp, producing 9 drops of saliva, etc. When this series of conditioned reflexes is practised day after day, always in the same order and with the same intervals between stimulations, a stereotype of nervous processes is obtained.

After this, if only one of the positive conditioned stimuli (preferably a weak one) is used, and repeated at the same intervals of time as

[1] Pavlov-Gantt ii, 91; *Selected Works*, 281–2.

were the others, it alone will bring about the representation, in their correct sequence, of the same conditioned reactions (or inhibitions) that were previously obtained to the varied series of stimuli. For example, a stimulus that called forth a conditioned reaction expressed in 5 drops of saliva will now, on being applied first in the series, produce a much greater reaction than that originally obtained to it alone, and so on; i.e. the given single stimulus will, with each successive application, produce the different degrees of reaction that were obtained to the varied stimuli given in the original series.

In such cases, the specific extent of the effect is obtained, not as a reaction to the stimulus to which the reaction was originally worked out but to another stimulus. It is this latter that serves as the impetus, setting in motion traces of previously established conditioned connections. Since a specific degree of reaction is produced, in accordance with the place occupied by the given connection within the series of conditioned connections, it is not a question of isolated traces but of a system of traces set in motion in a strictly specific order. The example further indicates that not only excitatory but also inhibitive processes are retained in the form of a trace; moreover, definite relations between these processes are retained; if they were not, no regular functioning of conditioned reflexes would be possible and the subject's behaviour would be chaotic.

All this throws light on the foundations of recollection and retention of complex wholes (entities) composed of multiform parts. The production (elaboration) and retention of the subtlest interrelations between excitatory and inhibitive processes explains physiologically the formation and retention of motor habits.[1] Pavlov explicitly stated that the manifold states of the nerve cells are retained in the form of traces entering into the composition of specific systems.

> These countless states of the nerve cells are not only formed under the influence of acting stimuli, nor do they exist only during the action of external stimuli; they remain, in their absence, in the form of a system of intermittent excitation and inhibition of different degrees, and of greater or lesser stability.[2]

The traces of stimulations and conditioned connections do not remain in the cortex unchanged, as do scratches on metal. Changes

[1] Pavlov's explanation is as follows: 'The cerebral hemispheres, as everybody knows, are continuously intervening in the smallest details of our movements, setting in motion one, and suppressing another, as is the case, for example, in playing the piano; you can see how fractional is the degree of inhibition, if one movement of a certain intensity is effected, while in another, side by side with it, even the smallest of movements is inhibited.' *Selected Works*, 370.

[2] Pavlov-Gantt ii, 131–2; *Selected Works*, 429.

in the environment make necessary not only the formation of conditioned connections but also their obliteration:

> What is necessary, in order to attain the right relation of the organism to the surrounding world, is not only the formation of temporary connections, but also a constant and rapid readjustment of these connections when, under certain conditions, their existence is not justified in reality; i.e. their removal. The removal of temporary connections is brought about by inhibition.[1]

If a conditioned stimulus begins to signalize incorrectly, it loses its excitatory effect: the conditioned reflex dies away. Its extinction is due to inner inhibition in the cortex—some time later it may recover its strength. The extinction and restoration of systems of conditioned connections proceeds in the same way. The interaction of processes of excitation and inhibition, the concrete nature of which is conditioned by external agents, results in traces of excitation being either set in motion or remaining inhibited. Pavlov gave an example, when referring to Köhler's experiment with a dog. Meat was placed close to a railing and the dog ran vainly to and fro attempting to get it, without trying to use the gate; Köhler did not try to explain this behaviour.

> But with conditioned reflexes to guide us we can easily see how things stand. The nearby meat strongly stimulates the dog's olfactory centre, and, in accordance with the law of negative induction, this centre strongly inhibits the remaining analysers, the remaining parts of the hemispheres, thus causing the traces of the gate and the way round to it to remain inhibited; which means, speaking subjectively, that the dog temporarily forgets about them.[2]

The relations that arise during readjustment of an established system of conditioned connections are highly complex. During readjustment a short period of breaking up the system of connections produces only superficial modifications. Even when only a brief rest is allowed, owing to the development of a process of inner inhibition it is the new and less lasting conditioned connections that are the first to disappear, while a firmly established system of connections, which has remained in a semi-inhibited condition, will reappear [60]. These findings clarify the phenomena of forgetting, of changes in material retained in the memory, its coalescence with other material, and so on. In practice, material that has been learned does not remain in the memory unchanged; it is grasped more and more thoroughly,

[1] Pavlov-Gantt i, 331. [2] Pavlov-Gantt ii, 143; *Selected Works*, 445.

digested, enters into new connections, and is readjusted as new knowledge accumulates. If this extremely complex process is examined as an aspect of memory to which a physiological explanation must be given, the facts and laws adduced above will provide a guide to a genuinely scientific interpretation.

IV

The Joint Functioning of the Two Signal Systems

The development of speech in the child means that conditioned connections begin to be formed not only to concrete stimuli but also to words. Pavlov regarded words as 'just as real a conditioned stimulus as any other that man has in common with the animals', but all-embracing, and therefore qualitatively different. Conditioned connections formed in response to words, while obeying the fundamental laws governing higher nervous activity, have their own peculiar characteristics.

The role of speech in the development of a child's higher nervous activity can best be seen if we examine the period of transition from the undivided domination of the first signalling system to the rise of the second. Before this stage, the word already serves as a signal producing a definite conditioned reaction, but it has not yet become an all-embracing stimulus.[1] At the age of approximately eighteen months, a word to which a certain number of conditioned connections have already been formed, produces the correct reaction from the first time a new combination is used. For example, a child may have developed a definite reaction to the word combination: 'put down your doll', and may also perform the requisite actions in response to the words 'bring me the clown'; but he has never heard the word combination 'make the clown sit down', nor performed the corresponding action. But if these words are said, the correct reaction takes place, even though it has not previously been established.

In this reaction are to be found the rudiments of abstraction and generalization, which will develop in depth and breadth of range as the second signalling system develops. Even at this transitional stage it is clear that the nascent second system plays a major role so far as memory is concerned. The connections formed earlier now function, not only when activated by the customary stimuli, but also under the influence of other specific stimuli: viz. a new combination

[1] According to Koltsova's experiments [28], a word, in the first months of the child's second year, causes only the single specific reaction that has been established to it. But, on being included in a new complex of stimuli, the word will not lead to this reaction; in order to obtain the reaction it must once more be established to the new complex of stimuli.

of words. Moreover, earlier connections have now become the basis for effecting new reactions 'from the very first time'.

The close and continuous interaction between the first and second signal systems is of particular importance. Investigations under the direction of Ivanov-Smolensky, with children of 8 to 10 years, have shown that when a motor conditioned reaction has been formed to a specific concrete stimulus (the ringing of a bell) the same conditioned reaction can, immediately, without any previous establishment, be obtained to the word 'bell' [18]. Control experiments showed that no other word called forth the given motor reaction. It was also established that, if a conditioned reaction is formed to a given word, and the subject is then shown the concrete stimulus of which that word is the sign, the latter produces the same reaction, though it had not previously been connected with this reaction. These, and other, investigations show that conditioned connections formed within the first signal system function if the stimulus used is the corresponding word; and *vice versa*. Generalizing the results obtained, Ivanov-Smolensky advanced the hypothesis of 'elective generalization' (as distinguished from simple generalization, the customary generalization of conditioned connections). What takes place is elective irradiation of the process of stimulation within the framework of a single dynamic structure, formed in the cortex, which comprises all the three kinds of conditioned connections; namely, motor reactions connected with (1) a concrete stimulus, (2) an oral stimulus, (3) a written word symbol.

Explaining the phenomena described, Ivanov-Smolensky writes:

> This reaction occurred because the impressions in the cortex of all three stimuli had been interconnected in the child's past experience, in the course of the development of his higher nervous activity. Therefore, if the sound of a bell enters into a conditioned connection with a particular reaction, it must be remembered that it has already been linked, associated, in the subject's cortex with impressions of the oral and written word symbols of this stimulus. If now we substitute for the conditioned stimulus—the bell—the *word* 'bell', we will obtain the conditioned reaction in response to this word, even though this word has never formerly been combined with this reaction [17].

Researches into conditioned-reflex connections between words of similar and different degrees of generalized meaning are also of outstanding importance. These show that, if stabilized connections have been established between a series of words—names of birds, for example—and if, subsequently, a conditioned reaction is formed to one of these names, the other names that have earlier been connected with the selected name will produce the same reaction; no other names of birds will produce any effect at all. But should the child hear the word 'bird', designating a species, this gives rise to the intensive conditioned-reflex reaction which has been established earlier to a specific name of a bird. Krasnogorsky notes that this

> is evidence that in the speech system there exist integrating symbols of higher orders—in the case in point of the second order—unifying a group of differentiated primary symbols (of the first order) and having a direct, conditioned-reflex connection with each one of them [34].

The presence of this type of connection, specific to the second signal system and reflecting also the comprehensive character of the word as a conditioned stimulus, is of fundamental importance to the interpretation of phenomena of memory. Impression is considerably facilitated because it is grounded on connections of a wide range conditioned by the abstracting and generalizing function of the word. Moreover, it becomes possible for traces to be set in motion from many starting points. Favourable conditions are created for the rise of complex systems of connections which cannot take place within the framework of the first signal system alone. Finally, these researches throw light on the physiological bases of conscious operations of recollection.

It should not be forgotten that a single word also leaves a trace in the cortex. Pavlov pointed out that 'speech, especially and primarily the kinaesthetic stimulations, which proceed from the speech organs to the cortex, constitute a second set of signals—the signals of signals'.[1]

We may suppose that the word is first impressed in the form of a trace of kinaesthetic stimuli originating in the organs of speech; and that words audible and visible to man also leave traces in the corresponding groups of nerve cells. Thus, the functioning of the second signalling system is effected not only as a result of the direct action of verbal stimuli—kinaesthetic, aural or visual—but also in the form of their traces.

Thus, the comprehensive nature of the word as a conditioned stimulus is, in part, manifested in the fact that various previously formed connections are brought into action; and that, owing to this, and without any preparatory establishment of the required connection, the given conditioned reaction may be obtained. Moreover, new connections easily arise which in turn become the basis for the formation of further connections. In the course of a man's life, multiform,

---

[1] Pavlov-Gantt ii, 93; *Selected Works*, 285.

widely ramified, and intricately interlaced connections are accumulated and perfected within the first signal system, between the two signal systems, and within the second signal system. These data, in some measure, throw light on the complexity and mobility of processes of memory.

[The paper concludes with two further sections. The first is concerned with the development of research on memory. The processes of memory are a part of the whole analytic-synthetic activity of the cortex, contributing to the maintenance of the organism's life. This means that memory must be studied in its connection with the living activity of the subject; this is particularly important in work with schoolchildren, in view of the great influence of education on the development of the child's psychic processes. If memory is studied in this way, its artificial separation from other psychic phenomena such as emotion (an example of intellectualism in psychology) can be overcome.

[In the final section, the author criticizes idealist theories of memory, in particular those which posit two types of memory ('lower' and 'higher', the latter beyond the reach of scientific explanation), the theories of Gestalt psychology and those of 'physiological idealism'. On the other hand, Pavlov, by disclosing the underlying physiological mechanisms, provided the basis for a scientific interpretation of the various phenomena of memory.]

THE FORMATION OF ASSOCIATIVE CONNECTIONS: AN EXPERIMENTAL INVESTIGATION [1]

BY

A. N. LEONTIEV AND T. V. ROZONAVA

I

The Theoretical Background of the Investigation

PAVLOV USED THE TERM 'association' to denote the temporary connection with indifferent stimuli which is the basis of the mechanism of cortical linking. Although associations may be formed in animals, the associative activity of the cerebral cortex reaches its full development in man. An essential condition for the formation of temporary connections, in both the animals and man, is the presence of an active state of the cortex.

In animals the cause of such an active state may be external influences which evoke an orienting reflex. Among animals, the anthropoid apes have the highest potentialities for forming associations, owing to the 'exceptionally high development of their exploratory reflex' [50: 68]. Because it has highly mobile extremities, the ape

is capable of entering into very complex relationships with objects in its environment. This is why a mass of associations develop in the ape which are not to be found in other animals. Since these motor associations must have a material substratum in the nervous system, in the brain, the cerebral hemispheres are more developed in the ape than in other animals, a development closely connected with the diversity of its motor functions. [2]

Pavlov repeatedly drew attention to the importance of specific selectivity in the forming of associations; to the fact that connections

[1] *Sovetskaya Pedagogika*, No. 10, 1951, pp. 60–77 (translated by N. Parsons).
[2] *Selected Works*, 561.

are strengthened only if they lead to successful achievement, if they 'are confirmed'. The formation of associations in man shows quite unique features when compared with the same process in animals. Ivanov-Smolensky has demonstrated that associations can be developed in man on the basis of verbal reinforcement, which gives rise to the activization of previously established connections. He has shown that certain peculiarities of the formation of associations in man are connected with his possession of an 'exceptional supplementary', the second signal system [20: 17]. However, it is not yet sufficiently clear how the formation of associations depends on the conditions and content of concurrent activity. The investigation here described is concerned with further study of this question.

Psychological investigations have shown that the effectiveness of 'involuntary recollection' of different material depends, not only on the character of the recollected material (the number and order of repetitions, etc.) but also upon the content of the individual's activity and the place the given material takes in this activity. Thus Zinchenko [68] has demonstrated that recollection of perceived objects is most effective when the subject's activity is directed to these in the same way as it would have been if he had had a definite aim of his own. Smirnov [61] has also confirmed the dependence of memory on the activity during which memorizing occurs. In these researches, however, no particular attention was given to the laws governing the formation of the actual associations underlying this interdependence; nor was the method used in the experiments adequately explained.

The present investigation set out to consider the data provided by these researches from a specific point of view; namely, how are the associative connections underlying so-called 'involuntary recollection' formed and activized? This called for methods of investigation that would provide a purely objective way of establishing the laws governing association, in the case of associations arising from the subject's activities in an experimental situation.

II

Method and Procedure

The methods used may be outlined. The subjects who carried out specific tasks in the experimental situation, were subjected to many stimuli, all of which were strictly controlled. But they were not warned that they would have to recall anything. It was then ascertained which elements of the situation could be recalled. An elaboration of the method in parallel experiments was as follows: while objective elements of a situation (i.e. stimuli affecting the subject) were kept identical, the content of the subjects' actions was altered by confronting him with *differing* tasks; alternatively, subjects were given *identical* tasks in *differing* experimental situations.

In the basic experiments the stimuli were circular cards with words written upon them. These were laid out on a board in a specified order. In some experiments, subjects were required to remove cards bearing words beginning with a specified letter; in others, they had to *find* the letter which appeared most frequently as an initial letter on the cards, and so on. After carrying out the required action, subjects had to give the initial letters of the words, to say which words started with a given letter, where these were situated, etc. The elements that were recalled indicated which elements had entered into associative connections, formed on the basis of the subjects' action. In a supplementary series of experiments, subjects carried out tasks with a different set of cards. This general scheme was varied in the different experiments. All the methods, however, had the following characteristics:

(1) Experiments were carried out as laboratory experiments under relatively simple and completely controlled conditions. The subject was affected only by specific stimuli, presented in a specific order, for a specified length of time. Chance influences were almost entirely excluded, so reducing the probability of chance connections being formed.

(2) The experimental situation and the content of the task were planned so that the subjects' existing associations could have no appreciable effect on the results. This relative levelling of individual differences made it possible for the facts established with one subject to be accurately reproduced in the case of others.

(3) Since the intention was that each subject should carry out only one specified action, and be unaware that he must recall particular elements of the situation, only one experiment was carried out with each subject.

There were, in all, 160 experiments performed with adult subjects, all of whom had received a higher education.

III

Basic Experiments, Series I–III

The first task was to establish that recall of the elements of the experimental situation (i.e. the forming and activizing of associative connections under the influence of verbal instructions) depended on the nature of the activity undertaken in the given situation. To clarify the nature of this dependence, several series of experiments were carried out which differed only in the task set; all the other conditions being identical.

On a table before the subjects lay a square board on which were drawn 16 rings (4 rows of 4 rings each); inside the rings lay smaller circles of cardboard (cards), each with a word written on it. Each card was in exactly the same place in all the experiments. (See Figure I.) The words were so chosen that they were about equally familiar to the subject; all were four-letter words, printed in identical type.

FIGURE I [1]

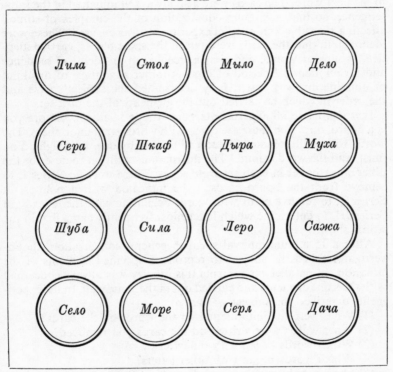

The investigator first read the instructions describing the required action with the cards; the subject then carried this out. After an interval of 15 minutes, the subject was asked questions which required the

[1] Saw   Table   Soap   Task
Sulphur   Cupboard   Hole   Fly
Coat   Strength   Pen   Soot
Village   Sea   Sickle   Cottage
ы is a single Russian letter (trans.).

recall of specified elements of the situation in which he had acted, and which he must have perceived in carrying out the given action.

To exclude chance visual stimuli the room was blacked out; only those cards which the subject had to perceive to carry out his task were illuminated. This procedure also served to create strictly equal conditions and complete control. The subject saw only the outline of the square board and the cards on it; the darkness prevented him from reading the words on the cards except when one was illuminated by the investigator. The illumination of each word continued for the same time—2 seconds—after which the light proceeded immediately to the next word. The cards were also always illuminated in the same sequence, so that maximum equalization of the complex of stimuli affecting the subject in parallel experiments was ensured. These were identical, in that the cards were put in the same places, carried identical groups of words, and were perceived in an identical sequence and for an identical period of time. Another advantage of this kind of illumination was that it fully determined the subject's gaze and the order in which he carried out the elements of the task set.

Instructions in all experiments were strictly identical. 'Before you is a board, on which there are cards with words written on them. The words will be illuminated in succession, one by one, by a light. You must read the words aloud.' The instructions went on to describe the different tasks set in each separate series. These were, in Series I, to remove from the board cards to be indicated with a pointer; in Series II, to remove cards with words beginning with the letter S; in Series III, to determine which letter most frequently came first in the words shown.

After a 15-minute interval spent in general conversation, the investigator asked the subject to reproduce specified elements of the situation. In parallel experiments this inquiry was always concerned with the same elements and carried out in the same way. In the experiments described the subject was asked:

(1) What were the initial letters of the words on the cards?
(2) What words were written on the cards you removed?
(3) Which words began with the letter S?
(4) Which words began with other letters?
(5) Show me, by putting your fingers on the board, the position (rings) of the cards you took away.

A verbatim record was made of the course of the whole experiment, including the investigator's questions and the subject's replies. There were ten subjects in each case.

In Series I, when the subjects had removed the six cards indicated by the investigator, not a single subject was able to reply to any of the questions listed above. All met the questions with a puzzled look, showing that they were not trying to recall anything. Two even maintained that they were unable to recall the words because they had not really read them, but had only followed the pointer; though, in fact, they had read every word aloud. After five experiments in this series, further trials were discontinued, since the results for all subjects were identical: none could recall a single one of the elements required.

In Series II, after the subjects had removed cards with words beginning with the letter S,[1] the results were quite different. All were able to point out the position from which they had taken cards, whereas in Series I none had been able to do this. Five subjects gave all six positions correctly, and five others showed five places correctly and confused one position with that next to it; apart from this there were no essential differences in recalling the material. But, as in Series I, subjects were unable to recall any of the first letters of words, apart from the letter S given in the instructions; and of the six words beginning with S, they recalled on an average only one—this invariably being either the second or third word (*Sera* or *Sila*), no other being recalled.

How is such a sharp difference to be explained? All the conditions were identical, except that the subjects' actions (removing cards) were governed by a different signal. In Series I the subject had to respond to the investigator's indication of a card, while in Series II he had to respond to cards with S. It was clearly this that determined the difference between results.

To illustrate more exactly how fixation and recall of relevant elements of the experimental situation depend upon the content of a concurrent action, we carried out a third Series of experiments. This time the subject was not required to perform a specified external action (i.e. removing the cards indicated); he was only asked to say which letter came first most frequently in the words written on the circles (this was the letter S).

In Series III, all ten subjects recalled the first letters of all the words. Nevertheless, subjects recalled, on an average, only one (whole) word beginning with S (either *Sera*, the second such word, in order of illumination, or else *Sila*, the third); nine subjects failed to recall a single word beginning with other letters; one recalled a word beginning with M (it should be added here that the latter was not sure until the end of the experiment which letter came at the beginning of the words most frequently, M or S). Subjects rarely recalled the positions of words with S (three could not point out a single place correctly, and others could only point out one, either the penultimate or the last). Thus, of all the external stimuli influencing the subject while he

---

[1] A card carrying a word beginning with S (or any other letter) will be referred to in future as a 'card with S', a 'card with U', etc. (Ed.).

carried out these tasks, only initial letters proved to be fixated; the degree of fixation of all other elements was negligible.

In comparing these results a clear distinction emerges between the first two Series and Series III. Whereas in Series II all the positions of cards with S were recalled, in Series III this was not so; on the other hand, something was recalled in this series which was quite forgotten in Series I and II—the initial letters of words (cf. Table I). It should be pointed out once again that these distinctions cannot in any way be attributed to the stimuli operating, since these were always identical.

The conclusion must be that the fixation of elements of the experimental situation in which a subject carries out a given task takes place selectively, depending on the content of the action performed.

But why does fixation of different stimuli take place in the carrying out of different tasks in a completely identical experimental situation? Underlying the fixation of any stimulus is the formation of a new associative connection, the prerequisite for which is the presence of an orienting reflex to the stimuli entering into the association; in other words, subjects can only recall stimuli that have evoked orientation. However, the formation of associations underlying the stimuli fixated in Series II and III cannot be understood as the formation of temporary connections based on an unconditioned orienting reflex to the 'novelty' of the stimulus. It seems that the recall both of card positions (Series II) and of initial letters (Series III) took place because of the formation of new associations, based on the conditioned-goal orientation which man possesses by virtue of his second signal system.

The subject is oriented in the experimental situation by means of a verbal instruction, which, as Ivanov-Smolensky has shown, creates and activizes a specified complex of temporary connections. Owing to the excitation of this complex of temporary connections, orientation is evoked only by specified stimuli affecting the subject; there is inhibition of orientation to other stimuli. The stimuli evoking orientation enter into connection with this excited complex and can therefore be recalled by the subject. Thus, when different tasks are carried out, different stimuli are fixated, because the task set in the instruction activates different complexes of connections, which give rise to different orientations.

IV

Control Experiments, Series I–IV

There remain more concrete questions which require an answer. First, what is the essential orienting element in the task? Second, which stimuli evoke orientation during the performance of a task?

To throw light on these questions we conducted four series of control experiments. The same methods were used as in the basic series, except for two features: (1) the board with 16 rings was replaced by one with 36 rings (6 rows of 6 rings each), (2) different words were written on the circular cards. Of these words, eight began with the letter U, and four in each case began with the letters V, G, L, M, O, S, T; eight signified animals (wolf, goose, fox, fly, sheep, elephant, tiger, duck). The words were distributed on the board as follows:[1]

глаз	труд	очки	угол	лужа	вилы
снег	муха	утес	лето	герб	весы
узел	тень	слон	окно	урок	мост
лист	волк	утка	град	мера	обоз
тигр	удар	сруб	мазь	овца	утро
спор	гусь	вода	торф	улей	лиса

With the 36-card board, the larger number of rings reduced the chance factor in recalling the positions of the cards with the appropriate words, while the change of apparatus made it possible to check whether the results of the Basic Series I–III depended upon the nature of the words themselves. Five subjects performed the experiments.

The results of the experiments in Control Series I confirmed those of the basic series. Of five subjects who worked through a series analogous to the Basic Series I (removing cards as indicated by the investigator), not one could answer any of the questions.

In Control Series II subjects had to remove all words beginning with U. All could recall with certainty the positions of the cards they had taken away, but not one could recall a single initial letter apart from the letter U given in the instruction. Of all the words read out during the experiment, subjects recalled, on an average, one.

Control Series III (specifying which letter came first most frequently) also repeated the results of the basic series. Four subjects recalled all eight initial letters, one subject recalled five.

In an additional control experiment, Series IV, subjects were required to collect all cards with words denoting animals. In initiating this series, we started from the supposition that complete memorizing of all these words could be obtained by a specific change in the task

[1]
Eye	Work	Glasses	Corner	Puddle	Fork
Snow	Fly	Crag	Summer	Coat of Arms	Scales
Knot	Shadow	Elephant	Window	Lesson	Bridge
Leaf	Wolf	Duck	Degree	Measure	Baggage
Tiger	Blow	Frame	Grease	Sheep	Morning
Quarrel	Goose	Water	Peat	Hive	Fox

set; if this were so, it would prove that the failure to recall words in the first three series was determined, not by the words themselves,

TABLE 1

Experimental Data for the Basic Series I–III—16 Cards Used

Name of the series	Average number recalled per subject		
	Initial letters	Positions of cards	Words
Series I Removing cards indicated by experimenter	0	0	0
Series II Removing cards with words beginning with S	0	5·5 out of 6	1 out of 16
Series III Specifying which letter comes first most often	5 out of 5	0·7 out of 6	1·1 out of 16

TABLE 2

Experimental Data for the Control Series I–III and Series IV—
36 Cards Used

Name of the series	Average number recalled per subject			
	Initial letters	Positions of cards	Names of animals	All other words
Series I Removing cards indicated by experimenter	0	0	0	0
Series II Removing cards with words beginning with U	0	8 out of 8	—	1 out of 36
Series III Specifying which letter comes first most often	7·4 out of 8	—	—	2 out of 36
Series IV Collecting all cards with words denoting animals	—	4·6 out of 8	7·6 out of 8	0·2 out of 28

but by the nature of the tasks performed, i.e. by the content of the subject's activity.

Whereas in Control Series I–III not one subject reproduced any of the animal words met with in the experiment, in Series IV subjects recalled almost all the words: three recalled all 8 words, and two others 7 out of 8.

The positions of the cards with animal names were also recalled (three subjects correctly recalled 5 positions, two recalled 4). It is important to note that the subjects, pointing out a particular position, could say exactly which word had been there; the association between position and word always proved correct in this series. Only one subject recalled a word not denoting an animal—*Ulei* (bee-hive)—and he had tried to remove this word from the board in collecting cards with animal names; it is obvious that he had extended the task to this word as well.

The results obtained in the Basic and Control Series may now be summarized (cf. Tables 1 and 2).

In Series I (removing cards indicated by the experimenter), subjects could not recall the words on the cards, nor their initial letters, nor the position of the cards on the board. In Series II (collecting cards with S or U), the positions of the cards removed was recalled, but the words on the cards and initial letters were not, in general, recalled. In Series III (determining which letter came first most often in the words occurring in the experiment), initial letters were recalled, but the words and positions of specified cards were not fixated. In Series IV (collecting cards with animal names), words denoting animals were recalled, and in a considerable number of cases their positions also.

As has already been emphasized, the parallel series of experiments differed only in the nature of a subject's action in the given situation. Consequently, in comparing the different series of experiments, differences in the material recalled can only be explained in terms of differences in the actual actions performed. How, precisely, did these actions differ? Above all, they differed in their outcome. The action in Series I resulted in the removal from the board of cards indicated by the investigator; in Series II in the removal of cards with S (or, in the Control Series, with U); in Series III in specifying the most frequent initial letter; in Control Series IV in the removal of cards with words denoting animals.

The variations established by our experiments may then be explained in terms of differences in orientation. The actual setting of a task informs the subject of the result he has to achieve by action in the given situation. In mastering the task, corresponding associations are formed and activized in the subject. The different requirements of the instructions naturally form and activize different systems of connections. It becomes the subject's aim to achieve the required result, and his actions are based on associations aroused by this aim. According to differences in the systems of connections activized by different purposes, the subject develops a different orientation in the experimental situation and plans his action accordingly. The situation, therefore, also turns out to be different for him; in other words, he extracts different elements from it.

Thus subjects had, primarily, a sure memory for the result of the action they had just completed, but it was not only the elements that entered directly into the result of their action that they remembered. Subjects doing Series III could name not only the initial letter they had singled out as the most frequent (S, U), but also other initial letters of words entering into the experimental situation. In Series IV, subjects recalled not only that they collected words denoting animals, but also the precise names of these animals. It is, therefore, the elements of situations that are fixated, not the actions leading directly to the result. Obviously the elements fixated are determined not only by the outcome of an action, but also by its *content*.

In Series I it was found that, of the elements of the experimental situation, subjects only remembered what they had been told in their instructions; other associative connections, such as those corresponding to the positions of the cards on the board, could not be activized. This suggests inhibition, either of the orientation to these situational elements, or of the emerging connections. What were the features of the subject's action determining this?

The action consisted in removing cards indicated by the investigator; the subject, after noticing the pointer on a certain card, performed the required external movement. The connection between the response-determining stimulus (the pointer) and the removed card was not set up by the subject, but was contained objectively in the investigator's instructions. It was not, therefore, the subject who set up the relationship between the elements of the situation: it was only the investigator's pointer that evoked orientation, the card remaining unconnected with the position it occupied on the board, with the word written on it, etc. Since all these stimuli remained in the background for the subject, orientation towards them was inhibited and they were not fixated.

In Series II the subject behaved differently. He had to find and remove all cards with S. Cards with certain words were thereby distinguished, especially according to the position a given card occupied relative to the whole board. But why was there no fixation of other initial letters, and of the words themselves, when the subject selected words with a specified initial letter (S)? Clearly orientation was evoked by all initial letters, but, as soon as a letter was determined not to be S, action and corresponding connection were inhibited and the letter was not remembered; that such non-remembering is due to inhibition of emerging connections is made clear by further experiments described below. The words themselves did not evoke orientation and were not fixated because the subject did not interact with these objects of the situation.

Analysis of Series III and IV confirms that orientation is supported only by those objects with which the subject establishes relations (i.e. with which he acts), while there is inhibition of orientation to other elements of the situation.

In Series III the task was to specify which letter most frequently came first in the words on the cards. The subject's action consisted in making a comparison between initial letters to determine which was most frequent. Each one of the initial letters might have been needed to give him the required result. Therefore there was no inhibition of associative connections based on orientation to these letters as in Series II, but rather fixation so that the letters were remembered. No other stimuli were remembered, since these were background features only; orientation to them was inhibited.

In Series IV subjects were required to collect all 'animal' cards. In order to remove these cards the subject had to establish a relation between the meanings of words, i.e. to put words in a group of animals or in a group of non-animals, selecting them according to their meaning. Orientation was evoked not only by the position of the selected cards, but also by the words themselves. Though the subject acted in relation to all the words written on the cards, connections evoked by words not relevant to the task were inhibited as 'non-confirmatory'. Only those connections were strengthened which resulted in words being put into the required category ('animals'). This explains how one subject came to recall the word *Ulei* (bee-hive). Although he did not remove this card, inhibiting the act of movement, yet at a certain moment this word struck him as being connected with the required group ('animals'), and the connection produced was strengthened.

In Series IV, as in Series II, the positions of cards that had been removed were recalled. The reasons are the same as for Series II, the subject selecting from amongst all the cards only certain specified ones, and thereby connecting the card with the position it occupied on the board. However, whereas in Series II all the positions of removed cards were recalled, in Series IV only half of these positions were remembered. This reduction is probably due to inductive relations between the first and second signal systems.

In this connection some further points may be made. The positions

175

of the cards removed were fixated more fully in some experiments than in others. Thus, all the cards carrying words beginning with the same letter were restored to their proper positions (8 out of 8), whereas only half the 'animal' cards were correctly replaced. Sometimes subjects talked during the experiment, saying that they remembered that the card specified lay, for example, last but one from the end. In this way, recall was made part of a verbal system. After reproducing one or two positions in this way, however, subjects declared that they were unable to show where the remaining cards belonged. Only when the investigator insisted did they agree to show him, and then as if guessing at random. But, to their own surprise, they subsequently showed the positions of three or four more cards correctly, and the rest without erring by more than one place in a row.

It seems that this double recall indicates the sequence of formation of first-signal connections. This is also suggested by the fact that the connections underlying recall of card-positions are inhibited when there is pre-eminent concentration of activity in the second signal system. If the subject recalled the words on the cards, then he was unable to give their positions; the only exceptions were the few cases cited above in which subjects verbally recalled card-positions. It is clear that first-signal connections, on which memory for the positions of the cards usually depends, is inductively inhibited by the excitation of the second signal system which appears when the meanings of words are distinguished and recalled. This would explain the lower indices for recall of card-positions in Control Series IV ('animal' cards), since this series entailed even greater activization of second signal system processes.

If this explanation is correct, then a weakening of the activity of the second signal system must lead to a reduction of inductive inhibition in the first signal system. The following experiment was carried out to test this supposition. The words on the board were replaced by differing sets of dots. Eight cards had one dot each, and 2, 3, 4, 5, 6, 7 and 8 dots were each drawn on four cards. The task was to remove the cards with one dot. The number of correctly remembered positions was higher than in the series requiring the removal of cards with words.

The following fact is also of interest. If subjects who had done the series with dots, instead of being asked to show on the board the positions of the cards removed, were asked to *say* where these were, they were not only unable to do this, but also were subsequently unable to *show* a single position correctly. Inhibition of connections of the first signal system by the second signal system appears here even more clearly.

These facts are cited not only to support the explanations given, but also because we consider them to be important both from the theoretical point of view and for methodology.

V

Additional Experiments, Series V–IX

We have seen that stimuli fall into two groups: those evoking orientation, and those which are neutral and background. But stimuli that evoke orientation are not always strengthened, since some connections arising on the basis of orientation are inhibited as not leading to success. Evidence of this could be provided by changing an action, so that a connection previously inhibited became reinforced and *vice versa*. To this end we introduced special experiments (Series V, VI and VII) in which the tasks performed by subjects were identical but the elements of the experimental situation were changed. The method was technically the same as in the experiments already described.

A 36-ring board was used. In different series, either the words on the cards or the distribution of words on the board differed.[1] The instructions for all series were as follows: 'You are to collect cards with words which have the same initial letter—the initial letter that occurs most frequently. You will be shown every word twice. The first time you must determine which is the required initial letter, the second time you are to collect the cards.' The words were accordingly shown to each subject twice in succession: the first time each word was illuminated for 2 seconds, the second time for 4 seconds.

In Series V subjects carried out the task set in the same experimental situation as before. The most frequent initial letter was U. All ten subjects recalled all or almost all of the initial letters of the words shown (six subjects recalling all 8 letters, four 7 out of a possible 8), and were able to show the position of all the cards with U which they had removed. But the *words* on the cards were scarcely recalled at all: three subjects failed to recall a single word, five recalled one word with U, and two others each recalled two words with U, so that the average recall was just below one word out of a possible eight.

Another group of subjects carried out the same task in a different experimental situation (Series VI). New cards were substituted with other words and beginning with other letters. The number of words beginning with any given letter and their distribution on the board

[1] The tables have been omitted. The words used in Series V were the same as those used in Control Series I–IV, and were arranged in the same way. Those used in Series VII were the same words arranged in a different order. In Series VI, a different set of four-letter words was used (Ed.).

corresponded to the same elements in the Series V experiments. But while in Series V there were 8 words with U and 4 each with V, G, L, M, O, S and T, in Series VI there were 8 words with K and 4 each with B, Z, I, N, P, R and SH.[1] The results of Series VI exactly repeated those of Series V. Differences in the elements of the situation did not, therefore, lead to any difference in the formation of associative connections; the letters subjects had to isolate and the words they had to read aloud were of no significance.

Finally, in Series VII, the experimental situation was altered to give the same set of cards as in Series V, but differently distributed. Whereas in Series V, cards with a given letter were evenly distributed all over the board, in this series the cards with U were concentrated in the first two rows. There were five such cards in the first two rows, which also contained cards with the letters G, T and O. In the remaining four rows words beginning with various letters were distributed more or less evenly. Results were as follows. The words written on the cards were not recalled—just as in Series V and VI. All ten subjects remembered only the initial letters of words in the first two rows, i.e. U, G, O and M; not one recalled an initial letter which did not occur in the first two rows. Recall of the distribution of cards with U was similar to that in Series V and VI, but even more exact.

This peculiarity in the formation of connections was evidently due to the different concentration of cards with U in different parts of the board, for it was only in this respect that the distribution had been altered. Did this difference in the formation of associative connections depend only on changes in the situation itself? This could be determined by altering the task given in Series V and VII, and then comparing the results anew. Six subjects, therefore, were set the task of collecting all cards with U in the Series VII situation; and the same task was set to six others in the Series V situation. No differences were found in the results of these two series of experiments. This shows that the differences in association-formation in Series V and VII were not determined only by differences in the situations. The only possible explanation is that, in carrying out the same task in different situations, subjects act differently, and that for this reason the emerging associative connections are not identical.

How did subjects act in Series V and VII? The process of selecting the necessary letter was determined by the concentrations in which words with the same initial letter were distributed. The easiest method of selection is to find out which letter occurs most frequently in the first rows of the board, and to draw a conclusion about the degrees of frequency with which initial letters are repeated over the whole of the board. Determining how often separate letters occur in the first

---

[1] SH is a single letter in Russian. (Ed.)

parts of the board becomes a new, practical goal related to the task. In Series V all letters were encountered in about the same numbers. Each letter evoked orientation and connections were strengthened as potentially successful, because each initial letter might be the one sought for. Only at the end was there a final selection of the letter U, as the initial letter occurring most frequently. In Series VII the subject's goal was the same; every letter in the first row evoked orientation and was fixated. But thereafter they proceeded differently; from the first rows they not only selected U as the letter occurring most frequently, but also distinguished it as the desired letter. Letters which did not appear until the four lower rows, were therefore not fixated.

Another experiment was then introduced which shows that this failure is connected with inhibition of emerging connections. The situation was changed so that words with M, instead of being evenly distributed, were concentrated in the last four rows; five subjects then carried out the same task as in Series VII. All recalled the same letters, G, O, T and U, with the addition of M, but none recalled any of the other initial letters (V, L and C). Why was M also recalled in this case? Subjects often hesitated in deciding which initial letter to choose. Thus one subject said after the experiment: 'At first I thought I would collect words with U, but then there were a lot of words with M, so that I could have collected both.'

If the failure to recall letters in the lower rows had been a consequence of inhibition of orientation, then the concentration of words with M would not have led to the formation of a new connection. Clearly all letters continued to evoke orientation, and it was only the connections that were inhibited. When the letter M began to be repeated frequently, the connection emerging on the basis of orientation was reinforced as leading to success; subjects developed the hypothesis that M might be the commonest initial letter. The difference between the formation of associative connections in Series V and in the parallel Control Series is, therefore, due to a change in the experimental situation leading to change in the subject's action.

In these cases, the situational elements that influenced the course of the action undertaken were the proportions in which each letter was concentrated in different parts of the board. The situational elements provide the conditions in which the action takes its course, and differing elements of the situation are decisive according to the subjects' tasks, i.e. the differing actions required.

To confirm these indications of dependence we carried out two further series of experiments, Series VIII and IX. The identical instructions for both series were to collect all cards with words denoting invertebrate animals. But the material was different. In both experiments 36 cards were set out on the board. In Series VIII six cards denoted invertebrates but none of the others denoted animals, while Series IX included the cards for the six invertebrates, as well as cards for six vertebrates. There were five subjects for each of these experiments.

Comparison of results showed the following differences. In Series VIII all subjects recalled the words on the cards they had removed (those with the names of invertebrates), but not one subject could recall a single word apart from these. In Series IX, on the other hand, subjects recalled not only the six invertebrates, but also the vertebrates, i.e. twice as many words. Thus differences in the experimental situation led to differences in the resulting associative connections. The recall of the vertebrates' names obviously occurred on the same basis as the recall of the word *Ulei* by the subject in Series IV.

In Series IX, the subject's action, directed to removing cards with the names of animals, involved classifying words as denoting either invertebrates or other animals; that is, it involved a differentiation of words. Accordingly, all the words recalled had evoked a conditioned orientation. In Series VIII only those connections based on orientation to names of invertebrates were reinforced, all other connections being inhibited. But in Series IX connections based on orientation to names of vertebrates were also reinforced because they led to success; the subject could not remove them immediately to the group not requiring a response—though he inhibited the motor act of removing the appropriate card.

But these variations of the experimental situation resulted in no differences in the associative connections brought about by actions directed towards goals not requiring the isolation of words of defined meaning; thus there were no differences in the associative connections resulting from actions with the same sets of cards, when the instruction was to remove all cards with K. We may, therefore, conclude that there is also reinforcement of those elements of the situation which determine the way in which the subject acts and the course of such goal-directed action.

VI

Additional Experiments, Series X

The stimuli which become fixated may include other elements besides those we have distinguished. Sometimes 'background' elements are fixated. To illustrate this, we may turn to another series of experiments (Series X).

One of the cards on the 36-ring board was replaced by a card with the word outlined in Indian ink, and, in this situation, nine subjects were required to carry out various tasks; three were asked to remove cards with U, three to determine the most frequent initial letter, and three to remove names of animals. All subjects recalled the word outlined with Indian ink, though this word had never previously been recalled in any experiment when it had not been outlined. The fact that an outlined word was so recalled, irrespective of the action the subject performed, is evidence that its fixation took place, not because of a conditioned orientation based on the instructions, but simply because it attracted an orienting reflex as to a 'novelty'. Thus connections may develop during an action which do not depend upon the content or conditions of the action; 'neutral' stimuli may evoke an orienting reflex in the subject and may be fixated.

VII

Conclusions

The principal aim of our investigation was to demonstrate experimentally some of the laws governing the formation of associative connections during the performance of simple actions. We set out to study, not the general mechanism of connection-formation, but its special features in conditions where connections relating to differing elements in the situation, and to the action itself, are fixated. We reached the following conclusions.

First, that fixation and recall only appear in the case of certain of the stimuli which are elements of the experimental situation and which influence the subject. When there is a change of task (i.e. of instructions) and thereby of the subject's action, then different stimuli are fixated,—the subject forms other associative connections. Differences in the nature of the stimuli do not determine which stimuli are fixated by the subject; control experiments were carried out in an identical situation, the only feature that differed being the task to be performed. Therefore, the origin of the differences in associative connections is to be found in the content of the subjects' actions.

Second, analysis of the connections formed showed that these develop on the basis of that higher type of orientation made possible by the second signal system. This leads to a consideration of the differences between associative connections, formed in carrying out different tasks, in relation to differences in the subjects' orientation in an identical external situation. To carry out their instructions subjects acted in accordance with particular stimuli; these stimuli evoked an orientation reaction which affected the formation of corresponding connections, yet other stimuli in the situation remained neutral, mere background features.

These experiments show that orientation to relations between stimuli which do not lead to success, i.e. are not 'self-confirming', does not produce fixation, the connections between them being inhibited. Conversely, connections which secure the achievement of a goal, i.e. are 'self-confirming', are fixated and may be reproduced.

Those associative connections which were strengthened in the course of action, and which could be reproduced, can be divided into four groups.

(1) Connections based on orientation towards a goal. These lead to fixation of whatever is achieved by the action.

(2) Connections which are formed and grow because they ensure achievement of a goal, but which do not enter directly into the composition of the connections on which the achieved result is based. Such connections may explain why the positions of removed cards were fixated, and why, after the instruction 'Determine which letter comes first most often', all the initial letters were fixated, with the exception of U and C, which entered into the result; the same might be said about the fixation of the words denoting animals. Among these connections must be included those first signal connections which elicit the subject's motor action, but which are in most cases inhibited by the second signal system.

(3) Connections based on orientation to stimuli which constitute the conditions of the required action.

(4) The formation of connections in these three groups depends on the subject's action. A fourth group consists of connections, also formed in the course of action in a particular situation, but based on a reflex orientation to the 'novelty' of stimuli and not depending directly on the content of the subject's action.

These results can only be regarded as preliminary. But certain of the propositions and deductions advanced have a definite theoretical significance in that they contribute to a strictly psychological interpretation of the formation of temporary connections in man. They also have a bearing on education, in particular insofar as they suggest ways in which tasks can be assigned in order that pupils may distinguish and consolidate specific material.

PART IV

CHILD PSYCHOLOGY [1]

BY
A. A. SMIRNOV

[P]ROFESSOR SMIRNOV BEGINS by saying that more research is devoted to child and educational psychology in the U.S.S.R. than to any other branch; and enumerates many research projects. The scientific foundation for all such investigations is the physiological teaching of Pavlov; its philosophical foundation is dialectical materialism. Research takes place in special research institutes and in the psychological departments of higher educational institutions. Every effort is made to acquaint teachers with this work, in schools and colleges and through special courses for practising teachers who wish to add to their qualifications. Parents also show a keen interest in the subject. In fact, these branches of psychology owe their rapid development to the solicitude for young people's upbringing shown by Soviet society as a whole; evidenced in a desire to further the all-round development of the individual, to provide youth with a broad range of knowledge, to foster those traits of personality that correspond most closely to high moral demands. This paper, however, is concerned, not with educational psychology, but with some of the theoretical premises that inform research into the child's psychic development.]

I

It is of primary importance to any theory of psychic development to answer the question: what determines this development?

[1] Paper given at the 'Journées Internationales de Psychologie de l'enfant', Paris, April 1954 (translated in the U.S.S.R.).

Psychic development is the development of the brain. This is a cardinal thesis of materialist philosophy. It goes without saying that there are inborn, individual differences in higher nervous activity. But these inborn differences do not predetermine psychic development in an absolute way. The individual's brain also functions under the influence of his surroundings, and his mentality, being a reflection of objective reality, is also formed and developed under this same influence. Individual behaviour is not, therefore, the simple expression of natural endowment, independent of external influences. It has a physiological basis in the system of temporary connections formed as a result of the influence of the environment and the individual's response; these are not inborn but acquired during the individual's life experience. Moreover, Pavlov's researches have demonstrated the extreme flexibility of the nervous system in forming these connections, which constitute the basis of human psychic activity and are always strictly determined by objective conditions. 'The *chief*, *strongest*, and most *lasting impression* we get from the study of higher nervous activity . . .', wrote Pavlov, 'is the extraordinary plasticity of this activity, its immense potentialities; nothing is immobile, intractable, everything may always be achieved, changed for the better, provided only that the proper conditions are created'.[1] It follows that his conditions of life play the decisive part in man's psychic development. These always depend on society and are determined, not by the individual's biological inclinations, but by the historically determined material life of the society in which he lives. This is the fundamental premise when it is a question of investigating what determines man's psychic development.

The conditions of life do not, however, determine psychic development automatically, of themselves, simply by virtue of their existence. Under the same conditions development may take place in different ways; this depends on the place these conditions occupy in the life and activities of the individual, the way in which his life unfolds in them, and what is his attitude to them. Psychic development takes place in the course of interaction between human beings and objective reality. A man is not the passive object of the influences of his surroundings, but an active participant in them. Men create the conditions of their own lives, and the present or former conditions of a man's life do not absolutely determine his psychic development, any more than do the inborn differences of the nervous system. A change in the conditions of life entails a change in individual development. There is, therefore, great scope for man's psychic development if there is conscious and directed organization of his life and activities; i.e. if the necessary conditions for development are created. Similarly,

---

[1] Pavlov-Gantt ii, 144; *Selected Works*, 446–7.

there is great scope for influencing the child's psychic development through education, for education is primarily the organization of the child's life and activity, while his psychic development is not a spontaneous, internally conditioned process, taking place apart from educational influences; on the contrary, education plays a leading part in the child's development.

To what extent are these premises confirmed by practice? Compulsory secondary education has now been established in the majority of Soviet schools. What has it demonstrated? That, if education is correctly planned and promoted, all children (with the exception of a few pathological cases) can acquire a secondary education. This conclusion is widely at variance with assertions that the majority of children are incapable of profiting from secondary education, cannot, for example, master algebra; assertions made with the aid of alleged scientific facts but without consideration of social causes. Tens of thousands of Soviet teachers promote the normal advancement of all their pupils, ensuring that they have fully mastered the knowledge and skills required by the schools. This demonstrates clearly that education, correctly promoted, provides scope for extensive mental development, for the fostering of children's capacities, and so for their acquisition of knowledge. And this does not apply only to isolated, 'selected', children, supposedly endowed with 'natural abilities', but to all the children in school.

The work of the remarkable Soviet educationist, A. S. Makarenko, provides a vivid illustration of the decisive influence of education in the formation of personality. He demonstrated what outstanding successes can be achieved by rational organization of a child's life and activities; how effective is the role of the collective itself if the teacher so develops and guides the children's independent activity that they are not aware of any compulsion, if the children themselves struggle for a common cause, and if relations within the collective are based on respect by each member for the collective opinions and traditions and the respect of the collective for each of its members. Makarenko's work is of immense value, not only for education but also for psychology, because it showed in practice how a child's personality is formed under the influence of his conditions of life and activities.

This has also been the subject of research, in particular as concerns the formation of moral qualities: diligence, community spirit, sense of duty, sense of honour.[1] The aim of the investigations was to find which aspects of education, both at home and in school, have most influence on the development of moral traits of personality, and how these traits develop under the influence of conditions of life and

[1] Researches of Bozhovich and research conducted under my supervision.

education. Inquiries with children were coupled with a search for active means of developing personality, and it was demonstrated that the basis for the formation of such personality traits is the organization of practical moral experience for children. It was found that difficulties experienced in upbringing were not due to innate peculiarities, at variance with social demands, but to the circumstances of particular children and to mistakes in education. 'Difficult' children were those who had developed wrong attitudes towards their surroundings, school, or study, as a result of certain conditions of life. The first necessity, if such children are to be educated, if their attitudes are to change, is to change these conditions; to alter their 'position' *vis-à-vis* their surroundings so that a favourable soil is created for positive educational measures. To confront the child with authoritative demands will not serve; nor is a knowledge of moral codes sufficient. Practical moral experience is necessary, which can give rise, not to merely formal knowledge, but to real moral conviction and moral behaviour.

The importance of organizing the child's activity has also been demonstrated in the case of intellectual development. One investigation was concerned with children who lagged behind in their schoolwork, who created an impression of dullness because of intellectual passivity; this, despite a conscientious attitude to learning, impeded their studies.[1] The cause of this 'dullness' was traced to particular circumstances of their upbringing, and it was shown that intellectual passivity can be overcome by organizing the child's mental activities along certain lines.

II

In close connection with the researches described are investigations into the psychological peculiarities of different age levels.

Each stage of child development has certain common psychological peculiarities, which depend on the development of the nervous system and organism, and on certain common conditions of life. These peculiarities, however, are also determined to a considerable degree by the course of the child's life at the given period; and, since this may be different in many respects, considerable psychological variations are found in children of the same age.

This was clearly shown in investigations with adolescents. Adolescence is usually regarded as a period of severe crisis in the development of personality, one with many negative features which are attributed to biological peculiarities. But, though the physiological changes of adolescence influence behaviour and create certain educational difficulties, research has shown that the negative features of

[1] Research by Slavina (cf. p. 205—Ed.).

the 'crisis' disappear, or are considerably reduced, if certain changes are made in upbringing. It was found that one of the main sources of such difficulties is the contradiction between the adolescent's consciousness of his new potentialities and the kind of demands made upon him.[1] It is, then, the adolescent's conditions of life that play the decisive role. Similar conclusions were reached in the course of investigations into another 'critical' period—the age of seven [2] (the age of commencing school in the Soviet Union—Ed.).

The psychological peculiarities of different age levels depend, very largely, upon the activities during which psychic processes take place. Here there is a general regularity, or psychological law; each psychic process depends upon the concrete components, the aims and motives of the activity engaged in, and upon the child's attitude towards this.

To provide examples, I will refer to some of my own investigations, concerned with the dependence of the processes of memory upon activity. In one of these, voluntary memorizing (i.e. memorizing with the definite intention of remembering) was compared with involuntary memorizing (when there was no such intention). The relation between the two was shown to differ in accordance with the type of activity engaged in; while in some cases involuntary memorizing proved less effective than voluntary memorizing, in others it proved considerably more effective. In both cases, the results depended on the nature of the mental activity engaged in.

Other experiments have also demonstrated this dependence of memory upon activity.[3] For instance, a group of kindergarten children were required to memorize words read in the manner usual in experimental investigations of memory; later, a game was played which required the participants to memorize the names of certain objects. Under the latter conditions, the children memorized about twice as many words as in the former case. Again, considerable differences have been discerned in voluntary attention under experimental conditions and during play. Voluntary attention was maintained for a longer period during play, but the number of distractions from the activity and the number of errors made were greater than under experimental conditions.[4] The same dependence of mental processes on the activity during which they take place has been observed in investigations of musical ability, and of the motivated activity of adults.[5] The search for ways of compensating for defects arising from brain

[1] Researches by Levitov, Bozhovich and others.
[2] Researches of Volokitina and others.
[3] Those conducted under my supervision and those of Zankov, Zinchenko and Leontiev.
[4] Researches of Zaporozhets.
[5] Researches of Teplov; and of Leontiev and Zaporozhets and their collaborators.

injuries in movements of the hands, and in speech, reading, writing and counting has demonstrated the same: that a change in the aim and organization of the activity plays an important part in the restoration of a lost ability.[1]

The peculiarities of psychic processes depend to a great extent upon what the child does, what he remembers, what he comprehends and so on. It has been found that, in children of the same age, a similar mental process (of perception, memory, etc.) shows characteristics usually regarded as peculiar to different stages of development, depending upon what is the object of the child's activity.[2]

Many characteristics, customarily regarded as typical of a certain age, have not been confirmed as such when there has been an alteration of the aim set, the material presented, or the conditions of the experiment. For instance, children aged four to six years do not by any means confine themselves to enumerating the objects depicted in an illustration, as is usually affirmed; on the contrary, if the subject is sufficiently plain and comprehensible, if it calls to mind some personal experience, if the questions posed prompt a narration, then they attempt to give an interpretation of the picture. Again, the supposition that younger children are more 'sensitive' to colour than to form has not been confirmed; under certain conditions, children orient themselves exclusively according to the shape of the object. When familiar phenomena are explained to them, kindergarten children, despite assertions to the contrary, interpret cause and effect correctly and easily notice discrepancies in the facts or the explanation. In children of this age, mechanical memorizing does not, by any means, occupy the same place as it does in the case of younger infants. If the child's activity is properly motivated, the problem set is clear and definite, and material is offered corresponding to his knowledge and experience, then his psychic processes reach a much higher level than is indicated in many expositions of this subject. On the other hand, if these conditions are not complied with, then not only children, but even adults, show results which do not correspond to their actual capabilities.

Since psychic processes depend upon the activity during which they take place, it is impossible to establish any universal standards applicable to particular age levels. There is no single age characteristic that is divorced from the conditions in which the relevant psychic processes take place. What may seem to be an age peculiarity, may no longer make an appearance if the process takes place during a different activity, or if the child is offered more comprehensible material.

Tests based on universal standards, and designed to ascertain the

[1] Researches of Luria.
[2] Investigations conducted under the supervision of Rubinstein.

adequacy or inadequacy of a child's development are, therefore, unacceptable. The kind of tests used cannot serve as a basis for such an estimation. The aim a child is pursuing, his motives for fulfilling his task, and his attitude to the test as a whole, may differ so greatly, may influence the solution of the problem to such an extent, that it is impossible to judge what might be revealed under different conditions of activity, what are the child's real capabilities. If a child's psychic development is to be correctly judged, it is necessary to study him under conditions which create the necessary motivation for the activity and a definite attitude towards it. Only then is it possible to ascertain what abilities the child actually possesses. This is the path taken by psychology in the U.S.S.R.

Tests are also inadmissible (and this is particularly important) because they are restricted to a mere statement of the result, without disclosing why or how it was achieved, or what prevented it from being better. When the process itself remains hidden, its significant and qualitative characteristics undisclosed, then it is impossible to judge of the child's activity. The essence of the phenomena is not discovered; whereas the main concern of psychological research, employing strictly objective methods, is with psychic activity proper, its substance, structure, mechanisms, i.e. precisely that which is disregarded in the case of test investigations. The aim of Soviet psychology is to analyse the characteristics, the reasons and motives, the psychological mechanisms, of psychic activity; this procedure alone opens the way to discovery of the essence of the activity and to an understanding of its result. This is how Soviet psychologists interpret the subject of psychology and the purpose of objective methods of investigation.

This is the constructive way of solving the most important problems before psychology: to give effective assistance in the formation of man's personality, in the development of his consciousness, his cultural demands, his rich creative potentialities, and his high moral qualities. Psychology must assist men to develop their valuable qualities, and to form useful ones that may not always be adequately developed. People are the most precious capital in the world. To care for human beings is the sacred duty of every science and every scientist. The most valuable contribution that psychology can make towards solving the problems of mankind is to make scientific and realizable plans for the all-round development of personality; for the fostering of all man's powers and gifts, of all that is best, most truly humane, in people. This is how Soviet psychologists understand their task.

SOME ASPECTS OF THE PSYCHOLOGY OF TEACHING [1]

BY
N. A. MENCHINSKAYA

IN THE PSYCHOLOGY OF TEACHING, the key process now studied is the assimilation of knowledge, skills and habits in school, by children of different ages. This is not only a matter of interest so far as psychological theory is concerned; by revealing the general laws governing the learning of school subjects, and the individual differences displayed in the process, psychologists can assist in furthering more effective methods of instruction.

Learning implies conscious mastery of knowledge, skills and habits. Conscious awareness in learning is a basic principle of the Soviet school; this presupposes that children understand the purpose of their studies and strive to learn as well as possible. Such an attitude is of key importance in the process of acquiring knowledge, and, as investigations have shown, the nurturing of stable and socially useful motives can improve the quality of learning. [2] Study of the cognitive interests of children, which has brought to light the chief stages in the formation of these interests, occupies an important place in this work. [3]

The part played by evaluation of learning constitutes a special problem. Here, it has been demonstrated that approval or censure has, in itself, no real significance; these become important only when the pupil understands *why* his reply received a particular evaluation. [4]

In contemporary psychological literature, a great deal of attention is paid to the so-called 'law of effect', which is regarded as the basis of learning. It is taken to imply the necessity of reinforcing the pupil's

---

[1] Paper given at the 'Journées Internationales de Psychologie de l'enfant', Paris, April 1954 (translated by H. Milne). This paper has been slightly abbreviated.
[2] Bozhovich, Volokitina and others.
[3] Morozova and others.
[4] Researches of Ananiev. This point has received confirmation in the results of a special investigation conducted by Menchinskaya.

correct or incorrect actions by means of approval or censure. But, in the treatment of this law, an extremely important point is ignored, namely, that the real power of 'reinforcement' is only brought to bear when knowledge of a result is accompanied by understanding of the reason for the evaluation.

Many studies of the conscious assimilation of knowledge are concerned with scientific concepts, and investigations take place, not under laboratory conditions, but in the schools.[1] These are concerned to trace the main stages in assimilating concepts from different branches of knowledge, and they are bringing to light the peculiar features of this process in the case of different categories of concepts, the mistakes commonly committed, and the means of avoiding or overcoming them. Special attention is given to the application in practice of concepts of varying complexity, since the introduction of polytechnical education gives this process, and the unification of theory and practice in general, added importance.

I

A psychological analysis has been made of the difficulties pupils encounter when applying knowledge in practice, and of the methods of overcoming these. It has been found that one of the chief causes of these difficulties is a lack of variety in the visual material used as a prop for new concepts. For example, scholars find difficulty in applying geometrical concepts if only standard diagrams are used (e.g. right-angled triangles presented with the right angle exclusively on the base).[2] That visual material must be varied to guarantee a correct mastery of concepts is generally recognized; but how, and to what extent, has not been experimentally established. Evidently, it is impossible to present the whole gamut of experience underlying a particular branch of abstract knowledge. But the task is to reveal to scholars the possibility of going beyond the bounds of the given, limited, sense experience.

An investigation of the study of geometry by sixth-year pupils (12 to 13 years) has determined the variation of visual material necessary to give an understanding of the limitations of sense experience, and so to ensure mastery of the generalized content of a geometrical proposition. In one experiment, pupils were asked to draw a circle with diameters. One subject drew two diameters (in the position in which he was accustomed to see them in diagrams), and when asked 'How many diameters can be drawn in a circle?' he replied,

---

[1] This work is being undertaken by the staff of the Institute of Psychology under Menchinskaya, and by psychologists at the Leningrad Institute under Ananiev and Shardakov.   [2] Researches of Zykova.

relying on his drawing, 'Two'. The investigator drew two more diameters (still putting them in the customary position) and repeated the question. The pupil, again on the basis of his perception of the drawing, replied that it was possible to draw 'four diameters' in a circle. He was then shown another diameter, but in an unusual position. This time his answer was very different: 'Any number of diameters can be drawn in a circle.' What made the pupil change his reply? The fact that the diameter was drawn in an unusual position, one which he had seldom encountered in his past experience. This immediately *broadened* his ideas and prepared the ground for a generalized deduction.

But rational variation of visual material is not in itself sufficient. It is also necessary to express verbally, not only the general features of phenomena embraced by the given concept, but also their inessential features—those which may vary. The decisive importance of this was indicated in further investigations concerning geographical and geometrical concepts undertaken with primary and secondary school-children.[1] It was shown that rationally organized teaching requires the pupil to make, not one, but *two* deductions in the process of generalizing heterogeneous material. For example, when pupils are mastering the concept 'watershed' in the geography course, they must first formulate the essential features of this concept by giving its definition; but they must also express in words the principle of variation of the inessential features: 'the elevation may be slight or very great', 'the direction of the upper reaches of rivers may be different from the direction of their lower reaches', and so on. Abstraction does not only mean casting aside inessential features, as is usually supposed; the process also requires that the essential features be separated from the inessential and *set over against* them. This can only be done with the help of language, which directs and guides in relation to the perception of visual material.

These data suggest that it is necessary to change the formulation of one of the principles of teaching, the so-called 'principle of visuality'. It would be more exact to speak of 'the principle of the concerted action of language and visuality in instruction, with language playing the regulating role'.

The study of a number of school disciplines (e.g. arithmetic, history) shows that visualizing is a *temporary support* in learning a definite category of concepts; but also that this temporary support is essential if the pupil is really to master a concept. These investigations have made clear that the need for a sense support, in the conscious learning of innumerable concepts, is determined not only by the characteristics of the thought processes of pupils of differing ages,

[1] Research of Meller.

192

but also by the *nature* of the material they are studying and the method whereby they are required to carry out their tasks. Pupils who can work with abstract ideas when they are dealing with one kind of material often feel the need for a sense support when they go on to study new material.

My own investigations show that, after pupils of the first class (7 to 8 years) have learned to add by units without the support of actual objects, they must temporarily be brought back to perceiving objects when they advance to the higher stage of counting with groups of units; not in order to count out objects singly, as at the earlier stage, but so that they may determine the quantity of objects on the basis of direct perception of a plurality of objects. Again, when pupils of the third and fourth classes (9 to 11 years) have wholly mastered the abstract idea of number as regards whole numbers, they once more require a sense support when they go on, in the fourth and fifth classes (10 to 12 years), to deal with fractions. Thus the attainment of a new level of abstraction requires a corresponding broadening of experience in the perception of objective reality.

II

The ideas children form on the basis of their perceptions play an important part in the learning process, one that varies with the problem presented and the pupil's stage of development.

A mental operation of great significance in the assimilation of knowledge is the paraphrase of a text. In one investigation,[1] pupils of various ages were told first to think of a title for a text that had been read, then to paint a word picture of it, and finally, to make up a legend for this picture. The aim was to establish whether a pupil could make a paraphrase, in what forms he visualized the situation described, and finally, what influence the actualization of his images had on his subsequent thinking about the text. The overwhelming majority of first-class pupils (7 to 8 years), and a significant proportion of second-class pupils, could only make a paraphrase after they had mentally drawn a picture, that is, visually imagined the situation.

A characteristic report concerning a first-year girl may be quoted: The first part of the story was read: 'Beetle's legs were weak, she was quite unable to move, for three days she lay hungry under the porch.' Then the child was asked: 'What can we call this part of the story? How can we say quite briefly what the story is about?' The child answered: 'Beetle's legs were weak, she lay for three days hungry under the porch, she was quite unable to walk.'

The experimenter: 'But you have repeated everything I read. You

---

[1] Conducted by Lipkina.

mustn't repeat everything, but say briefly, in two or three words, how you would name what has been read.'

The pupil: 'Beetle's legs were weak and she was quite unable to walk.'

Experimenter: 'Say still more briefly what was wrong with Beetle.'

Pupil: 'Beetle's legs were weak and she lay hungry!'

Experimenter: 'But what picture can you draw of what I read, how can you show in the picture what was wrong with Beetle?'

Pupil: 'I must draw a little house with a porch, and Beetle lying under the porch'.

Experimenter: 'And what must you write under the picture?'

Pupil: 'I must write: "A sick Beetle".'

This record shows that 'the strengthening of the image-link', that is, the actualization of the images underlying the words, assisted the child to express her thoughts in a more generalized form.

The results of this investigation, and of many others with junior and senior schoolchildren, are at variance with the accepted view that the transition to adolescence involves a change in forms of thinking. It is often said that a junior schoolboy thinks in concrete terms, while the adolescent possesses the power to think in abstractions. This assertion is, to say the least, inaccurate. In reality, both the generalizing component and the imagery of intellective activity change substantially as children grow older. Moreover, the development of the power of generalization and of abstract thinking is directly connected with enrichment of the imagery components of intellective activity.

III

A partial explanation has been given of the role of perception and imagination in the conscious mastery of abstract knowledge. But the understanding of new conceptual material is also governed by previously assimilated concepts which themselves represent the outcome of complex abstraction. These now fulfil a new function; they, in their turn, become a *concrete support*. Thus knowledge, in respect of its concrete or abstract quality, has a dynamic character, that is, it changes in the course of instruction. For example, arithmetical operations with numbers call for a complex process of abstraction and generalization, and at first have to rest on manipulation of objects. But the position changes radically when problems are set, when pupils must not only perform mechanical operations with numbers but also work out what these operations are to be. The former abstract operation (multiplication, addition) now becomes, as it were, the more concrete link, the link whereby a practical solution is achieved. The abstract link is now the formulation of the questions that the problem involves, which includes a decision as to which particular arithmetical operations must be performed. An analogous function is performed by numbers when the pupils go on to use letter symbols in the study of algebra.

In the process of consciously mastering habits also, there is a smooth transition from certain modes of action to others; we have conducted many investigations into this question. It has generally been held, in educational psychology, that connections must be formed from the outset in the way in which they will later operate. Our findings cut right across this principle; indeed, so far as the formation of complex habits is concerned, they confirm the *opposite* principle, that the associations underlying a habit must *not* be made in the form they will later assume. In the process of instruction there takes place a successive, qualitative, transformation of earlier acquired associations, that is, a transition from one form of association to others.

Our investigations demonstrate that the acquisition of many habits, even elementary ones, is a complicated process. The essential connections (associations) are not made at once, but by means of a series of intermediate connections which gradually lead to the end action (end connection), and fall out once the habit is established. Thus, in acquiring the habit of multiplication, the pupil learns to add equal items before multiplying directly. This method ensures conscious mastery of the content of the operation, and provides the pupil with a check in the case of future difficulties. Similar considerations apply to the learning of reading and writing,[1] and to all cases of learning procedures based on rules. Initially, rules must be remembered in their entirety; then they can be produced in a progressively more abbreviated form until, finally, they are not brought to mind at all. At this stage in the acquisition of a habit, actions are performed without conscious recall of the rule, but on its basis; this results from the formation of a special type of connection—the generalized connection—which arises from the assimilation of a general rule.[2] This comparatively complex process means that pupils themselves acquire the capacity to manipulate their habits and to modify these in a flexible manner.

Some of our investigations concerning the psychology of teaching have been described, and it has been indicated that the method chiefly used is that of studying pupils under instruction in school. In 'teaching-experiments', designed to clarify stages in the learning process, psychologists themselves often undertake the instruction; this means

[1] Researches of Egorov and Gurianov.
[2] The formation of connections of this type has been studied by Shevarev and his collaborators.

that they must be closely acquainted with programmes of work and educational methods, and act in close collaboration with the teaching profession. But many teachers also study psychology; and besides acting as consultants in such experiments, themselves draw up reports which contribute substantially to the solution of key problems; problems of interest both to education and to general psychology.

THE DEVELOPMENT OF CHILDREN'S SPEECH AND THOUGHT [1]

BY

A. A. LIUBLINSKAYA

[THIS PAPER OPENS with a brief discussion of the importance of mastering language. In the course of the child's varied personal experience, many changes take place in his understanding of phenomena and objects with which he has long been familiar. At different stages of development, these, though continuously denoted by the same word, are reflected in quite different ways; that is, there is a change in the conception the word denotes in its generalized reflection of phenomena of the environment. Study of these changes reveals extremely complex dynamic relationships between the child's sensory experience, his practice, and his mastery of language, on which depends the development of abstract thought. Therefore, data relating to the development of children's speech and thought throw light on the interrelationship between language and thought as an aspect of the general theory of knowledge. Mastery of vocabulary and grammatical structure is an indispensable condition for the development of abstract thought and for proficiency in logical operations, including the higher processes of analysis and synthesis. The paper summarizes the results of recent experimental research on this question.]

I

The development of sensations, in particular of discriminatory sensitivity in children, is inseparably connected with the intervention of the second signal system. Long before the end of the first year of life, the infant's whole sensory apparatus is carrying out the complex function of analysing experience. At the age of six months, the infant is capable of quite fine differentiation between stimuli from the outside

---

[1] *Speeches at the Conference on Psychological Questions, July 1953* (Moscow, 1954), pp. 124–38 (translated by N. Parsons).

197

world, and towards the close of the first year it is possible to establish a differentiated conditioned reflex with any analyser [26]. The introduction into perception of a word denoting the stimulus perceived—its colour or quality—causes a fundamental reorganization of the whole nature and nervous mechanism of the process of discrimination or differentiation. The development of the child's speech is possible only on the basis of the functioning of the first signal system. It is only on the basis of simple conditioned connections and a fine analysis of speech sounds that the connections of the second signal system can be formed. Then the child can master words as signals, which generalize a whole group of similar stimuli by abstracting the essential common features.

This view has been convincingly proved by research with children of pre-kindergarten and pre-school age.[1] In children aged one year one month to two years seven months a conditioned reflex was produced to the colour (in another case to the size) of a paper cap, under which the children found a sweet as reinforcement. With the experimental group, the successful solution was accompanied by verbal designation of the distinguishing feature ('red' colour, 'small' size); with the control group, the differentiating feature was not named. The results were as follows:

(1) Initially, children in the experimental group required from 9 to 15 presentations for the formation of a temporary connection between the colour of the cap (or its size) and the corresponding food reinforcement. Children in the control group required 2·5 to 3 times as many presentations, the number rising to 45 or 50.

(2) The connection produced on the basis of food reinforcement and verbal accompaniment proved very persistent in the experimental group of children, and there was ready recovery after a 5 to 7 day break. In the control group, the connections produced with such difficulty were extremely unstable and were found to be extinguished even on the following day.

(3) When the distinguishing feature (colour or size) was changed, children in the experimental group showed a quick, even immediate carry-over of the reflex to other objects, i.e. stimulus generalization. For example, after experiments with a red cap, the children lost no time in looking for the sweet under a red cup, a red box, or a piece of red material. No transfer of reflexes was observed in children of the control group; in each new situation they had to produce the necessary conditioned connections anew. Here was a striking example of the role of a word as a signal, making possible abstraction and generalization both of an object and its features.

[1] Carried out at Leningrad University by Yu. Shipinova and M. Surina, and in our laboratory.

(4) The number of presentations was considerably reduced when conditioned connections had previously been formed to some one distinguishing feature. Thus children who knew the colour red needed only 2 to 5 presentations to form a connection to the colour yellow. The same reduction in the number of presentations was observed in the experiments with the control group, though, again, results were considerably less positive than for children of the same age in the experimental group.

(5) Both the speed with which connections are formed and their stability was found to increase somewhat with age. This is obviously a consequence of increased and varied experience, especially as concerns the child's verbal communication with those around him. Words become more efficient as signals for older children as compared with the younger ones. In the control group, abstraction of a factor on the basis of a sense-perception only, without a verbal denotation, was almost as difficult for the older children as for the younger.

In other investigations children were required to abstract the pattern (spots or stripes) from the colour of a butterfly's wings and to find a butterfly similar to the one given among a number shown to them. The experimental group were given a verbal label for the differentiating factor (the pattern), but the control group were not. Initially, however, neither group was given the verbal label, and at this stage children in both groups completely ignored the pattern on the butterfly's wings, being guided solely by colouring in choosing a pair. After the pattern had been denoted by fixed names ('spots', 'stripes', 'nets') even the younger members of the experimental group began to turn their attention away from colour and to compare patterns which were different in colour. The speed, accuracy and fineness of their distinctions was noteworthy; they were also able to explain their choices readily and intelligently, using various verbal labels, but always noticing exactly the features of the pattern, i.e. the essential identifying factor. Thus children described 'that butterfly' (the specimen) as having the same 'dots', 'frin ge s', 'sots', 'crumbs', 'waves', etc., as the one they chose as being similar. In the reorganization of perceptual differentiation, which occurred on the introduction of language, there also emerged clearly the thinking process of comparison.

Results obtained with the control group confirm this conclusion; despite practice, even the older children could hardly distinguish the patterns. In control experiments carried out with an experimental and a control group, the children in the latter group made many mistakes, and did not understand their own rare correct solutions. Not one could explain his choice; to the question, 'How did you know that this was the butterfly to choose?' these children replied, 'I just knew', or 'I had a good look', etc.

The series of investigations showed that:

(1) The introduction of a word signalizing the distinctive factor (colour, size, pattern) has decisive significance for its isolation and differentiation. Labelled with a word, such a feature becomes a powerful, really effective stimulus which acquires dominating significance in the complex of influencing stimuli. It becomes stronger still in the skills which the child uses in all his subsequent activity.

(2) An isolated feature designated by a word (for example, 'with spots' or 'red') acquires the significance of a generalized feature. The child begins to find it easy to isolate an analogous feature (colour, size, pattern) in any other object. This is of decisive importance for the improvement of the child's orientation in the environment.

(3) The introduction of language into the process of visual discrimination re-structures the whole activity of the analyser and the whole process of sense perception. There is no doubt that this is related also to other aspects of sensitivity. Simple differentiating— discriminating—turns into a reasoning operation, that of comparing. The child learns to isolate common and distinguishing features in two similar stimuli. This confirms Pavlov's view that the second signal system 'builds' the first. To know how to compare is to master a thought-process essential for knowledge of any subject.

(4) Not every sign whereby the child orients himself in his differentiating activity is reflected in the second signal system, is verbalized, i.e. perceived by the child. This was clearly illustrated by the experiments in choosing butterflies by their patterns. These had to do with the complex, changing relationships between the first and second signal systems, which exist at different levels of child development and in adults, when phenomena of diverse content are reflected.

(5) When children compare two similar patterns and distinguish between them, without applying a word to the differentiating feature, this does not lead to any noticeable change in the actual process of visual perception. In spite of training, the child learns essentially nothing, and his sensitivity scarcely improves during the period of instruction.

Further investigations traced the role of words in the functioning of the motor analyser, i.e. in the substitution, mastery and abstraction of action by the small child. Sechenov considered that an essential part in the development of the small child's thinking is played by his muscular sense, evolving as kinaesthetic perception in the solution of problems of movement. We investigated the influence of language on changes in kinaesthetic perceptions.[1] Results showed how the use of language enables a young child's specific actions to become generalized and abstracted from the single concrete situation with which they

[1] The description of this series of experiments has been omitted (Ed.).

were originally associated. It was demonstrated that an action, when generalized in language, becomes an early form of problem solving for the child. The enormous significance of this is easily understood. The word denoting an action makes possible its abstraction and generalization. The action is thereby reflected in the child as an object of knowledge, as a means of solving new, strange problems; this is done 'on the spot', because the child applies the known action to the solution of all analogous problems.

II

A fundamental role is played by the verbal designation of objects perceived by the child. Language is distinct from all other signals in that it signalizes a whole group of objects in a generalized way by abstracting their common features. This makes perception intelligible. The process is well illustrated in an investigation carried out by Lukina. A child aged 12 to 14 months connected the word 'ribbon' only with the ribbons on her bonnet, and did not relate the word to the ribbon by which a celluloid parrot dangled before her eyes. In another case, the familiar word 'cup' was the 'name' of one cup only —a small, pink cup with white spots. When a large white cup, to which the child did not yet relate this word, was placed before him, and he was asked 'Where is the cup?', the child waved his hands about and looked at his mother with a puzzled air; his perceptual knowledge did not yet have a generalized character. In such cases a word is a signal of the first system. Only as his experience becomes richer does the child relate one and the same word to many different objects of the same kind.

What takes place during this time? How does the child's knowledge of his environment change?

(1) Above all, converting a word into a signal of the second system means changing the reflection of the object itself. Initially, every cup is perceived by the child as a new and special object, whereas later he perceives any cup as a representative of a whole known group of objects: in the particular he sees the general. Later, he will be able, on this basis, to isolate the particular.

(2) There is, then, a change in the meaning of a familiar word. Initially, the word is connected with one concrete object, having a number of particular characteristic features which belong to it alone (e.g. white spots on a pink cup); the same word later signalizes features common to a multitude of objects which, though different in many ways, constitute a single group. While at first the word 'cup' signalizes a combination of features belonging to the object fortuitously as well as essentially, later the word signalizes the essential

feature of the object, irrespective of changes in secondary features. This essential feature, found in the concrete and single instance, remains unchangeable and common for all objects of the same kind, and is the means of distinguishing them from other similar classes of objects. Only at this stage has the word acquired for the child that 'comprehensive' character distinctive of signals of the second system, which 'cannot be compared either quantitatively or qualitatively with the conditioned stimuli of animals' (Pavlov), i.e. with signals of the first system. So the content of a word which the child has known for a long time changes; it becomes broader, more interesting, rich, exact and elastic.[1]

III

The part played by language in the development of children's thinking appears most clearly in the way objects and phenomena are reflected in their connections and interrelations. Spatial connections can be perceived only by perceptual contemplation, but even so they are only understood when given a verbal designation. The remaining connections are reflected indirectly, through speech.

In his daily activity the child constantly meets with various interrelationships between phenomena. As soon as he has acquired the words 'because', 'in order to', 'early', 'yesterday', 'next to', 'about', etc., he is capable of understanding the various ways in which one thing depends upon another; the connections themselves become an object of knowledge.

A distinguishing characteristic of verbal signals, which denote and generalize different connections, is that the child at first masters these as a whole. Though not yet able to isolate them, the child nevertheless understands spoken words and the thought they express, carries out commissions correctly, and starts composing proposals himself, changing the form of words and using various joining words to express his thought. The reflection of a phenomenon or object in its connections with other phenomena is a specific quality of developed thought. To master the elements of the grammatical structure of his mother-tongue is both a condition and a means of development of the pre-school child's thought. An investigation into this question may be cited here [25].

Prepositions and adverbs, denoting position and spatial relationships between objects, were used as the grammatical categories to be mastered. Instruction in the correct use of appropriate words was

---

[1] The author goes on to describe further experiments, designed to trace the change in the child's perception of an object when a word is introduced to designate it. This section has been omitted (Ed.).

conducted by means of didactic games; these were directed to teaching the children to see the location of an object, to distinguish and interpret the posture of a man and to discriminate spatial interrelations between things represented on a picture or with the help of toys. This understanding of spatial interrelations was fixed in correctly constructed sentences including prepositions and adverbs (on, in, towards, under, behind, near, above, next to, etc.).

The children were offered the same pictures to look at before and after the instruction given in the didactic games. A control group of children had no instructional activities. In the first experiment, before any of the children had been instructed, the majority confined themselves to naming separate objects, or establishing private local connections between them, which did not enable them to give a correct interpretation of a whole picture; whereas, in the last experiment, the reports of children in the experimental group reflected the whole situation represented in a picture, correctly stated its content, expressed its relation to what was represented, and gave suitable generalizing names for each picture.

Substantial changes in the children's speech were observed. There was an improvement of its general structure, a particularly sharp rise in the number of extended simple sentences, and an increase in the number of more complex sentences. Table 1 compares the number of prepositions used by children in the experimental and control groups, in their reports about the pictures, before and after the instruction

	TABLE 1 Use of prepositions				TABLE 2 Use of adverbs			
Picture	Experimental group		Control group		Experimental group		Control group	
	Before	After	Before	After	Before	After	Before	After
1	77	125	101	95	31	29	23	27
2	81	120	53	49	34	46	41	27
3	110	155	68	79	32	51	20	23
4	111	164	114	109	30	52	22	23
	379	564	336	332	127	178	106	100

carried out with the experimental group. Table 2 gives analogous data on the use of adverbs.

Qualitative analysis of these results showed that the change was expressed not only in the increased number of prepositions and adverbs used, but also in the new accuracy with which the children designated connections. Adverbs such as 'here', 'there', 'still', were no longer used in an imprecise and amorphous way, but with the most diverse meanings. For example, of 28 meanings of the preposition 'on' in the Ushakov dictionary, the children indicated 18; and 15 of the 21 meanings given for 'in'. This enrichment of the children's speech, and the change in its structure, are direct pointers to the higher level of thinking attained. Nothing comparable was observed in children in the control group.

Though the exercises carried out concerned the mastery of only one category of connections, spatial connections, they also led to the use of a wide variety of joining words: i.e. to discovery of the most varied connections in the perceptual situation. The child began to interpret a whole picture as a complete situation and to give it the correct generalizing designation.

This investigation indicates that, in children:

(1) The development of cognitive activity, beginning with perception and concluding with abstract thinking, requires familiarity with the mother tongue. The mastery of language appears as a condition of generalized human reflection of objects, their features, activities, and so on.

(2) The development of sense perception is inseparably linked with the development of thinking. The improvement of sensation, perception and conception *is* the deepening comprehension of the visually presented phenomenon, object, or whole situation. The more complex the situation as an object of perception, the stronger is the influence of the developing mechanisms of thinking in re-structuring the child's perceptual knowledge.

(3) The mastery of words, signalizing different relations among the phenomena of the objective world, is of particular significance for the development of perceptual activity. This means that the child must master the grammatical forms for constructing sentences. Expressed in a grammatically correct sentence, the child's thought gradually becomes an increasingly accurate and complete reflection of reality, of all the diverse connections and relations between the objects and phenomena of nature and society.

This short and incomplete survey of recent work on the psychology of early childhood throws some light on one of the most complex problems of the theory of knowledge: the relation between perceptual knowledge and thinking. The study of the role of language in man's reflection of nature throws light on these relations. Our data, modest though they are, show convincingly that Sechenov was correct to make the study of the child's perceptual activity a key method of studying the laws of human psychic development.

SPECIFIC FEATURES OF THE INTELLECTUAL
WORK OF UNSUCCESSFUL PUPILS[1]

BY

L. S. SLAVINA

THE INVESTIGATIONS DESCRIBED in this paper were undertaken in the department of educational psychology for children of school age at the Institute of Psychology. In the course of analysing cases of backwardness in pupils of Class I (7 to 8 years), the hypothesis was advanced that the children showed 'intellectual passivity', a negative attitude to intellectual work, chiefly as a result of incorrect mental training. In the light of this, the experimental method used was that of organizing a system of educational measures designed to remedy both the general and the specific backwardness. The first series of experiments was directed to overcoming the 'intellectual passivity' developed by the subjects in the course of school tasks. Didactic games, involving number calculations, were introduced, with the object of transforming the subjects' motivation. When problems that could not be correctly solved by ordinary means were solved in play, the subjects' negative emotions towards mental work began to be replaced by positive emotions and a lively cognitive activity. Initially, however, this new intellectual activity, and the resultant successful solution of the arithmetical problems set, was confined to the particular play situation and not transferred to school tasks. But by the fifth and sixth day, a significant improvement in this direction was registered, indicating that the new cognitive, problem-solving activity, stimulated at first by play, quickly became permanent and was engendered in other than play situations. Nevertheless, when an attempt was made to encourage the subjects to use only the more abstract methods of calculation, calling for greater intellectual activity, this was not successful. It was found that the subjects lacked the number skills essential to an understanding of the processes of addition and subtraction. Special teaching was then provided to discover

[1] *Sovetskaya Pedagogika*, No. 1, 1954, pp. 91–101 (translated by J. McLeish).

the particular gaps in their knowledge of number sequence; and a comparison was made between the performance of the experimental group and that of successful pupils in the same class. The conclusion was that the 'intellectually passive' children had not acquired, at the appropriate time, the intellectual knowledge, habits and skills, mastered by the majority of the class, which form the foundation of school instruction. A systematic experimental course in arithmetic was, therefore, introduced, with the aim of remedying the specific deficiencies discovered; this was undertaken with five children, all of whom shared the same shortcomings; each child was treated individually. This remedial course is described in the section of the paper printed below, reference being made, for greater clarity, to one typical subject, Vova B.]

I

In the first place we ascertained that Vova, like the majority of the other subjects, had mastered a single habit; he knew the names of all the numbers in order from one to ten and their written symbols. But he knew nothing else about number sequences. We therefore introduced problems using cut-out figures, which were distributed in order from one to ten. As a result the boy learned to find any number mentioned, to point to it, then to the number which followed or was second from it, and so on; he also learned to count, taking any number as a starting point, instead of counting only from unity. As soon as we removed the cut-out figures, however, Vova became quite helpless and was unable to solve similar problems in his head. We had, therefore, to teach him to complete mentally those operations which he had already fully mastered with the numbers in front of him. We used a special method, which proved extremely effective and became the basic procedure in the remaining experiments.

Since Vova could carry out number operations when the figures were arranged in sequence before him, but was unable to complete these same operations when the numbers were not visible, we decided to introduce an intermediate stage. In problem-solving he was to rely, not on the figures placed in front of him, but on a mental representation of them. This was achieved by leaving the figures on the table but asking Vova to solve the problems *without* looking at them, in fact with his back to them. The investigator, however, helped him to find his bearings in relation to these figures, and in any difficulty invited him to look at them to verify his results. Soon Vova gave up turning to the numbers altogether, and at this point they were removed. After completing several tasks in this way, he solved all the problems enumerated above in his head, quickly, clearly, and faultlessly, and did not seem to differ in any way from the successful pupils in mastery of the technique.

At the same time we taught Vova to count forward in correct order from any number in the sequence, and to name the number standing one place, two places, and so on, from it. These problems he also learned to solve correctly. In this way, we slowly taught him to count in inverted sequence from ten to unity, and, beginning from any number, to name the next in the inverted sequence. But even when he had mastered all these processes, Vova still had not thoroughly assimilated the fact that one of two numbers standing in succession is always greater or less than the other by unity. Obviously, without thorough knowledge of this fact, he was not in a position to master mental addition and subtraction, since these consist at the outset precisely in adding or subtracting unity.

We again applied the same method. First, Vova performed the external operation by means of objects, then these same operations aloud representing the objects in his imagination; only after this did he go on to mental calculation in the strict sense. Initially he was instructed to arrange the figures in order and to place under some of them the corresponding number of sticks. In this way he was convinced that it was necessary to place one additional stick under the next number to have the correct number there. After several repetitions of this exercise, the subject began to understand that the difference between any two numbers in immediate sequence is always unity. To enable him to grasp this fact, and to avoid his counting through the sequence each time, we had allowed him to perform the action externally, and then according to an imaginary schema, before compelling him to make use of the strictly mental process.

For example, leaving the numbers on the table in the correct order from one to ten, and pointing to the number seven, the investigator would ask: 'Do you know how many sticks we must place here'? Or, she began by placing the appropriate number of sticks under some number, then—without giving the child an opportunity of counting them—placed some sticks under the next figure and asked how many more or how many less than before had been placed on the table. The subject did not count the sticks at all, nor did the investigator count them off in his presence; the number of sticks was taken up, arbitrarily, precisely to obviate counting and, so that the subject should neither see nor count them, the investigator covered them with her hand or a piece of paper.

Thus, though the subject had seen the sticks earlier on, in this exercise he was already proceeding almost in accordance with an imaginary schema. This stage could not be omitted without a deleterious effect on the quality of the mental processes. The investigator's attempt to go straight on to tasks without sticks, after Vova had carried out those in which he actually counted up the number involved, was not successful; this applied also to all the other subjects and problems. The final transition to activities using an imaginary schema was only accomplished gradually. The intermediate stage in the transition took place when the child's imaginative processes depended on the actual presence of objects but were already free in relation to the actual *number* present. Such imaginative freedom depends on specially developed conditioned connections which permit the quantities named to be reproduced in imagination.

After these exercises, all the sticks were cleared away and the subject solved the same problems without sticks, actually using a strictly imaginary schema, counting aloud and having only the figures in front of him, but behaving as though he could see the sticks. If he made a mistake at this stage in solving the problem, the investigator suggested that he convince himself of the correct answer by reckoning up the number of sticks. However, in general, the subjects made few mistakes after instruction had been carried out systematically in the stages described.

By about the sixth session, Vova had acquired all the facts about number sequence necessary for mental addition and subtraction; his instruction was completed. Exactly similar results were obtained with the other four subjects. Only four instead of six tasks were necessary for two of the children; seven tasks for another, while another required ten tasks.

II

We then proceeded to teach the subjects the mental addition of unity to any number up to ten. All the facts about number, including the method of adding unity, were mastered without any special difficulty. After one explanation the subjects carried out the required activity mentally, without error. We then proceeded to the addition of other numbers.

The method of adding unity is substantially different from that of adding any other number, even when the latter is accomplished by counting up in units; it consists only in naming the next number, or in other words, carrying out a process which had become automatic for our subjects. The addition of any other number is, however, a new process demanding special instruction.

We deliberately taught this process using only a single illustration— the addition of two to a given number. We had good reason to assume that if the subject were to master the process of addition by adding successive units to the first number until the second number had been added, illustrating the process by means of one augment, he could adapt the method to the addition of all other numbers. When the subjects had mastered the method of adding two's therefore, we suggested, without any supplementary explanation, that they add three, four, and so on. The extension of the method, without any additional explanation whatsoever, was taken as proof that the subjects had mastered it.

The method of instruction used previously was also applied here. We instructed the subjects, first, to carry out an external process with the aid of objects, corresponding to the mental activity we wished to teach; second, to carry out the complete process aloud in an imaginary schema; and, at the third stage, to carry it out mentally, abbreviating and omitting all the intermediate stages. The investigator began by telling the child to add to a given number of sticks (the first number) two more sticks (the second number), moving them one by one and calling out the result of adding each. To enable the subjects to master this process (counting aloud) it was necessary to repeat it a large number of times (from 15 to 20). After the subjects had learned this complete process of adding by units with objects, we passed on to the next stage.

Now the children carried out the same process without objects, maintaining the structure of the external process, but guided solely by the image of the objects and counting aloud as though adding imaginary sticks. Only certain subjects graduated straight away to this method, others reached it only by the gradual omission of activity with objects.

The process was intentionally gradual. First, it was controlled by the fact that not all the sticks were removed immediately from the subject; initially, we made him complete the process without the sticks corresponding to the first number; then, when he had learned to solve the problem under these conditions, we removed the remaining sticks.

Second, the transition to counting aloud, according to an imaginary schema, was also accomplished in stages. Though removing the sticks, we took care to preserve temporarily the hand movements which the subject made in using them. At first he carried out the full hand movement, stretching out towards the normal resting place of the sticks, meanwhile counting aloud; then this movement was attenuated until the subject neither moved his arm nor changed his position, but only made slight movement with his hand; finally, even this was discontinued and only counting aloud remained. When the subjects had learned to count in imagination, without objects and without external activity, they proceeded gradually to mental reckoning without difficulty. If they could not manage this independently, the investigator suggested that, in answering, the subjects should count in a whisper, and afterwards only to themselves. It is noteworthy that if the subjects omitted this stage in the imaginative scheme and began to count silently after several exercises, they did not usually fully master mental counting; we had then to revert to this particular stage of the process.

After mastery of mental counting we checked how far the subjects were successful and found that all had fully mastered the method we had taught them. The check questions were solved correctly and without difficulty, though this was the first time they had been encountered.

Parallel with the teaching of addition went the teaching of subtraction, using exactly the same method of counting off in units; there is no need to dwell on the data since no differences were disclosed here. The processes of mental addition and subtraction by the method of augmenting or decreasing by units were mastered by the subjects, though they had not been able to master these processes by the ordinary methods of instruction. But the question remained, whether the mastery of these and a number of other processes under experimental conditions constituted a proof that we had evolved a successful method of overcoming 'intellectual passivity' under school conditions, even in relation to arithmetic.

III

We had tried to overcome the 'intellectual passivity' of our subjects in two ways. First, by overcoming their negative emotional attitude to intellectual activity and replacing it by new positive emotions. Second, by exercising them in all those mental habits and skills necessary to the securing of knowledge—in this case, mental counting. Both these problems require solution if 'intellectual passivity' is to be effectively overcome. If our subjects could now learn completely new school material, demanding both the application of previously learned intellectual operations and the mastery of new ones, this would prove that the problems had been solved.

We therefore instituted a control experiment, concerned with mastery of the process of multiplication, under the guidance of the class teacher, using ordinary scholastic methods. All our subjects had learned to count, quickly, sensibly, and almost without error; and could add and subtract as far as twenty. Before beginning the experiment they were taken through 18 to 20 problems. Then the teacher took each child individually; but, to provide additional proof that the subjects had acquired the capacity to master new material, her explanations were made more complex than those used in class. For example, when explaining multiplication by two, she demonstrated the substance of this process only in relation to certain numbers (2, 3 and 4); without further explanation or demonstration the subject was asked to multiply the other numbers up to ten, by himself. To exclude the possibility of calculation by addition, the problems were given in random order (2 by 5; 2 by 8; 2 by 10; 2 by 7; 2 by 6; etc.). All the subjects in the course of this experiment mastered the method of multiplication; the teacher was unable to distinguish any difference whatever between them and the remaining members of the class. We further asked her to verify carefully how far each subject had mastered counting habits. Her examination showed their sound knowledge, correct methods of counting, and—this she particularly noted—their awareness of the habits.

The control experiment, therefore, demonstrated that the experimental subjects, who had been specially taught the simplest methods of counting, (1) were in a condition to master new and relatively complex school material, (2) had the capacity to master new methods of calculation demanding active intellectual work.

In our earlier experiments, we began by using the normal, school methods of instruction; that is, employment of objects in external actions. But, at the outset, it was recognized that supplementary conditions would be necessary if we were to teach the subjects to count mentally. The difference between the method we evolved and those normally used in school is that the subjects carried out a correct external action with objects analogous to the mental process we were teaching. Only after they had fully mastered the correctly constructed external process was it possible for them to make the transition to the next stage of their instruction.

In school instruction, mental counting follows immediately after activity with concrete objects. But we became convinced that this transition, in one step, to mental counting was not accomplished by our subjects. We therefore introduced an intermediate stage in the process, which involved carrying out the fully developed activity, but guided by the subjects' images of the objects and by oral counting. In practice, this second stage is usually omitted by the majority of teachers. In teaching 'intellectually passive' children, however, great significance must be attached precisely to this second stage; for our subjects, a progression to the abbreviated process of mental counting without this intermediate stage was demonstrably impossible.

Our investigations, therefore, confirmed the original hypothesis: that in the phenomenon of 'intellectual passivity' in children we must distinguish, first, the general attitude to intellectual activity, and second, the absence of appropriate knowledge, habits and skills required for the realization of the given intellectual activity. Strictly speaking, the latter appears to be a consequence of 'intellectual passivity', but to overcome it both of these aspects must be remedied. Modification of the motivational side does not of itself create the conditions for acquisition of the appropriate knowledge, habits and skills.

AN EXPERIMENTAL STUDY IN THE
FORMATION OF MENTAL ACTIONS [1]

BY

P. YA. GALPERIN

TO DISCUSS MENTAL ACTIONS [2] concretely, is to ask what is involved in the process of solving various problems, in a more or less generalized form, 'in one's head'. This is one aspect of the broader question of human conscious activity, considered not in the philosophical or social-historical sense, but in its concrete psychological meaning.

It has long been known that, as we master a psychic process, it becomes automatic; in current terms, it becomes a dynamic stereotype and 'drops out of' consciousness. This applies particularly to mental actions. When these have become complex and habitual, they are hidden from direct observation, leaving only an end product, whose properties give no indication of the character and content of the process that has occurred. At the present stage of psychological research, the best way of finding out about the structure of a mental action is to study it in the process of formation; indeed, there can be no true understanding of mental actions without study of this process.

The content of our cognitive processes comprises images of the external world, its objects and events, and our mental actions in relation to them. Thus mental actions comprise only a part of cognitive phenomena. But, since they include everything that we can do 'in our heads', they form so important a part of the content of consciousness that a true understanding of them is essential to an understanding of the psyche as a whole.

This is demonstrated by the whole history of bourgeois psychology, which has been divided into two camps on this question. The first—

---

[1] *Speeches at the Conference on Psychological Questions, July 1953* (Moscow, 1954), pp. 188–201 (translated by N. Parsons).

[2] The word is *deistvii*, which can be translated as 'action', 'operation', 'activity', or 'skill'. The term 'action' has been used throughout this article, as it seems most accurately to represent the meaning in this context (Ed.).

that of the empiricists, and, later, the so-called physiological psychologists—denied the existence of mental actions, and reduced the psyche to an association of images. But, since images of this ideal character cannot act of themselves, consciousness, consisting purely of such images, can have no real practical significance; it is turned into an epiphenomenon—a useless duplication of, a meaningless exception from the rest of the world. The second school of psychology recognized mental actions, but only as primary 'spiritual acts' which could not be analysed. In practice this amounted to denying their existence as natural phenomena and ruled out any possibility of studying them scientifically. Thus, both trends in bourgeois psychology adopted the same basic view of mental actions as supra-scientific processes; but while one recognized them openly, as such, the other, on similar grounds, denied their existence. The outcome in both cases was that the psyche became a subject for mysticism. But there can obviously be no true understanding of the psyche unless there is a concrete study of the nature of mental actions. Herein lies the theoretical significance of the problem.

Its practical significance lies in the fact that mental actions make up a considerable part of what children are taught in school. Mathematical reckoning, calculation of the ways physical bodies interact, learning how to write words and phrases correctly, the analysis and evaluation of historical events—all these are different aspects of mental actions. Mental acts do not, of course, exist in isolation; they are always inseparably linked with knowledge and concepts of one thing or another. But such knowledge itself only acquires real significance, full value and effectiveness, in connection with particular mental actions. An understanding of the concrete structure of mental actions, of the laws governing their formation and the conditions for their effectiveness, of the different disturbances and methods of recovery—this is the prerequisite of successful teaching.

I

In our experimental investigation, we wanted to study mental actions which were simple and clear in content, and which could be kept completely under control during their formation, depending entirely on the instruction given. After preliminary discussion, we decided on the most elementary mental actions in arithmetic, and our subsequent researches were concerned with their formation and composition in pre-school children of varying ages, and children of the first class (7 to 8 years).

In general outline, the method of research consisted in setting the child an arithmetical task requiring a specific degree of knowledge and ability, and finding out whether he could carry out this task 'in his head', aloud, and with objects; how he did it by himself, and whether he could do it when methods were suggested to him; to what extent these methods were generalized; and how far they were mastered, i.e. how readily they were applied and could be interchanged.

Several investigations were carried out on these lines, isolating stages of particular importance in the chain of mental actions, and then systematically investigating their formation.[1] The principal conclusion drawn from these researches was that, during learning, an action may change simultaneously in four relatively independent directions.

(1) *Generalization.* An action may be generalized to a greater or lesser degree: one child could perform a particular action solely, or more easily, with particular apparatus, while another found it just as easy whatever the apparatus; one child found no difficulty in doing addition with numbers from 1 to 10 (e.g. $4 + 3$), but could not add numbers from 11 to 20 ($14 + 3$), while his classmate could add easily in any numerical range, and also do 'carrying'. There may obviously be a different *measure of generalization.*

(2) *Completeness* (Abbreviation). An action may be performed not only with a differing degree of generalization, but also with differing completeness, with a complete or incomplete structure of operations. One child, for example, will carry out addition in the most extended form: he makes up each number separately, then joins them together in one group, and finally counts this out afresh one by one from the first to the last. Another child works rather more briefly: taking the first number as a whole he counts the second on to it in ones. A third does addition in different groups, adding each one according to the table of additions. There can obviously be differences in the *measure of completeness* with which an action is performed—how extended (complete) or how abbreviated (incomplete) it is.

(3) *Mastery* (Familiarity). Furthermore, forms of one and the same action, differing in degree of generalization and abbreviation, may be learned by the child to a differing degree. For example, a child may often, at his teacher's request, carry out an action by the best method, but he may not use this method when working on his own because he has not mastered it sufficiently. On the other hand, weak pupils often show a high level of mastery of simple action-forms, such as exceptionally quick addition (or even subtraction) by directly counting

---

[1] By Hippenreiter on counting in pre-school children; Davydov and Golomshtok on arithmetical processes in children of the first class; Davydov on children's ability to perceive a number as a whole; Stepanian on the role of apparatus in the generalization of an action; Morozova on how the method of mastering a task influences success in a subsequent action.

objects one by one, and they make these automatic; such premature automatization is a great obstacle to the learning of more advanced abbreviated and generalized forms of an action. Thus the *degree of mastery* (familiarity) of differing forms of an action is a special index of the action, and may stand in differing relations with the other indices.

(4) *Assimilation* (Level of Mastery). But, in addition to this, a child may perform an action on differing planes: with the aid of objects, 'speaking aloud' but without using objects, or 'speaking to himself', 'in his head'. In the first case, the child can only perform the action with the help of objects; in the second, objects are no longer indispensable, but talking aloud still is; in the third, the child can dispense with both external objects and audible speech. This is a measure of his independence of various external aids. Here we have a new parameter—different degrees or *levels of assimilation* of an action.

There is a highly variable relationship between this latter parameter and others. The lowest level of assimilation (action with external objects) may be combined with quite a high degree of generalization and abbreviation; while on the other hand an action 'in the head' may be combined with the most extended form or with limitation to some particular apparatus, though this, of course, is only represented 'in the head'. But a given series of levels of assimilation are always related to each other in strict succession, since a higher level always assumes the presence of all the preceding ones. It is true that there appear, at first sight, to be frequent exceptions to this rule. A child may, for example, perform an action 'in his head' but be unable to do it aloud; or he may perform it aloud and be unable to do it with objects. But, in these cases, investigation always shows that the action is being performed 'formally', i.e. that the child is recalling some part or other of the action without understanding its real content. These, therefore, are only apparent exceptions to the rule of the succession of levels.

Levels of mastery (assimilation) are successive degrees on a separate parameter. But, since they signify not so much quantitative as qualitative changes of action, it is preferable to call them *levels* of mastery (assimilation), to distinguish them from measure or *degree* of mastery (familiarity).

The measures of generalization, abbreviation, familiarity, and the levels of mastery of an action are, then, relatively independent parameters. For the formation of a fully effective mental action, each one must be worked through in a definite relation with the others. But, of all the parameters, it is the change of levels which leads in a direct line from action with external objects to action 'in the head', that constitutes the fundamental line of development of a mental action as such. It is, accordingly, with changes along this parameter—the level of mastery (assimilation) of an action—that this account is principally concerned.

II

There is an initial stage when the child cannot act himself, but follows the explanations and demonstrations of his teacher, so getting a preliminary idea of the action he is to learn; the learning of every mental action then passes through the following five basic stages:

(1) Creating a preliminary conception of the task.
(2) Mastering the action using objects.
(3) Mastering the action on the plane of audible speech.
(4) Transferring the action to the mental plane.
(5) Consolidating the mental action.

Within each stage an action follows a specific course of development, but the present account will be confined to the general characteristics of these stages.

(1) *Creating a Preliminary Conception of the Task*

We became increasingly convinced of the special importance of this neglected and vaguely defined stage. Two methods of becoming familiar with a task have been discovered which differ profoundly in their effect on the subsequent formation of an action.[1] First, after the teacher's initial explanations, the child immediately proceeds to make himself familiar with the material by his own efforts (though under the teacher's direction); second, the child does not himself perform any action for a long time, but takes an active part in the teacher's explanation by prompting his next operation or naming its result. We expected that the first method, which appears to be more active, would give the better results, but in fact the second proved rather more productive.[2]

How can we account for this? We can only surmise that the second method frees the child from the task of performing the action physically and at the same time organizes his orienting activity, his attention; this results in a more thorough acquaintance with the object and a fuller and more correct conception of it, which in turn enables the child to master the task more quickly, easily and correctly.

Though the preliminary conception of an action is of great significance, its actual application by the child is limited in principle by the potentialities of previously acquired abilities. In other words, it does

[1] Researches of Morozova.
[2] An investigation by Zaporozhets, into the formation of motor skills, has shown analogous results.

not include ability to perform the action, nor that knowledge of the properties of objects which is acquired through practical activity, but only knowledge of the external aspect of the new activity; it is not actual knowledge, therefore, but only the condition for its discovery.

(2) *Mastering the Action using Objects*

The child cannot learn a new action by means of a single observation, 'purely theoretically'; he first becomes familiar with a new action in the course of activity with external things—he learns to count, add and subtract with objects. Thus an action that must in due course become a mental action is not originally formed as such, but as an external and material action.

This material action is, of course, built up in continuous verbal intercourse with the teacher, under the guiding influence of his instruction, explanations and corrections. But, at this stage, the role of speech, in the case of both teacher and pupil, is limited to indicating objective features of the goal, the objects available and the methods of dealing with them. These instructions, however important, do not take the place of action; the action can be completed only on the level of things, being based on them and determined by them, and remaining essentially an external, material action.

Psychic processes naturally have their part in this external action: in conceiving the goal, controlling the virtually fluid action, and regulating it in accordance with the task set. But this psychic activity constitutes only a part—an important one, but yet only a part—of the external action actually performed. This is because, at this stage, a child can carry out the reorganization which constitutes the content of every action only with external objects, and only by reconstructing them in a material way; he cannot do this in thought or imagination. Therefore, his action only exists at this stage in the form of an external action of this kind.

The kernel of the matter is that this material form of action is not only the inevitable initial form of a child's independent activity, but also the origin of the content and structure of the mental action subsequently elaborated. As has been noted, preliminary conception of the task includes only the external indications of what is to be achieved and how the initial material should be used. It does not include knowledge of the properties of things and the relations between them; still less does it include the necessary skills for dealing with them. The actual properties and relationships of objects and instruments (including the 'natural instrument' of the arm) are first manifested in practical activity with objects in efforts to reorganize these in the direction of the goal set. It is not surprising, therefore, that the child discovers the objective content of an action, in full measure and in the real world, not as a result of his preliminary conception of the task in the light of the teacher's explanations, but from his own action with things. Only in the collision between the material properties of object and instrument in the performance of a task, does a child perceive the objective logic of things and of his own action. This has been demonstrated by experiment, in a very simple, even naïve form. A child, counting buttons, takes them away singly with his fingers. A mitten is put on his hand, and, as the next 'unit', he takes at one go as many buttons as he can cover with the mitten. When the mitten is removed, the child at once returns to counting the buttons correctly, removing them with his fingers one by one.[1]

An action with objects is strictly determined by the properties of the objects and, at the same time, is substantially supported by them: they seem to prompt and direct the action. Because of this, action with material things is exceptionally easily and has incomparable advantages over all other forms. The facts incline us more and more to the view that the basic reorganizations of an action, as it evolves towards a fully effective mental action—generalization and abbreviation, testing, explanation and proof, correction and re-learning where required, and the actual formation of new conceptions—that all these should proceed, either directly at the level of activity with material things, or with a fresh approach to this level.

It would be incorrect, therefore, to attribute the advantages of activity with external objects only to its visual graphic nature. Such activity is significant, not because it illustrates a mental action, but because the child discovers the objective, concrete content of the action for himself, and achieves his first practical mastery of this content.

(3) *Mastering the Action on the Plane of Audible Speech*

When an action has been sufficiently mastered with objects, it is transferred to the plane of audible speech: the child learns to count aloud without the help of objects. This frees the action from the constant necessity of manipulating external things, but above all it represents a full advance to action with concepts.

Research has shown that, while an action remains on the plane of material things, words relating to it (in our case numerals) act mainly as indications of the objects. These signs may be well generalized and finely differentiated. A child may fetch any 5 objects, know by how much 5 is more than 4 and less than 6, and readily continue counting from any number; but when he is given a problem, say 5 + 4, he does not use '5' as a directly given number but begins counting it over again to recall it. To this end he turns to objects at hand, and counts

---

[1] Investigation by Hippenreiter.

them off or, if there are none, tries to imagine them. Only when he himself reaches the number given does he go on to add the second number to it.[1] At this stage, the numeral represents for him only a sign for a specified aggregate of units and he returns to these units again and again in accordance with the sign. A numeral has not yet become a fully effective concept, which is itself a specific object of mental activity; it is not yet a meaningful sign for a certain quantity conceived as a simple whole.

It would appear that our belief in the child's ability to grasp the first item as a whole may be just as fallacious as our view of the child's other arithmetical actions. A child can be taught to add a second number directly to the first, given verbally or as a written figure, but if the number is simultaneously given in objects, he once more starts counting these out. In this case, the number or verbal sign serves only as a signal 'to count further', without denoting the nature of the first item as a simple whole, and the manipulation of numbers is 'formal'.

To turn a word-sign (in this case a numeral) into a real concept, it is necessary to enrich its meaning. This calls for a fresh return to objects and for additional work with them. If the addition of a second number is taught in this way, with actual objects, the action is immediately carried over to the spoken or written numeral. This shows that it has acquired full value in the sense indicated.

Arriving at a concept, therefore, requires a further return to objects; without this, words cannot acquire their proper meaning and provide an adequate foundation for a theoretical action 'in the head'. But the use of language in the course of action with objects, though it creates the essential conditions for a transition to the verbal-conceptual plane, does not of itself bring this about. When an action is performed only with objects, the failure to work out new concepts is clearly demonstrated by the child's inability to give an accurate account of his action. At first sight this picture seems strange: the child can act correctly, and with obvious understanding of objective relationships, yet he cannot give a comparable account of them and of his action. But this observed inability accounts for a familiar phenomenon: the delay between ability to perform an action and ability to give a verbal account of it, the 'retardation of the transition to the second signal system'.

(4) *Transferring the Action to the Mental Plane*

When a full reflection of a material action has been achieved on the plane of audible speech, the stage of transference to the mental plane begins. The child is now taught to count in a whisper, then silently, to himself; he is advancing to action 'in the head'.

[1] Researches of Davydov.

Of course, even 'in the head', he continues to use language and sense-images. The fundamental question is: How must the relation between concepts and sense-images be changed in order to ensure fully effective transfer to the 'mental plane' in different tasks and with different material (arithmetic and geometry, physiology and literature)? But from all the variations a rule gradually emerges: a perceived, and in this sense full-scale action 'in the head'—one which can be used accurately and confidently—forms only after the action has been thoroughly practised on the plane of audible speech.[1]

By virtue of its method of transfer, an action 'in the head' is initially an accurate reproduction of the final form to which the action evolved at the preceding level. But this action 'in the head' is now, of course, reproduced only in accordance with its own objective content and quickly proves to be a mere recollection of the former external action. The more habitual this recollection becomes, the more easily and automatically it takes its course, the more it becomes apparent that this is not really the action any longer, but rather a flow of concepts about it. However, that the process becomes automatic in its later stages should not blind us to the fundamental fact that, at the right time, we learn to reproduce this recollection; to reproduce it in exact correspondence with the course of the objective process and then to carry it out just like any other action. In short, this is a real action, even though it occurs 'in the head' and has become automatic.

(5) *Consolidating the Mental Action*

Representing an action correctly 'in the head' (i.e. so that it corresponds with objective objects) is naturally more difficult than performing it with things, or even with concepts spoken aloud. Things can be seen and can guide our action; words spoken aloud can be heard, as if they were those of another person, and their guiding power is even greater; whereas 'in the head' we have to imagine both the objects themselves and the actions to be performed with them, and also to check that both are correct. But, for the most part, it is not essential to reproduce all this fully. As a result, an action 'in the head', after becoming an accurate reflection of the final form of action reached at the preceding stage, is inevitably abbreviated or compressed and proceeds to the final stage, consolidation of the mental action.

Since an action recalled, or conceived 'to oneself', is one that has

[1] This appeared alike from our own investigations, from those of Slavina (carried out before our own and independently of them) and from those of E. I. Ignatiev (undertaken primarily for purposes other than investigating the development of mental actions). Ignatiev showed that practice on the plane of audible speech is indispensable if sense-perceptions are to be formed capable of providing a full-scale foundation for drawing objects.

previously been carried out in reality, the correctness of the recall or conception can only be checked by returning to this external action; but it soon becomes evident that there is no point in following through the whole course of an action 'in the head'. We know the result in advance, and surveying the intermediate stages adds nothing. Equally, nothing obliges us to make such an inspection: omitting it evokes no negative reinforcement, nor does carrying it out evoke a positive one, so that the intermediate stages of the action gradually begin to drop out. At the conclusion of this process the course of an action runs as follows: having received instructions about initial data and what is to be done with them, we proceed immediately to the result, which is known as a result of frequent repetitions in past experience. Such an abbreviation fundamentally changes the character and 'external appearance' of a mental action. In 'external appearance' it loses the remnants of sense content, so that introspection cannot now reveal its actual course.

As for the character of the mental action, this is changed insofar as nothing is now produced beyond affirmation of what the end result would be if the corresponding external action had been carried out; whereas it formerly reorganized and performed, the action now anticipates and warns. As a result of this change, a mental action is placed in a new relation to its practical prototype. Having absorbed the experience of the latter, it now begins to orient this (not only, as previously, during the actual course of the action, but also up to and including its final results) and thereby discloses new possibilities for practical action. At the same time, the mental action shows a certain dependence on practical action and even rests upon it. As a result of this change in form and function, a mental action at last realizes its 'specifically psychic nature', or, as we are accustomed to put it, makes its appearance in 'direct experience'.

III

This, then, is the process of teaching a mental action: it begins with the task of learning something, a task usually set by other people; on the basis of demonstration and explanation, the child builds up a preliminary concept of the action as seen in the external action of another person. He then makes himself familiar with the action in its external material content, and gets to know it in practice, in its application to things. The first independent form of such activity in the child is, thus, inevitably the external material action.

Next, the action is separated from things and transferred to the plane of audible speech, where its material foundation is fundamentally changed: from being objective, it becomes linguistic, verbal. But the crux of this change is that, from being an action with things, it becomes an action with concepts, i.e. a genuinely theoretical action.

Finally, the action is transferred to the mental plane. Here, having undergone its final changes, it assumed that purely 'psychic appearance' revealed in introspection, which has so often been taken to be its real nature.

The first independent form of the child's new action is a material one; the final form is 'mental' ('conceptual'); the whole process of transition, from the first form to the last, consists in the formation of a series of qualitatively different reflections of this material action, with consequent abstraction of a particular aspect, and the transformation of a material reorganization of things into a means of thinking about them; a material phenomenon is turned into a phenomenon of consciousness.

Marx, contrasting his method with that of Hegel, writes, 'For me, on the contrary, the ideal is nothing else than the material world reflected by the human mind and translated into forms of thought'.[1] The formation of a mental action is a particular instance of the process to which Marx refers. The order of the basic stages of a mental act given here is envisaged as a more developed account of the 'reflection' of the material in the human head and of its further transformation there, insofar as one aspect of man's consciousness—mental actions—is concerned.

Another aspect of the matter may be briefly considered. The stages in which a mental action is formed are also stages at which a new theoretical ability is acquired. As we have seen, this process is by no means a simple reinforcement of such an ability in one and the same form; on the contrary it comprises a series of successive and qualitative changes in it.

But understanding—becoming mental—is only one parameter of the new ability. A mental action may be made up in different ways, both correct and incorrect, and in the end may not prove to be very effective. Whether it attains its full value depends, not only on the level of understanding reached, but also on other parameters—on the way it is generalized, abbreviated, and duly mastered in the course of instruction. In general, the quality of the final mental action is determined by the following factors:

(1) Whether, at the first stage, there is formed a correct conception of the task, of the content of the action to be mastered;

(2) whether the material form of the action is fully developed and its objective content mastered at the outset;

(3) whether all the operations of the action, and the action as a whole, are generalized at the right time;

[1] *Capital*, i, xxx.

223

(4) whether proper and timely abbreviation also takes place;

(5) whether there is a careful and timely transfer of the action to the plane of audible speech,

(6) and the same careful and timely transfer to the 'mental plane';

(7) whether, in the course of all these changes, the intermediate forms of action are duly mastered. By 'duly' is meant, sufficiently to ensure the free application of the new forms of action, but not to such an extent as to interfere with the transition to higher forms; for, while it is important that each form of an action should be mastered at the right time, it is no less important that it should be given up at the right time for the following, more advanced, form;

(8) whether the final form of the action is consolidated, and whether this mastery is carried to the point of becoming fully automatic.

This system of requirements provided us with a scale for evaluating the mental actions mastered by children, and so for diagnosing success and failure in school and determining remedial measures.[1] When the latter are necessary, pupils should first be taken individually, with the aim of raising their level of achievement. In practice, in the schools, attempts to remedy qualitative shortcomings in the mental actions of retarded children lead to a paradoxical situation: these pupils are given additional activities but these only mean additional practice and further reinforcement of precisely those defective methods of action from which they are in prime need of being freed.

Slavina's systematic experiments, and our separate but parallel attempts to make good the qualitative shortcomings in children's mental actions, have so far resulted in unsuccessful children becoming successful. There is nothing surprising about this, since we had a clear picture of the nature of these shortcomings. We obtained this picture on the basis of the scale of parameters and their indices given above; then, still using them, we systematically remedied the particular deficiency. To do this, we took the children back to the preceding stage in the formation of a given action—almost always to its material form, but sometimes even to the explanation of the task—and then systematically conducted them up the ladder of the requisite changes to the conscious 'action according to formula'. Thus the children mastered the full-scale mental action; and found that they were able to carry out corresponding tasks; the results drew approval and surprise from their elders and comrades, and it was worth seeing the

[1] Davydov analysed the arithmetical knowledge and skills of retarded children in the first class; Slavina undertook an earlier analysis without making systematic use of the above criteria. Golomshtok extended this analysis to all levels of children's achievement at the end of their first school year; his data show that, for one and the same achievement (and all the more for a failure), the qualitative shortcomings in arithmetical mental actions are often extremely varied and so require various remedial measures.

change in their attitude to arithmetic, a subject towards which they had previously felt nothing but dislike!

Both this work and Slavina's were carried out with individuals; a modification of method is, of course, required when working with a class. But, whether instruction is individual or collective, formation in stages remains the essential content of the process of mastering new skills. Precisely the same scale of basic parameters can be used in the evaluation of a mastered action, whatever the factual content and other qualities of the instruction. It may be hoped that knowledge of the way in which mental actions are formed stage by stage will provide a firm theoretical foundation for the development of effective teaching.

THE NATURE AND FORMATION OF HUMAN
PSYCHIC PROPERTIES [1]

BY

A. N. LEONTIEV

TO INVESTIGATE man's psychic properties and the laws governing their formation is one of the most difficult tasks of psychology. If it is to be undertaken in a scientific, materialist way, the
psychologist cannot rest content with a mere statement of the different
properties and their more common interrelations, nor with a descriptive study of their gradual development in children. Psychological
investigation must rather be directed to discovering the origin and
significance of the actual mechanisms, in whose functioning, properly
speaking, the various psychic properties are revealed.

This approach derives from the view that all man's psychic properties and processes are the product of dynamic systems of cerebral
connections, that is, conditioned reflexes built up in the course of life.
It has long been established that the mechanisms underlying even
such a simple and universal property as the ability to see objects can,
under certain conditions, be quickly and radically altered. A striking
example is the changing of the central nervous mechanism of visual
perception, described by Stratton; if, with the aid of an optical device,
images projected on the retinae are reversed, the subject, after a relatively short time, begins once more to perceive objects normally. A
great deal of experimental evidence of this kind has been accumulated
in both psychology and physiology; this paper is concerned with certain investigations bearing on the subject.

I

A detailed investigation of the mechanisms underlying simple
psychic abilities has been undertaken with patients suffering from

---

[1] Communication to the Fourteenth International Congress of Psychology,
1954; published in *Voprosy Psikhologii*, No. 1, 1955, pp. 29–36 (translated by
H. Milne).

astereognosis caused by injury to the hand.[1] The displacement of surface tissues, considerable deformation of the muscles and changes in the joints, lead, after a lengthy immobilization, to a 'blinding' of the hand; though an elementary sensitivity is preserved, the patient loses the power to perceive objects by touch.

In a large number of the cases studied, this phenomenon was conditioned by changes that had taken place in the localization of the receptors of the hand. As a result of these changes, the system of connections between tactile-kinaesthetic and optical stimuli, formed during ontogenesis, becomes inadequate, suffers inhibition, and ceases to function. It must be stressed that this is manifested in many ways; patients lose the Charpentier illusion, there are characteristic changes in the afferent impulses following from movements of the hand and so on.[2]

On the other hand, the formation of new reflex connections between tactile-kinaesthetic and optical stimuli in the new situation (where the sense organs of the hand are displaced) leads to a more general effect, manifested simultaneously in all the gnostic (cognitive) and motor functions of the hand. We have to do here with a system of cerebral connections which serves a whole series of processes and, in this sense, acts as a sort of special cerebral 'physiological organ'— an organ of stereognostic (kinaesthetic space) perception. It is noteworthy that, even in cases representing appreciably different morphological changes in the sensitive periphery of the hand, the formation of such a system of connections produces a qualitatively identical end result. This indicates that there is very great scope for replacing certain elements in the system of connections being formed, by other elements, without substantially modifying its general function (the so-called phenomenon of intra-system compensation).

The conditioned-reflex nature of such systems has been clearly indicated by experiments directed to the study of the mechanism of spatial localization of sound.[3] The methods used may be described. An electric bulb and an invisible sound membrane were set on the perimeter of a circle with the subject as centre. In the initial experiments the bulb and the membrane were on the same line with relation to the subject. After the light stimulus (the flashing of the bulb) had been repeatedly linked with the sound of the membrane, the bulb and the invisible membrane were moved apart. As a result of the connections which had been formed, the light stimulus now caused the

---

[1] Research of Leontiev, Zaporozhets and collaborators (1945).

[2] 'Charpentier's bands' is the name given to alternating light and dark fan bands seen when a band of light is moved across the retina (Ed.).

[3] Conducted by Yu. A. Kulagin under the direction of E. N. Sokolov, Department of Psychology, Moscow University.

subject to perceive the sound as considerably displaced in the direction of the bulb. Further experiments demonstrated the generalized character of this phenomenon, and also the possibility of training the subject to differentiate between and wipe out previously formed connections.

These and other similar data show that the mechanisms with which we are concerned—the functioning of which is manifested in such common and universal psychic properties as the ability to perceive spatial qualities visually, to localize sounds in space and so on—are unquestionably of a conditioned-reflex nature. Since they are formed under the influence of conditions which affect everybody in an identical way, in normal circumstances they are the same in everyone. This unique universality, and the stability they acquire, give them the functional properties of specific *mechanisms* of psychic activity, arising during ontogenesis.

These simple and universal properties differ substantially from those properties that are not common to everybody. The peculiar characteristic of these specific properties is that the reflex systems of which they are a function are formed only under certain definite conditions; they do not, therefore, always develop, and, in the case of different individuals, they may have a different structure. As a result, the functioning of such specific properties often seems to be a manifestation of inherited powers, powers which are lacking in the natural endowment of certain individuals. Study of these properties is, therefore, of crucial importance.

An example of a very simple special ability is the power to reproduce sounds of a given pitch correctly; teachers of singing find that certain pupils are quite unable to do this. The writer has undertaken a special investigation with children incapable of reproducing orally their aural perception.[1] Pupils were chosen whose results in initial tests were completely negative; not only did they fail to reproduce orally a sound of a given pitch or a short melody, but they could not even 'attune' their voices to a continuously sounding note. The aim of later experiments was to create a correct central recording of the phonation of their vocal apparatus (according to pitch) by forming the essential aural-oral connections. The given sound was produced by an electrical sound generator; this, and the sound reproduced by the subject, were recorded on an oscillograph.

The subject had first to attune his voice to the pitch of certain sounds, fed as continuous notes into the earphones by the sound generator; when he had consolidated this achievement, another series of experiments was begun. After the subject had begun to vocalize a sound of a given pitch, the sound generator was switched off, and he

[1] In cooperation with Yu. B. Hippenreiter (1954).

continued to 'sing' independently. Finally, the subject had to reproduce a sound of a certain pitch after an interval of up to 6 seconds,
that is, to sing 'from memory'. There were 8–10 sittings with each
subject. Subsequently attempts were made to train the subjects to
reproduce very simple melodies, and certain additional experiments were undertaken with the aim of providing supplementary
material.

The general result of the main experiments was as follows: after
the subjects had gone through the processes outlined, the initial tests
in which they had originally failed were repeated, and positive results
were recorded for all subjects.

Why, if progress during the experiment was so rapid, had prolonged training in singing failed to produce any substantial measure
of success, so that the subjects had been persistently classified as incapable of vocalizing sound according to pitch? The answer is that
they did not possess the necessary ability which, in the majority of
cases, is formed without any systematic training—in the course of
everyday experience. The mechanism underlying this is an extremely
simple system of aural-oral connections, but one of a special kind.
The connections that make up this system are peculiar in that, under
normal conditions, they are formed in response to complex sound
stimuli in which the *pitch* of the sound plays the part of the so-called
'powerful' component. This distinguishes them from aural-speech
connections in which this component is not the main one. The essence
of our experiments was to form precisely such connections in our
subjects. For this reason we used sound stimuli that were varied in
pitch but identical as regards their other components.

The formation of these connections is, of course, only the first link
in the complex system which underlies correct vocalization of musical
sounds. But it was precisely the absence of this link, which had not
developed in the subject under consideration because of certain circumstances, that led to their failure to sing separate notes and
melodies correctly. Our experiments restored this 'lost', but absolutely essential link and guaranteed the speedy success of the concluding experimental-educational exercises.

We consider that the foregoing has an important general significance. The point is that, in the course of development of all psychic
properties, there are a series of successive stages; during these stages
the separate links are formed that are essential to the building up of
the final mechanism which comprises the basis of the property in
question. Certain of these links, however, usually develop 'of themselves', unseen, and outside the control of the educator. Therefore,
in those cases where some preceding link has not developed, or
has developed wrongly, the inevitable result is a typical picture of

incapacity. But if such a 'lost' link is discovered and formed, development begins to proceed normally.

II

Of particular theoretical and practical importance in this connection is the question of the nature of man's higher intellectual properties and processes. An investigation of the processes of recollection, carried out by the writer as early as 1930, gave rise to the hypothesis that internal mental processes are formed by means of the transformation of processes which initially take the form of actions based on external objects.

This hypothesis has been confirmed and clarified in a new way as a result of more recent investigations.[1] These involved a detailed study of the conditions and stages of formation of such processes as mental arithmetic, operations involving geometrical relations, and so on. It was demonstrated that the formation of internal mental processes does, in fact, begin with mastery of external actions with objects. For example, addition is done at first in the form of an external movement—by means of actually shifting one group of objects and joining them to another; after this the child 'counts them together'. Initially this is done by external movements of the finger or ruler, accompanied by a verbal naming of the ordinal numerals. Then these movements are replaced by movement of the eyes. Later this whole process is modified; the child goes on to counting groups of things, but at first still preserves the same method of operation with external, real material.

At the second stage the process progressively loses the character of an external action with objects. It is mastered in external speech, then in internal speech, and, as a result of this, is abstracted from the concrete material conditions and acquires a more generalized character. Even here the structure of the process does not change, but reproduces that of the corresponding external operations. For example, when the child begins, for the first time, to count 'to himself', he often still uses the method of adding by units, although now in a purely oral form.

The decisive change comes only at the third stage, and consists of a specific shortening of the whole process, which simultaneously becomes automatic and is transformed into a dynamic stereotype. It is at this moment that the mechanism of the corresponding 'psychic function' is formed.

This abbreviation of a process that has already become internal

[1] Carried out during the last few years by Galperin, Davydov, Morozova and others, at the Department of Psychology, Moscow University.

radically changes its structure. For, when ideas and concepts (which are only the generalized reflection of things) are being manipulated, there is no need to reproduce all the phases necessary when one is working with real things. Many links of the process become superfluous, are not consolidated, become inhibited and fall out. Thus, a child who has learned to add numbers from one to ten by means of recounting in his head, will, in future, begin to count by passing straight from the numbers to be added to their sum. This specific shortening of the process is accompanied by a strengthening of the corresponding system of reflex connections, which has already been sharply reduced, and which now takes the form of a stable stereotype.

These successive, strictly regular changes give the process the appearance of a momentary 'psychic action'; it is now difficult to recognize it as the product of the original external actions the child learned to perform. Such 'momentary' actions seem to be the manifestation of a special capacity of the mind for grasping quantitative, spatial and other relations, and for passing directly from primary data to 'awareness' (insight) of the solution. In reality, these actions are nothing but the product of past experience, reflected and transformed in the mind of the individual, i.e. of former actions which have been assimilated. It must be strongly emphasized that these actions are *assimilated* by each individual, that is, they are acquired through learning from others; but the actions themselves are created through social practice in the evolution of human society.

The method of formation of complex reflex systems, the functioning of which is manifested in the form of a capacity for this or that intellectual action, has been described here only in the most general terms. In reality it is much more complex and can vary in each individual case. In particular, these very systems can acquire different structures in the process of their formation, and these structures are sometimes inadequate. Thus pupils sometimes advance to more complicated intellectual operations without having mastered the necessary methods, and perform these operations by the primitive methods characteristic of an earlier stage. At first they attain the required result by using these more primitive methods—for example, addition with the help of direct counting. Since, in school practice, the quality of the performance of a task is often judged solely by the result arrived at, such pupils appear for a time to be successful; but, when the next step is introduced, they cease to be able to cope with their school tasks and show a complete inability to master the succeeding skills.[1] This situation usually arises when, in the course of education, a consolidation of the operations takes place at one of the intermediate stages, but in an insufficiently generalized form; or again,

[1] Research of Davydov.

when some necessary link is 'missed', and so fails to develop at the proper time.

Investigation of cases of inability to perform fully certain definite intellectual actions shows that this is only a question of an incorrectly formed functional system which can be successfully reconstructed. To do this, as experiments have shown, it is necessary to bring to light the undeveloped or incorrectly developed links, and to take the pupil back to the stage at which the links in question are formed in their elementary external form.[1]

The general conclusion to be drawn from this experimental work is that human psychic properties, both general and specific, do not represent the manifestation of certain special 'powers', the presence or absence of which can only be stated, but are the product of ontogenetic development. This does not mean that anatomical (physiological) differences between people play no part; it simply means that psychic properties and peculiarities cannot be directly inborn, that they are always formed in the process of the individual's development and education, and that knowledge of the laws of their formation makes possible the conscious direction of this process.

Investigation of the laws governing the formation of psychic properties serves a great practical aim: the fullest possible development of the capabilities of every individual. Soviet psychologists see this as one of their most important tasks.

[1] Researches of Slavina (cf. p. 205—Ed.).

PART V

A CONTRIBUTION TOWARDS THE DEFINITION
OF 'SKILL' AND 'HABIT' [1]

BY

E. I. BOIKO

I

THE FIRST SUCCESSFUL ATTEMPT to present a picture of the whole complex activity of man, from the point of view of the reflex principle, was that of I. M. Sechenov, a leading physiologist who founded the scientific school of Russian psychology. In *Reflexes of the Brain* (1863), Sechenov made a vivid sketch of the psychic development of the child, and, by analysing typical examples taken from real life, revealed the general reflex nature of purposive human action. His principal aim, in his own words, was to give a determinist explanation of 'the activity of a man . . . with an ideally strong will, acting in the name of some lofty moral principle, and realizing clearly at every step what he is doing—in a word, activity which represents the highest type of voluntariness' [56: 52]. Sechenov's work has not lost its scientific significance. A key task of contemporary psychology is to develop the theory of purposive, volitional action, which represents the clearest and most characteristic expression of the human psyche.

The basic psychological attribute of this higher sphere of psychic phenomena is that all human actions are, in one way or another, preceded by conscious intentions, and that a man is responsible before society for the realization of these intentions. Karl Marx, in his analysis of the labour process, pointed to man's ability to foresee and plan the results of his future actions as the most characteristic

---

[1] *Sovetskaya Pedagogika*, No. 1, 1955, pp. 41–55 (translated by H. Milne).

phenomenon of human life.[1] Science must give an exact description of this extremely complex psychic process, and disclose its inner mechanism, in all its detail, with all its connections and mediating structures.

We know from the physiology of the central nervous system that the so-called voluntary movements, at the basis of which lies the mechanism of the motor conditioned reflex discovered by Pavlov, are characteristic of both man and the higher animals. But the conditioned-reflex activity of animals does not usually go beyond a more or less exact adaptation of the organism to its environment. Such an adaptation has a biological, and only a biological, character. On the the other hand, our ape-like ancestors gradually transformed their whole nervous activity during the age-long adaptation of their organisms to the conditions of life in developing society. With the appearance of the second (verbal) signal system (the development of which is inseparably connected with the development of labour) there were formed in man qualitatively new behaviour reactions, alien to animals, and characterized by conscious purposefulness. The second signal system became 'the highest regulator of human conduct' (Pavlov), and conditioned-reflex adaptation to the environment took the form of premeditated, planned changing of this milieu, in conformity with man's developing needs and consciously advanced aims. Henceforth all human conduct is motivated, not only by foreknowledge of the direct results of this or the other action, but also by consideration of other people's opinion of it.

Such a psychological characterization of human activity, placing consciousness of purpose and premeditation in the foreground, must in no respect contradict the principle of determinism, that is, recognition of the objective, causal, conditioned character of human aims and deeds. A radical defect of most former theories of will was not that their initial description of psychological facts was mistaken, but that their authors were unable and unwilling to explain the phenomena of conscious purpose within the framework of a determinist world outlook. In this connection, Sechenov's work was particularly important, for he placed this psychological problem on the firm scientific ground of the reflex theory.

Though the concept of 'purpose' cannot explain any biological facts whatsoever, it must not be wholly excluded from the scientific

[1] 'We presuppose labour in a form that stamps it as exclusively human. A spider conducts operations that resemble those of a weaver, and a bee puts to shame many an architect in the construction of her cells. But what distinguishes the worst architect from the best of bees is this, that the architect raises his structure in imagination before he erects it in reality. At the end of the labour-process, we get a result that already existed in the imagination of the labourer at its commencement.' *Capital*, 157. Ed.)

vocabulary. A specific group of phenomena covered by this term undoubtedly exist and insistently demand a severely scientific investigation; only the successful accomplishment of this task can finally rid psychology of all remnants of idealism and metaphysics.

Psychologists have long been concerned with analysis both of the typical volitional action, and of the formation of the various human skills which enable a man to act successfully in changing circumstances. They have also been concerned to discover how modes of activity, acquired through experience, are perfected by practice, so changing their original structure and becoming transformed into habits of different kinds—connected with play, with the individual's mode of life, with school or work. At the theoretical level, the formation of skills is only one aspect of the wider question of voluntary action; while habit—not to extend the meaning of this term unduly—is only a part of the problem of skills. In tackling all these questions, general psychology and educational psychology are very closely linked, for the study of the general laws governing the formation of skills and habits is of equal interest to both theoretical psychologists and practical educationists.

Nevertheless, though extensive experimental work has been undertaken, the theoretical implications of this problem have been insufficiently elucidated; indeed, in certain important particulars the problem has not yet been concretely stated. For example, there are no generally recognized definitions even of the terms 'skill' and 'habit'. As a result, the very complex manifestations of psychic activity accompanying the formation of a conscious skill are often quite incorrectly subsumed under 'habit', and so remain unanalysed. Equally, attempts to assign a definite physiological base to these psychological concepts have inevitably tended to be one-sided and arbitrary. One of the main objects of this paper, after a preliminary survey of the relevant facts, is to attempt an exact definition of the content and limits of the terms 'skill' and 'habit'.

II

In everyday usage the concepts 'skill' (*umenie*) and 'habit' (*navyk*) are almost indistinguishable,[1] but in psychological literature the term

[1] The word *navyk*, as used by Soviet psychologists, means 'habit' in the sense of a skilled repetitive action making a minimum demand on the performer. It is distinguished from *privichka* ('habit'), a more colloquial word used, for instance, in the sense of 'bad habits' (e.g. the habit of continually whistling, twiddling objects when talking, inserting linking words into conversations: 'so to say', 'I mean', 'you know'). *Umenie* means 'skill', but it emphasizes the intellectual component of a skill, corresponding to *savoir*, i.e. 'knowing how' an operation or a series of actions is performed (Ed.).

'habit' alone is generally employed; analysis must begin, therefore, with a critical examination of the existing definitions of this concept. Two interpretations of the term should be noticed. The first, borrowed from biology, was introduced into psychology by the behaviourists, the term being taken to cover any individually acquired reaction, of an animal or human being, in response to external stimuli. According to J. B. Watson, 'Any definite mode of acting, either explicit or implicit in character, not belonging to man's hereditary equipment, must be looked upon as a habit.'[1] So also Clark Hull, another well-known American behaviourist, has written: 'The organization within the nervous system brought about by a particular reinforcement is known as a habit; since it is not directly observable, habit has the status of a symbolic construct. Strictly speaking, habit is a functional connection between stimulus and response.'[2]

Behaviourists regard the training of animals in special labyrinths, with several blind-alleys and one exit, as the classic example of the development of a habit. 'Problem cages', with specially designed bolts which open from the inside have a similar purpose. In the experiments an animal is put into the labyrinth or locked into the problem cage, and it has to get out through its own efforts by means of numerous 'trial and error' attempts. In certain modern modifications of these experiments, the animal must at first 'by chance' press on some lever or other, as a result of which food is automatically introduced into the cage. The reactions produced in this way, without any indication of further differentiating marks, are regarded as 'habits'.

More, behaviourists include the most complex forms of human activity (e.g. Tchaikovsky's 'Queen of Spades', the discovery of the differential calculus) under this same heading. It is unnecessary to comment on the uselessness for psychological purposes of this undifferentiated approach, one which lumps together, under a single heading, the most varied phenomena.

The second interpretation of the term 'habit' goes to the opposite extreme, narrowing the concept down to 'a secondary automatism', or to 'an automatized component of activity'. In Russian psychological literature this point of view was defended in detail by K. D. Ushinsky [67], and it has been adopted in modified form by leading contemporary psychologists. Here, the 'automatism' is often defined by a purely subjective criterion, namely its relation to consciousness. Automatized actions are said to be those which, as a result of a large number of repetitions, have passed out of consciousness. 'The most essential property of automatisms', according to N. A. Bernstein [3],

[1] J. B. Watson, *Psychology from the Standpoint of a Behaviourist* (Philadelphia and London, 2nd ed., 1924), 291.

[2] Clark L. Hull, *Principles of Behavior* (New York, 1943), 387.

'is the fact that they are unconsciously regulated.' More cautious authors speak of the 'partial' or 'incomplete' unconscious nature of the automatized components of activity, without realizing that these formulations are also subjectivist.

Such interpretations are as unsatisfactory as they are vague. That the subjectivist-psychological criterion is incapable of fixing the meaning of the concept 'habit' is indicated by the fact that there are two, directly opposed, points of view regarding the relationship of learned movements to consciousness. Here it may be noted that many authors, from Sechenov onwards, have vigorously denied the unconscious character of man's voluntary movements and have identified these with learned movements. 'The more learned a movement is', wrote Sechenov, 'the more easily is it subjected to the will. . . .'; or again, 'A voluntary movement is *always conscious*' (my italics—E. B.) [56: 25, 55]. Citing the example of experienced knitters, who can read while they are working, Sechenov elaborated his view as follows:

This does not mean, however, that the movements are produced *automatically*, without any control; a certain fraction of attention must be directed to them by the worker, otherwise the work would be impossible. . . . Even when she is reading a book the worker follows the movement of her hands. . . . She must *feel* the needles in her hands and *feel the measure of the movements she is making* (my italics—E. B.) [56: 522].

Some modern theoreticians of physical culture hold similar views. Thus Professor A. N. Krestovnikov speaks of 'the *seeming* absence of conscious analysis of movements at the stage of automatization' (my italics—E. B.) and of 'the illusion of the absence of consciousness' [35: 246]. This is confirmed by the observations of specialists on the actions of outstanding athletes. 'All the movements of an athlete, for example the movements of one of the best high jumpers in the country, Yu. Iliasov, are thoroughly automatized. But after his jump he can describe with almost complete accuracy every detail of his performance' [54]. Thus, the criterion of relationship to consciousness, as an indication of the automatization of a habit, turns out to be unsatisfactory in its application to the motor components of a voluntary action. Still less is it applicable to so-called 'sensory' and 'mental' habits, which will be dealt with below.

Meanwhile the variety of definitions of the concept 'habit' dictates recourse to the following method of analysis. First, the ordinary meaning of this term, that accepted in everyday life, may be dealt with and compared with the concept of 'skill' as accepted by educationists. Then, after examining data taken from laboratory and other observations, it may be possible to isolate the essential features of these concepts, and so to arrive at more precise definitions.

III

In common usage 'habit' is usually taken to mean habitual actions; that is, actions, practised continually, and so performed easily, quickly, and relatively speaking, perfectly. There is a firmly established connection between this concept and that of 'skill', and this connection must attract attention. Usually these ideas run parallel, but they can, as it were, fuse completely and become identified with each other, particularly when the method of performing some complex action, developed by experience, is under discussion. On the other hand, there is good reason to assert that the concept of 'habit' does not completely cover the concept 'skill', as it is made to do in the definitions of the behaviourists. In this connection an article by N. A. Rykov, 'Concerning the Formation of a Skill' [55], is of particular interest. The author notes at the outset that 'there is no universally accepted idea of skill in modern educational theory', and his subsequent argument is worth a full quotation:

Some people consider that a skill originates on the basis of the mastery of a system of habits, and recognize it as something higher and more complex than habits (P. N. Gruzdev); others consider that a habit is a system of skills, and a skill something more elementary than a habit (P. N. Shimbirev, R. G. Lemberg); a third group reduces the whole of practical training to the fixing of habits, identifies habits and skills, and avoids using the word 'skill' (K. N. Kornilov and others); finally, a fourth group recognizes a habit as a skill, perfected as a result of exercise and repetition, and brought to the stage of an automatism (I. A. Kairov).

A skill, as a capacity [1] to act rationally, consciously, with deliberation, and not as an automaton, emerges on the basis of the mastery of some definite activity; on the basis of an analysis of the conditions controlling the solution of a practical problem. A habit is unquestionably also a skill, but a skill perfected as a result of repetition and training. Kairov gives a more accurate account of habits than other authors.

Habits, of course, arise in the process of learning, but the training of pupils for their future careers cannot by any means be reduced to the development of habits. How, for example, shall we classify a pupil's capacity consciously to perform some action; a capacity which arises, not through training a definite working

[1] *Gotovnost*, literally 'readiness', 'disposition', 'aptitude' (Ed.).

organ, but only through influencing the pupil's senses and intellect? What name shall we give to a capacity to perform new actions, which arises through borrowing from another's experience related verbally? Or to a capacity to solve practical problems, which arises only as a consequence of perceiving, under the guidance of a teacher, the actions of others?

Such a capacity consciously to solve a problem, a capacity acquired without specific training, we shall call a *skill*.

The questions here posed are timely, and clearly formulated. And the author's systematic observations of lessons, during which pupils actually acquired definite skills solely by perceiving and thinking over the actions of others, greatly add to the value of his analysis. The only matter for regret is that he did not generalize his observations in psychological terms; as a result, his definition of skill proves one-sided. Why did he take the development of a capacity for action without training as the essential mark of a skill? Surely this is not the main point. It is certainly true that many simple skills arise at once without prolonged training, in the course of oral communication between people (or, as the physiologists say, 'on the spot'). But this in no way lessens the important consideration that many kinds of skills (e.g. shooting, swimming, riding a bicycle) arise only through the medium of a habit, that is, by means of numerous and prolonged exercises. Moreover, Rykov's generalization tends to contradict his own assertion that 'a habit is . . . also a skill'.

Rykov is nearer to the truth when he speaks of a skill as 'a capacity to act rationally, consciously, with deliberation . . .' But again the most essential objective distinguishing feature is here veiled; for 'consciousness' and 'rationality' can only indicate the presence of a skill when they guarantee the *success* of some action. 'A skill', says N. D. Levitov, 'means the due performance of actions, when the correct means are chosen and applied, regard is had for the conditions under which the actions are performed, and the proper *results* are obtained' [46: 76]. If such results are not obtained, the most conscious and rational approach cannot be taken as indicating the presence of a definite skill.

Nevertheless, Rykov's statements provide a starting point for further analysis. First, we must categorically refuse completely to identify the concepts 'habit' and 'skill'. Second, we must emphasize the vital significance for human actions of *knowledge*; not of knowledge in general, but of specific knowledge about the *action*. Finally, we must take into account the supremely important role of *language* in forming all human knowledge and skills; it is precisely this factor

239

which sharply distinguishes human skills from the reactions of animals.

From these initial propositions, we may go on to consider further objective factors governing a correct use of these terms. Generally speaking, a scientific approach to psychic phenomena means 'establishing the nervous mechanisms of the process of reflection';[1] the content of any psychological concept remains schematic, indefinite, and incomplete without a knowledge of the corresponding physiological mechanisms. In this connection, the first relevant question concerns the regulating role of the second signal system in the process of forming and performing all human actions.

In psychological literature this question is usually treated only when language and thinking are studied. But, as has been noted earlier, any purposive human action is primarily an action regulated physiologically by the connections of the second signal system. Obviously this point applies wholly to 'skill', but the precise role played by the second signal system in the mechanism of 'habit' is not nearly so obvious. It is logical to suppose that, at various stages in the forming of a habit, the interrelation of the two signal systems changes; and that, in actions which have been well 'automatized', the regulating role of the second signal system is reduced to a minimum. Thus physiological analysis at once indicates that it is incorrect to identify the concepts 'skill' and 'habit'. To proceed further, many writers, taking as their starting point the everyday interpretation of 'habit', quite justly link their conception with a dynamic stereotype, in the sense in which this phrase was used by Pavlov. Further, there is no doubt that any stereotype presupposes the permanence, or, as Pavlov himself expressed it, the 'ability to be repeated', of definite conditions or the 'external stereotype'. But the most important point to emphasize about 'skill' (which according to the apt popular expression, demands 'knowledge of the business'), is the conscious adaptation of the action to the *changing* demands of the situation. In other words, to know how to do something means, primarily, to know how to adapt oneself to various conditions in order to attain a definite, useful result.

As Pavlov showed, the higher nervous activity both of man and of animals proceeds on the principle of variable signalling:

The world surrounding the animal is so infinitely complex . . . that the complex system of the organism only has a chance of coming into equilibrium with it if it also varies correspondingly. And so the fundamental and most general activity of the cerebral

---

[1] B. M. Teplov, 'Objective Method in Psychology', p. 246.

hemispheres is a signalling activity, with a countless number of signals and with variable signalling.[1]

All this must be taken into consideration when the general nature of skills is explained. Every purposive action can be performed under various conditions in the most varied ways, all of which, in the end, lead to one and the same general result. The concept 'skill' must, therefore, embrace all the possible variations of different actions, and all the connections acquired in the course of experience which make possible the successful practical employment of these variations. But the term 'habit' presupposes the repetition of definite conditions and the corresponding forms or methods of action. An action acquires the features of a habit only by being performed many times. It appears to be correct, therefore, to regard this same habit as a definite aspect of the corresponding skill. The precise elements which make up this aspect are discussed after a preliminary summing-up.

The principal objective basis for discriminating between 'skill' and 'habit' is the fact that any capacity for an action acquired through experience represents a complex adaptation of the organism to two sorts of conditions: on the one hand, to the inescapable variability of actual situations which call for variation in the methods of performing the action (variable signalling), and on the other hand, to the permanence and repetition of a definite part of the external conditions which produce the stereotyping of conditioned reactions or the development of 'working stereotypes'. It is more convenient to designate the capacity for an action, in all the possible variations which ensure the necessary success, by the broader term 'skill'; while the stable interconnection of the elements of the same action, reflecting the adaptation of the central nervous processes to the *recurring* conditions of experience, may be designated by the term 'habit'.

It is hardly necessary to add that the direct physiological basis of a capacity for any purposive activity is composed of systems of conditioned or temporary nervous connections, built up in a definite way. From this point of view, the concepts 'habit' and 'skill' are seen to be related to each other as a part to the whole; under 'skill' must be understood the whole of that system of second-signal and first-signal connections which ensure the successful performance of an action in changing conditions; under 'habit' only that positive element which is introduced into this system by numerous repetitions. There is no habit apart from a skill, but the features of a habit are not expressed in identical form and identical degree in every skill. In some cases a genuine skill arises only through habit; in many others

---

[1] Pavlov-Anrep, 15.

habit only 'crowns the matter', adding the character of full completeness and technical perfection to forms of action which have already been built up.

IV

We may now go on to examine the separate aspects, or elements, which go to make up the special features of a skill as a habit. In order to discuss this question concretely, it is necessary to examine the changes introduced into an individual's activity by repeated practice. The following are the most important:

(1) As a result of repeated practice the mutual drag, clash, or 'interference' of the several separate actions which go to make up more complex activity, are gradually removed. The basic cause of this drag is the phenomenon of negative induction, which is gradually weakened in the course of training. If it is a question of a sufficiently large number of operations which have been mastered for the first time, in particular if these succeed each other in various orders, the process of forming a skill must necessarily take place through habit. Examples will make this clear.

Let us suppose that a craftsman explains to his pupil, and then demonstrates, a series of more or less complex methods of work on some machine. After the first demonstrations, the trainee's attempts to reproduce, on the spot, the whole complex action usually fail, even when he has been well prepared theoretically and knows what he must do and how he must do it. The reason is not solely lack of the necessary 'dexterity' in the movements of his hands, but primarily the unaccustomed situation which renders difficult the combination of different actions and operations which plainly hinder each other. This is particularly striking in the case of first learning to drive a car, or pilot an aeroplane.[1] Though the plan of action as a whole, and the sequence of the separate links, may be quite clear, in practice the immediate result is not 'everything together'; here, something has escaped notice, there, the right moment has been missed, a point has been forgotten, a simple movement has been bungled, and so on.

Again, to repeat accurately a phrase of seven to eight words in a completely strange tongue is almost impossible. The unfamiliar combinations of sounds cannot be 'stored' in the memory. But the repetition of separate elements (syllables and even words) presents no particular difficulty; obviously the elements forming a phrase at first interfere with each other, and only after sufficient repetitions is this temporary interference gradually removed. Similar phenomena are found in physical training (wrestling, boxing, fencing, etc.) where,

[1] A good description of this process is found in the article by E. V. Gurianov, 'Habit and Action' [14].

together with the elaboration of separate techniques, the skill of combining complicated movements, and of moving quickly from certain
reactions to others, is also required; at first this proves very difficult.

(2) In the course of training in any form of activity, a gradual
shortening of the time spent in performing separate operations and
complicated actions is observed. But at the highest levels of habit this
time tends to remain constant. That actions based on a stable habit
are performed easily and quickly is a general formula. This is a
common-place in actual experience, and there is no need to deal with
it in detail.

(3) When some activity is pursued for a long time, a gradual
specialization and sharpening of the corresponding perceptions takes
place and sensory differentiations become more exact. Thus perception of certain classes of objects is highly perfected in representatives
of those professions which call for constant and intense exercise of
the organs of sense; for example, tasters, proof-readers, and goods
inspectors. Insofar as such delicate perception is developed by practice, and controls specialized actions, there is every justification for
classifying it as habit (the so-called sensory habit).

(4) In the course of practice it is often observed that simple objects
in a perception are grouped into 'units of a higher order'; that is, into
simultaneous and successive sensory complexes. Thus, when reading
swiftly we do not separate out individual letters, but grasp whole
words, or even groups of words. The formation of successive sensory
complexes, with anticipatory thought (thought running ahead), takes
place when any series of movements, directed towards external objects and demanding visual control, is in course of development, for
instance, in learning to play musical instruments. The physiological
basis of this phenomenon is the formation of progressively more new
conditioned connections between the stimuli entering into the action.
This last point is extraordinarily important. It indicates that, as a
habit develops, there takes place not only further reinforcement but
also reconstruction of the operative temporary connections. This consideration is very relevant to the development of so-called mental
habits such as mental calculation or the solving of problems.[1]

(5) At the first stage in the development of motor skills, superfluous movements and unnecessary muscular tension tend gradually to
disappear. Unskilful movements are not only uneconomical, but also
tend to include a number of wholly extraneous elements which disappear step by step as the habit becomes established. Parallel with
this process, there takes place a strengthening of new combinations
of movements (simultaneous and successive) as motor coordination

---

[1] The process as applied to reading has been studied in detail by T. G. Egorov
[10].

becomes increasingly exact. As a result, the movements of the trainee acquire certain qualities, such as dexterity and sureness of aim. An important part in this process is played by the ever-increasing concentration of nervous processes (and exactness of differentiation) in the motor analyser.

(6) As a habit is developed, a lowering of 'sensitivity' to external disturbances and distracting circumstances is observed. A man who has thoroughly mastered an action does not cease to perform it when his attention is distracted by external circumstances, but, as has been suggested above, even reveals a capacity to combine it with others. Thus, among other things, the development of a certain 'immunity' to external inhibitory influences indicates the presence of a stable habit [31: 47].

(7) In the course of development of many skills, a tendency to the displacement of attention from the process to the result is revealed. This may be explained as follows. A trainee learning some new method is initially compelled to watch his own movements as he carries out an instruction or copies a demonstration. But at the next stage he can follow the objective of the action more attentively, disregarding the individual movements and details of the method he has mastered. A reconstruction of the system of operative temporary nervous connections evidently underlies this shift.

(8) A further improvement, proceeding from the same causes, is expressed in the capacity to reproduce complicated and delicate movements without looking at the object, guided solely by 'muscular feeling' (writing separate letters and words in darkness, playing the piano, typing). The investigations of A. N. Krestovnikov [36] suggest that visual control does not wholly give place to muscular-motor control, but continues to be exercised by the peripheral zones of the retinae of both eyes.

(9) All developed habits lead to a certain lessening of fatigue, and the emergence of a characteristic feeling of 'easiness'. The physiological changes underlying this complex process are governed by many factors, consideration of which lies outside the scope of this article.

When all these phenomena, which show how different types of activity change under the influence of repeated practice, are combined, the concept of 'habit' is, in the main, fully explained. It is evident that all the forms of functional adaptation to the recurring situations described above are characterized by one common feature; namely, a tendency to seek the maximum amount of harmony and coordination among the elements of the activity practised. Therefore the results of practice in any sphere can never be described merely in terms of quantitative changes, but in each separate case must receive a qualitative evaluation.

Under 'habit', therefore, we should understand the adaptation of the structure of an action to recurring conditions; resulting in a harmonization and connection of elements which at first hindered each other, a speeding up of performance of the action, more precise and specialized perception, the elimination of certain superfluous sensory-motor elements, and more accurate motor coordinations.

It is also clear, that the usual conception of 'automatization', when subjected to objective analysis, cannot be reduced to any single principle, but embraces that whole series of complex phenomena summarized above. In its broadest sense, this concept embraces the whole process of development of a habit.

Equally, the assertion that automatized operations are, generally speaking, unconscious, is shown to be incorrect and to lead to insoluble contradictions. But it would be just as incorrect to assert that habitual and non-habitual actions are cognized in identical fashion. The first demand incomparably less attention in the usual everyday sense of this word. The particular operations involved require no special effort, and are cognized more in their results than in what goes before; therefore, in definite habitual situations, these are produced, as it were, without volition, or 'of themselves', though the whole context of the action, in all its psychically regulated links, is indubitably cognized. This appreciable difference in the subjective picture of the process has, as its objective cause, regular changes in the interrelations of the two signalling systems.

[The writer goes on to discuss the physiological mechanisms of skills and habits, which have been treated of in many specialist works. But he notes, as a general shortcoming, a lack of precise definitions and a resultant failure to recognize the substantial difference between 'skill' and 'habit'. The outcome is 'a marked and harmful tendency to reduce the most complex forms of analytic-synthetic activity of the two signal systems, found in the process of development of any skill, to the very general formula of the dynamic stereotype'.

[In order to suggest a more precise physiological meaning for this term as used in this context, the writer analyses in some detail the changing relations between the two signal systems in the formation of a motor automatism, and especially 'the progressive tendency to shift from coordinations of the second signal system to those of the first', which he regards as characteristic of the formation of a habit. He concludes, after citing various examples, that 'the problem of motor automatisms is primarily one of the complex, dynamic interrelations of the two signal systems, which function in various ways according to the nature of the dynamic stereotype and the changes in the conditions in which it develops'.]

OBJECTIVE METHOD IN PSYCHOLOGY [1]

BY

B. M. TEPLOV

[THIS PAPER OPENS with the question: 'Should, and can, psychology be a science using a strictly scientific method, or is the subjective method essential to psychological research?' Professor Teplov refers to Sechenov's stress on 'an objective attitude to the facts', as synonymous to a 'scientific attitude to facts'; and to Pavlov's view that the subjective method had been entirely unproductive and that an objective analysis of psychic processes is possible. These views were upheld at the Joint Conference called by the Academy of Sciences and the Academy of Medical Sciences in 1950, to discuss the physiological teaching of Pavlov.]

I

The term 'objective', as opposed to 'subjective', refers to that which exists outside and independently of human consciousness. Objective truth is that part of our knowledge which correctly reflects reality and does not depend upon the subject, i.e. on human consciousness and will. Objective method, therefore, means the method that leads to knowledge of objective truth. For materialism 'the recognition of objective truth is fundamental';[2] consequently all materialist science must be objective in method.

The special difficulty in psychology is that consciousness and will are the very objects of study. A scientific psychology must discover the objective laws underlying the conscious, voluntary actions of man. Dialectical materialism regards as objective those laws which are independent of man's consciousness and will. The first proposition is, therefore, that human consciousness and will are subject to immutable objective laws. There can be no objective method, no truly scientific psychology, unless this is recognized.

[1] *Sovetskaya Pedagogika*, No. 7, 1952, pp. 66–86 (translated by N. Parsons).
[2] V. I. Lenin, *Selected Works*, xi, 189.

Freedom does not consist in the dream of independence of natural laws [wrote Engels], but in the knowledge of these laws, and in the possibility this gives of systematically making them work towards definite ends. This holds good in relation both to the laws of external nature and those which govern the bodily and mental existence of men themselves—two classes of laws which may be remote from one another in our conception, but not in reality.[1]

By recognizing that all psychic activities are governed by objective laws and are therefore causally determined, we extend the idea of determinism to human psychic activity. This is not to deny human reason or purpose; as Lenin wrote,

the idea of determinism which establishes the necessity of man's actions and rejects the absurd fable of freewill, in no way destroys man's reason or conscience, nor his valuation of his actions. Quite the contrary, the determinist view alone makes a strict and correct judgment possible, instead of attributing everything one fancies to freewill.[2]

The struggle consistently to apply the principle of determinism is vital to the development of a materialist psychology. Idealist psychologists could never accept this principle. During the second half of the nineteenth century, when experimental psychology became relatively popular, investigations required the principle that psychic processes are determined by external stimuli. But all the leading psychologists, defending themselves from the materialist elements that were trespassing into their science, proposed one hypothesis or another postulating the 'freedom' or 'creative origin' of characteristic features of psychic life. In their systems all psychology derives from ultimate explanatory concepts such as 'creative synthesis' and 'creative activity', which are designed to ward off the terrible spectre of determinism arising from experimental results.

Sechenov was a powerful and consistent opponent of this idealist psychology which denied determinism. Taking as his starting point the ideas of the Russian revolutionary democrats, especially Chernyshevsky, he set himself the task of proving that both voluntary and involuntary movements were strictly determined, even 'activity that appears in the highest degree voluntary'. His famous book *Reflexes of the Brain* concludes with the words: 'Thus the question whether the most voluntary of voluntary acts is fully determined by internal and external conditions is answered in the affirmative' [56: 174].

[1] F. Engels, *Anti-Dühring* (London, 1934), p. 128.
[2] *Selected Works*, xi, 439.

Another work, *Who is Psychology for and How is it to be Studied?*, opens with the words: 'Psychic life is governed by immutable laws; in this sense psychology can be a positive science' [56: 222].

Pavlov continued the struggle for consistent application of the determinist principle in explaining psychic activity. His theory of higher nervous activity, based on extensive experiments, transferred Sechenov's brilliant hypothesis into an exact and ordered scientific theory. Pavlov held that determinism was the first basic principle of exact scientific research on which his reflex theory relied, and that recognition or non-recognition of this principle was the key criterion in distinguishing the materialist from the idealist approach to psychic activity. In an article directed against idealist psychologists in America he wrote:

> Although Leucippus of Miletus long ago said that there was no effect without cause and that everything was necessarily as it was, is there not still talk, leaving man aside, about spontaneously acting forces in the animal organism? As to man, do we not still hear talk about freewill, and is there not a rooted conviction in many minds that there is something in us that is beyond the reach of determinism?

It was the task of materialist psychology to shatter this conviction, which was incompatible with the data of modern science. Yet leading American psychologists actually supported it by every available means. With these in mind, Pavlov continued:

> I should not err greatly in assuming that this conviction persists even among some psychologists, masked by references to the *peculiar nature of psychic phenomena*, behind which, despite the appropriate scientific reservations, can be detected the dualism and animism that is still unreservedly accepted by many thinking people, to say nothing of religious believers.[1]

Pavlov did not, of course, deny the 'peculiar nature of psychic phenomena'; in other words, he was not a mechanist in this matter. But he held, in full agreement with dialectical materialism, that the 'peculiar nature of psychic phenomena' provided no grounds for excluding them from the general interconnection of phenomena and for denying that they were subject to the laws of causation and the principle of determinism.

Man can only control himself and his behaviour insofar as he takes

[1] Pavlov-Gantt ii, 126; *Selected Works*, 421–2.

into account, whether consciously or not, the objective laws which govern his consciousness and will, his thoughts and actions. It is the task of psychology to discover these laws and so to help people consciously to regulate their own and others' behaviour and development, in particular, the development of their children.

Objective method in psychology is then, above all, the method which relies on the principle of determinism and aims to discover the objective laws which govern man's behaviour and the phenomena of his subjective world. It requires that the psychological explanation of voluntary and conscious processes be as strictly objective as the explanation of natural and social phenomena given by other sciences.

II

The subject of study in psychology is the psyche—man's psychic activity and consciousness. But this cannot, of course, be equated with the concept of 'the subjective'. The subjective as such, taken by itself, cannot be the subject of any science. It is secondary and derivative, and cannot be studied or understood in isolation. It is the subject of psychology only in combination with the objective.

Sechenov's outstanding contribution to psychology was his challenge to the idealist separation of objective and subjective. For Sechenov sensations, imagination, feelings, etc., form the middle member of a reflex;[1] they represent the unity of the cerebral process with its subjective manifestation. But, even understood in this way, sensations, imagination, etc., cannot be regarded as independent objects of psychological study. The middle of the reflex, the 'mental element in the strict sense of the word', is not an independent phenomenon, but an 'integral part of the process'. The object of psychological study consists in the 'whole acts with their beginnings, middles and ends' [56: 238], that is, material processes in which the subjective appears only for a moment, though a moment of fundamental importance and necessity.

During the last years of his life Pavlov suggested the possibility and necessity of a 'fusion of the subjective with the objective'. He considered that realization of this principle in the study of psychic activity was 'the urgent task of science in the immediate future', and 'the most important scientific problem today'.[2] Ivanov-Smolensky has recently stressed the same point, and shown its fundamental importance for the methodology of research into man's higher nervous activity.

---

[1] Sechenov (and Pavlov) regarded the reflex act 'as a functional union of three essential components—the receptor, the central-coupling, and the effector'. Ivanov-Smolensky, *Scientific Session*, 118 (Ed.).

[2] Pavlov-Gantt ii, 72; *Selected Works*, 455.

The subject of a scientific materialist psychology is man's psyche, understood as 'the function of that particularly complex fragment of matter called the human brain',[1] which reflects objective reality existing independently of consciousness. The mind of man must be studied in its dependence on the objective conditions of existence and the objective activity of which human life is composed. This is the only approach which can lead to a scientific explanation of the phenomena of man's inner subjective life. In sum, the objective method in psychology requires that the subjective, being secondary and derivative, be explained in terms of the objective. Concretely, this means:

(1) Psychic activity *is* higher nervous activity. Psychic processes are inseparable from cerebral processes. There cannot be a psychic process as an independent process, one that is 'other' in relation to the cerebral process. A psychic process, once recognized as a product and function of the brain, cannot be opposed to cerebral processes as purely subjective, i.e. purely psychic, and only occurring in parallel with the cerebral process. It follows that the psychologist, in explaining any psychic process, must rely on the scientific principles of higher nervous activity discovered by Pavlov and now being elaborated; otherwise an exhaustive materialist explanation of psychic processes is impossible.

(2) Psychic activity is the reflectory activity of the brain. Our sensations, perceptions, conceptions and thoughts are images of the material world. This is the basic thesis of the dialectical materialist theory of reflection. As Lenin put it: 'outside us, and independently of us, there exist objects, things and bodies . . . our perceptions are images of this external world'. 'Sensation is a subjective image of the objective world. . . .' [2] Psychic processes are, then, more or less exact copies or imitations of objective reality. It follows that the psychic cannot be *reduced* to the physiological; a physiological description of a process of perception or thinking does not include the content of the images and thoughts, and is not, therefore, exhaustive.[3] In explaining psychic processes the psychologist must, therefore, pay attention to the objective reality they reflect. This means that the mind and consciousness cannot be studied apart from their content; that questions of *what* a man feels, perceives or conceives, *what* he wants and *what* he strives for are inseparably bound up with questions of *how* these mental processes take place.

(3) Psychic activity, like all other forms of living activity, is determined by the conditions of the organism's existence. The human

---

[1] Lenin, *Selected Works*, xi, 286.   [2] *Ibid.*, 167, 182.

[3] As Engels put it: 'One day we shall certainly "reduce" thought experimentally to molecular and chemical motions in the brain; but does that exhaust the essence of thought?' *Dialectics of Nature*, ed. C. Dutt (London, 1941), 175.

psyche and consciousness are primarily and decisively determined by the *social* conditions of existence. 'Consciousness is . . . from the very beginning a social product, and remains so as long as men exist at all.' [1] Man's life, his social being, is always reflected in certain aspects of activity—work, study or play. Consciousness is indissolubly bound up with activity since psychic processes arise in activity and are determined by its content and nature. An individual's psychic qualities, interests, abilities, character, etc., are formed in this way.

Analysing the labour process, Marx pointed out that man, by acting on the external world and changing it, 'at the same time changes his own nature'.[2] Engels reproached the science and philosophy of his day for neglecting the 'influence of men's activity on their thought'; he added: 'It is precisely *the alteration of nature by men*, not solely nature as such, which is the most essential and immediate basis of human thought.' [3]

It follows from these three points that explanation in psychology means:

(*a*) relating the subjective image with the objective reality it reflects,

(*b*) establishing the nervous mechanisms of the process of reflection,

(*c*) clarifying how the phenomena of consciousness depend on the social conditions determining them, and on the objective activity in which man's being is expressed.

There is nothing new about these principles, they have been formulated in psychological text-books and other scientific works. But their recognition has often been purely verbal, and they have seldom been consistently put into practice in research. For example, the term 'reflection' enters into most definitions of psychic processes in psychological text-books, but the understanding of psychic processes as reflection is often only formal and lacks organic connection with the examination of relevant facts and principles. Again, in the introductory chapters of such text-books it is emphasized that the psyche is the product of matter organized in a special way; in other words, that it is a function of the brain. Yet in particular chapters of the same books, psychic processes are treated as 'independent' processes, as if they could be understood without explaining their material, physiological basis.

Another typical, and very important, error is the one-sidedness with which the objective determining of the psyche is understood. For instance, acceptance of the 'unity of consciousness and activity' has led

[1] K. Marx and F. Engels, *The German Ideology*, 19. [2] *Capital*, 157.
[3] *Dialectics of Nature*, 172.

to much useful research using objective methods,[1] but an examination of this work indicates that here the objective determining of the psyche tends to be reduced to *one* thing, its dependence on activity. This approach leads to two main shortcomings: first, it makes a consistently objective study of the psyche impossible, and second, it leads to deviations from materialism as a result of ignoring the theory of reflection and failing to treat the psyche as a function of the brain.

Another sign of one-sidedness is the belief that a dual kind of explanation is possible in psychology: explanation by social conditions, *or* explanation according to the laws of higher nervous activity. In fact, social conditions and physiological mechanisms are not two separate causes, but two links in a single process. The influence on man's consciousness of social conditions—both material living-conditions and social ideas—is a completely material process, consisting of the effect certain physical stimuli (including language) produce on the brain *via* the sense organs. Pavlov's theory makes possible a concrete study of the laws governing the formation of the human psyche under the influence of certain conditions. Study of the material basis of psychic phenomena is an indispensable step in explaining the psychic processes, since this study can reveal the exact mechanism by which given conditions evoke particular 'ideas and feelings'. Nevertheless, in text-books and courses, the social nature and physiological basis of human consciousness still appear as two planes of psychological study that are parallel and never intersect. Here, too, there may be found, unsolved, the much-discussed 'two factor theory' of mental development—the social factor and the biological factor.

There are two main reasons for these deficiencies. First, inadequate mastery of Marxist dialectics and so of scientific method. 'Dialectics requires us to consider interrelationships in their concrete development from all sides, and not to pluck out a little bit of one thing and a little bit of another', wrote Lenin, and again: 'In order really to know an object it is necessary to grasp, to study every side of it, all the connections and "intermediate stages". We shall never achieve this completely, but the demand for all-sidedness is a safeguard against mistakes and rigidity.' [2] Of course, separate psychological investigations may, and sometimes must, be directed to studying only one of the relationships in which the objective conditioning of the psyche is expressed. But a scientific psychology can only be built on a many-sided consideration of the connections and intermediate stages.

The second reason is inadequate realization that Pavlov's theory

---

[1] E.g. Smirnov on memory, Volkov on perception, Leontiev and Zaporozhets on child psychology, Menchinskaya on the psychology of teaching, and Ananiev. Rubinstein and Leontiev have dealt with the theoretical aspects of the principle.

[2] Lenin, *Selected Works*, ix, 63, 66.

of higher nervous activity provided, for the first time, a firm scientific basis for the development of a consistently objective, scientific, study of the psyche. Pavlov's theory is concerned with the physiological mechanisms of the *reflectory* of the brain. It makes possible an effective and consistent understanding of the psyche as a function of the brain, and as the reflection of objective reality. This theory is also concerned with the work of the cerebral hemispheres, in maintaining 'a dynamic equilibrium between the functional units within the self-contained system of the organism and between the organism as a whole and its environment'.[1] Pavlov showed that 'all forms of living activity of the complex organism, including psychic activity, are determined by its conditions of existence'.[2] Finally, his theory of 'inseparably connected and permanently interacting first and second signal systems' [17: 65] creates the basis for understanding the physiological mechanisms by which human consciousness is socially determined.

By taking as its starting point the philosophical teaching of dialectical materialism and relying on the scientific foundation of Pavlovian doctrine, psychology can effectively and consistently overcome the harmful rift between 'physiological explanation' and 'social explanation'; in this way, without retreating from materialism, it can realize the principle of the unity of consciousness and activity.

III

[In this section, the subjective method in psychology is described, with reference to the officially approved texts of pre-revolutionary Russia: *A Text-book of Psychology* by G. I. Chelpanov of Moscow University, and *Psychology without Metaphysics* by A. I. Vvedensky of Petersburg. The essence of the views outlined is that psychic events can only be perceived in oneself; knowledge of them can only be obtained with the aid of introspection or self-observation; the subjective method consists in the use of introspection for scientific purposes, and this is the only possible method in psychological investigation. The practical outcome is that the psychologist can only interpret the psychic life, the thoughts and feelings of others, in the light of his own personal, limited, subjective experience. It is clear that this procedure is scientifically worthless. It rests on the belief that man has a special instrument for *directly* knowing his mind (the instrument of internal perception or introspection) and that there is no possibility of other, indirect knowledge of the mental. Sechenov strongly opposed this theory: 'There does not exist any mental sight as a special instrument

---

[1] Pavlov-Gantt i, 379. [2] *Scientific Session*, 171.

for investigating psychic as opposed to material processes' [56: 197]. Introspection can never throw light on the extremely complex psychic processes involved in remembering, thinking, understanding, deciding. Just as atomic structure cannot be seen with the naked eye, so the mechanism of psychic processes cannot be seen with the naked 'inner eye'. There must be an unqualified rejection of introspection, conceived of as an instrument for directly knowing psychic processes. The only possible approach is by way of indirect, objective research. All science is indirect knowledge. It is disregard of this fact that leads to continued attempts to 'see' a psychic process directly; and so also to a questioning of the power of objective method which, through observation of the objective conditions in which the psychic process arises and of its objective manifestations, gives a genuinely scientific knowledge of the actual process.]

IV

The view that the psyche can be known objectively is the most important methodological premiss of materialist psychology. Psychic activity is always expressed in some kind of action, movement, spoken reaction or change in the functioning of internal organs. If this is not understood, 'psychic reality' is inevitably replaced by 'psychic fictions' (Sechenov).

Sechenov was the first to advance the conception of the psyche as a reflector, and he rejected the idea of reflexes without an end-product. 'In all cases', he wrote, 'when conscious psychic acts lack outward expression, these phenomena nevertheless conserve the nature of reflexes'; in these cases 'the end of the reflex is an act fully equivalent to excitation of the muscular apparatus, viz. excitation of the motor nerve and its muscles' [56: 152]. Bykov and his collaborators have recently shown the extent and variety of the influences exercised by cerebral, and thereby psychic, activity on the work of all internal organs without exception. By establishing the regularity of these influences, Bykov has discovered another possible approach to the psyche. But, for the psychologist, the expression of psychic processes in man's external activity, in his actions, words and behaviour, is their most important manifestation.

Sechenov wrote, 'Man's psychic activity is expressed by external signs, and usually everybody—simple or learned, natural scientist or student of the mind—judges the former by the latter, that is, by the external signs.' 'Everyone without exception judges the character of a man by his external activity' [56: 70, 114]. Lenin made many clear statements on this question. 'By what tokens are we to judge of the real "thoughts and feelings" of real individuals? Naturally there can be only one such token, namely, the *actions* of these individuals.' [1] And again, 'A man is judged not by what he says about himself, nor by what he thinks, but by what he does—do you remember this Marxist truth?' It should be noted that Lenin is contrasting men's 'acts', not with their words in general, for statements can be acts, but with what men 'say about themselves'. The subjective method in psychology is harmful, not because it attaches significance to man's *statements*, but because it attaches decisive importance to man's statements *about himself* and his own experiences.

There is another side to this question. It is often thought that a subject's verbal statements, in the course of ordinary experiments concerning the senses and perception, are introspective evidence. This is a mistake. Evidence about what a subject sees or hears, senses or perceives, is evidence about things and events in the objective world. Only the subjective idealist could insist on classifying such evidence as self-observation. No one would say that a military observer reporting that 'an enemy tank has appeared on the outskirts of the wood' is engaged in self-observation and giving introspective evidence. When a subject answers such questions as 'Which of the two squares is the brighter?', 'Which of the two sounds is the higher (or louder)?', 'Is there a light circle in the dark area?' he is engaged, not in 'introspection', but in 'exterospection', not in 'internal perception' but in the most ordinary external perception. He is giving evidence, not about self-observation, but about objects and events in the external world. If it were otherwise, it would be necessary to agree that all scientific knowledge is built on evidence from self-observation, since no scientific experiment can dispense with perceptual judgments. The same is true if the military observer or scout gives evidence 'from memory', that is, evidence of what he has seen several hours previously. This evidence, too, cannot be called evidence from self-observation; it consists of statements about objectively real objects, not about one's self, though these statements make it possible indirectly to infer a judgment about the memory of the man giving the evidence.

Thus by no means all verbal evidence obtained in psychological experiments can be called evidence from self-observation. This description should only be applied to subjects' statements 'about themselves', their activities and experiences. Objectivity or subjectivity of method is determined least of all by the kind of reactions—speech, motor, vegetative—being studied. The most important condition of objective method is that there should be the strictest possible check on all influences affecting the subject and on all his reactions, and this relates also to verbal influences and reactions; not a rejection of these

[1] *Selected Works*, xi, 620.

influences, but an attempt to give a strict account of them, that is what the objective method requires.

V

During recent years most Soviet psychologists have held that self-observation, while not the only or even the basic method, is still an indispensable and important method in psychology.[1] This view cannot be considered to be correct. Introspection cannot be regarded as one of the methods of scientific psychology, although the evidence from self-observation (in the meaning of the term indicated) can be an important object of study in psychology, as also in many other sciences.

Here it is necessary to call attention to a terminological absurdity. Psychological methods are all named according to *what the experimenter does*: the method of experiment, the method of introspection, the method of analysing the products of activity, etc. If the investigator observes pre-school children playing at shopping, we call this the method of observation, not the method of playing at shopping. If children's drawings are studied for psychological purposes we talk of the method of analysing the products of activity, not of the method of drawing. But if the investigator collects and analyses subjects' evidence from self-observation, for some reason we speak of the 'method of introspection', though the investigator's method of working is in no way introspective.

Does not this terminological absurdity reflect a deeper confusion? Does it not sometimes mean that the experimenter, turning to his subjects' introspection, imposes his task on them? They, the subjects, are, as it were, sent to the 'place of the event' which is not accessible to the investigator himself in order to make scientific observations there, while the experimenter's job is merely to systematize and arrange the results of these observations.

If we reduce the psychic to the subjective and suppose that the subjective is accessible only to self-observation by the person experiencing it, then such a conception is inevitable. Then the task of scientific observation in a psychological experiment really does have to be entrusted to the subject; then one not only may, but really must, speak of the method of introspection.

But if we accept the thesis that the psyche can be known objectively,

[1] This view is expressed in Rubinstein's *Foundations of General Psychology* (2nd ed., 1946), in the first four editions of the psychology text-book for secondary schools by Teplov, in the text-book for teachers' training colleges edited by Kornilov, Smirnov and Teplov (1948), and in Kornilov's two text-books published in 1946. This position was recently defended by Samarin and Leontiev in articles in *Uchitelskaya Gazeta* (26th May and 9th June, 1951).

there is no reason why the subjects under study should turn into persons studying their own psyches, and it becomes senseless to call a method, the method of introspection, when it involves using the evidence of subjects' self-observation. Many sciences—medicine, literary history, the history of art—make use of people's evidence about themselves, their experiences and their work, and this is called 'evidence from self-observation'. But no one has yet suggested that medicine or literary history are based on the 'method of introspection'. The view that introspection is a special 'method' of investigation, specifically and uniquely psychological, is the most striking symptom of the subjective method in psychology.

While the objective method in psychology decisively rejects introspection as 'internal perception', as a special instrument for knowing psychic processes directly, it does not, of course, deny man's ability to give a verbal report to himself or other people (including the psychological investigator) about his actions and experiences. In this sense it is possible to speak of man's capacity for self-observation, while sharply opposing the terms 'self-observation' and 'introspection'. Self-observation, in the only acceptable sense of the word, is not the result of direct perception of one's own psychic processes or of the psychic features of one's personality; it is not 'internal observation'.

In contrast to the belief that man obtains all knowledge about himself through introspection, it may be stated that a man learns the most important things about himself indirectly, in the same ways that are open to other people. It is impossible, through introspection, to determine the 'stores' of one's memory, to know how much one remembers and knows. We must decisively reject the idea that memory is a storeroom where everything 'remembered' is kept, and which can be surveyed by 'inner sight'. Remembering is the formation of connections, a complete system of connections; recollecting is an activization of these connections, evoked by a definite stimulus and strictly determined.

In order to know whether or not a man has remembered something there must be a test to see whether it is recalled, given the stimuli and influences which appear to be connected with it in the particular man. Various kinds of questions and tasks can be 'influences' of this kind; the more varied the influences, the more reliable will be the result. The man who wants to know whether he remembers something acts in exactly the same way. He asks himself something about the thing, sets himself some 'task', and judges whether he remembers according to the result of this test. The means I use to find out what I remember are in principle the same as those other people use to determine the 'stores' of my memory. I find out about it, not directly by introspection, but indirectly, for there is no other way of finding out. It is the psychologist's task to turn this indirect way, naturally used by every-one, into a scientifically sharpened method.

Thus introspection is not a means of determining one's own know-ledge, abilities and skills. The only way to do this is to try 'doing'; that is, to use the indirect, objective, way. Internal perception is not the slightest help in the matter. If a man sometimes (though by no means always!) knows his capabilities better than others, it is only because he has more frequent chances of testing himself, and not because he has some special 'instrument' for knowing them. It is not by introspection that one knows such personal traits as temperament, character, capabilities and interests. One can make judgments about these only indirectly, according to the way one behaves in certain situations, how one acts and what one does. In this connection Marx made a very relevant observation: 'Man, not being born with a mirror in his hands, . . . begins to see himself, as in a mirror, only in another man.' [1] Man begins by learning to judge others, and only then learns to judge himself. He judges himself by the same basic means that he has evolved in learning to judge others. 'Not being born with a mirror in his hands', he has no other 'instrument' for perceiving himself as an individual.

Having refused to accept self-observation as one of the methods of scientific psychology, we must draw a sharp distinction between our position and that of behaviourism. Behaviourism also rejects the method of introspection, but it does so because it rejects the study of the psyche and of man's consciousness. The founder of behaviourism, J. B. Watson, wrote, 'If behaviourism is ever to stand for anything . . . it must make a clean break with the whole concept of con-sciousness.' 'Any student loath to give up "consciousness", with all its past complications, should find happier sailing on some other craft.' [2]

Though apparently the direct opposite of introspective psychology, behaviourism springs from the same essentially idealist view-point; the view that the psyche and consciousness are only accessible to in-trospective knowledge and so cannot be studied by objective method. According to Watson, 'States of consciousness like so-called spiritual-ist phenomena, cannot be objectively demonstrated, and can therefore never be the object of truly scientific research.' The first behaviour-ists were mechanical materialists, but with idealist elements; that is why the crude mechanism of early behaviourism turned so simply and quickly into an equally crude idealism.

Dialectical materialist psychology is directly opposed to behavour-

[1] *Capital*, 21n.
[2] J. B. Watson, *Psychology from the Standpoint of a Behaviourist*, viii.

ism. The basic task of Soviet psychology is to discover the materialist explanation of man's psyche and consciousness. Behaviourism has rejected the method of introspection because it has rejected consciousness; we reject introspection as a *method* of scientific research because man's consciousness can and must be studied by consistently objective methods.

VI

Evidence from self-observation, in the sense indicated—or self-evidence as it may now be called—can be correctly used in objective research only in the light of Pavlov's theory of the two signal systems. It should never be forgotten that self-evidence can only really exist as *verbal* evidence. Not every verbal statement is self-evidence, but all self-evidence is made up of verbal statements.

The importance of verbal statements, and especially of self-evidence, differs in studying different psychological problems. In the study of visual and aural sensations and perceptions, verbal statements have great significance, though these are not usually self-evidence. But in the study of many other psychological questions, evidence 'about the self' is essential.

An example is the question of motor and organic sensations. A report of these sensations is undoubtedly a report about what 'I do' and what 'I experience', and not about external things. Nevertheless, Sechenov had reason to refer to the 'dark muscular feeling' and the 'undefined dark sensations' from the interoceptors; the word 'dark' here meaning 'inaccessible to self-observation' [56: 132]. It is not, of course, the actual sensations which are 'undefined', but the verbal account of them, the cause being the transfer of these processes from the first to the second signal system; study based on self-observation has, in fact, produced no evidence about these sensations. Systematic scientific research into sensations from interoceptors began with Bykov's application of Pavlovian objective method to this question. The position regarding elementary feelings or emotional states (pleasant and unpleasant feelings, states of excitation and tension, etc.) is analogous. These experiences are, in the highest degree, 'dark' to self-observation, and here the technique of self-observation has proved useless.

Of special interest from this point of view is the study of imagery, the traditional object of introspection. Introspection, as we have seen, means a special 'internal perception'. But what is it that can really be 'seen by inner sight'—if this expression means anything—if not visual images? What can be 'heard by inner hearing' if not aural images? It is therefore instructive that, as the history of psychology illustrates, very little can be learned about imagery from self-observation.

Images, as defined by Pavlov, belong to the first signal system, though in their development they are usually inseparably connected with the second signal system. In the vast majority of cases, both our images and perceptions are connected with words. But is the whole content of images fully and adequately reflected in the second signal system, that is, in words? Definitely not.

M. N. Borisova's extensive experiments in our laboratory have demonstrated that if subjects are shown a picture of a leaf by itself for three seconds they can often recognize this leaf among ten similar leaves. Yet few could give a verbal account of the characteristics by which the leaf could be recognized, even when they were given ten seconds to examine it beside the others from which it was to be distinguished—that is, in incomparably easier conditions (reverse instances are also observed: a subject successfully manages the task of verbal description, but shows little ability for direct recognition). This shows that, though the object has been adequately reflected (as is proved by correct recognition), not all its features are always reflected in the second signal system and so can be described in words. Analogous instances are observed in everyday life. People recognize their friends' faces perfectly well, yet how many can give a verbal account of the signs by which they recognize them?

It follows that the study of imagery solely through verbal accounts, through the evidence of self-observation, cannot be fruitful. The basic way of studying images is to study their manifestations in recognition and recollection, in acts and movements. The simultaneous use of a verbal account of images (evidence from self-observation) is not excluded, but its purpose is to define which sides and moments of the image are reflected in the second signal system.[1]

Can we speak of 'unconscious' human sensations, conceptions and movements? We may do so if we are referring to occasions when a man cannot give a verbal account of what he senses or conceives, or of what it is that produces a movement; in other words, when the nervous process does not carry over to the second signal system. The question of making experiences conscious is a question of the interaction of the first and second signal systems, verbal evidence being an indication that the process is reflected in the second signal system. Human psychic processes are usually the result of the joint work of the first and second signal systems, but not all links and moments in these processes are reflected in the second signal system; a subject's verbal account of particular links in the process proves that these

[1] I. M. Soloviev, F. N. Shemiakin, N. N. Volkov, B. G. Ananiev and others have made objective studies of imagery on these lines.

links have been reflected in the second signal system. On the other hand the absence of a verbal account of a stimulus in sense and perception experiments, or a subject's 'negative' evidence (not hearing a sound, not having a conception of it), does not prove the absence of a corresponding process of sensation, perception or conception. These things only prove that the process was not made conscious by being reflected in the second signal system.

The authenticity of objective experimental data is in no way dependent upon confirmation by evidence from self-observation. If, for example, it is objectively established that subjects memorize material better in certain conditions than in others, then the subjects' evidence about the conditions most conducive to memorizing can neither confirm (as many psychologists think) nor refute this objectively established fact. The subjects' evidence is concerned with something altogether different: the way the relative difficulty, under different conditions, becomes conscious for them (the term 'conscious' being understood in the sense indicated above). This kind of evidence is not a confirmation of objective data, nor does it provide another *method* of studying the same facts, it is itself a special *object* of study.

The ability to become *conscious* of one's actions and experiences, and the underlying possibility of giving a verbal account of them, is an essentially human quality. Self-observation, as the realization of one's actions and experiences expressed in a verbal account (to others or to oneself), is an extremely important aspect of life. The man who is incapable of self-observation cannot answer for his actions and behaviour. Neither self-control nor self-education are possible without self-observation. Accordingly self-observation is important both for psychological research, and for education. Man, to use Pavlov's phrase, is 'a self-observing animal organism' [1] and must be studied as such. But this does not imply that self-observation is a method of scientific investigation.

VII

As long ago as 1911 Pavlov said: 'To examine all psychological concepts and compare them with our objective data to show to what degree they are fantastic and embody that crude empiricism which is an insuperable obstacle to an analysis of the subtle phenomena of higher nervous activity—this is the great task for which I am preparing myself.' [2] Pavlov was thinking of the concepts of idealist psychology. The principle underlying these concepts had been clearly expressed several years earlier by Lipps, one of the militant idealists in

[1] Pavlov-Gantt i, 151.　　　　　　　　　　[2] *Ibid.,* 179.

psychology, in his speech at the Fifth Psychological Congress. Psychologists, he said, must express consciousness in those concepts, and those alone, from which everything originating outside the sphere of consciousness is excluded. In other words, psychological concepts must be purely subjective; anything going beyond the sphere of the subjective must be excluded.

Soviet psychology proceeds from a directly opposite position: psychological concepts must not be purely subjective, since the facts of consciousness cannot be understood in isolation. Soviet psychologists, striving for the creation of a materialist psychology, have tried to realize this requirement. I have indicated the reasons why the task has not been completely realized; inconsistent application of the principle of determinism in psychology, survivals of the view that self-observation gives direct knowledge of psychic phenomena, and one-sidedness in understanding the objective determining of the psyche.

The definition of most of the perceptual processes as special forms of the reflection of reality, with specific objective signs, shows the progressive tendency of Soviet psychology, though many of these definitions are, in other respects, imperfect and incomplete. In psychological text-books, however, definitions are still to be found which do not satisfy these requirements and which are virtually an appeal to self-observation. For example, 'Attention is consciousness directed to a defined object';[1] 'Will is a psychic process which is marked by a unique effort and is expressed in human actions and behaviour directed to achieving consciously set goals';[2] the 'unique effort', which is the essential sign of the will, is subsequently defined as a 'special state of internal tension', an indication which is essentially only an appeal to the reader's self-observation. Moreover, references to particular nervous mechanisms are rarely made an organic part of definitions of basic psychological concepts.

Much fruitful work has been carried out by Soviet psychologists in analysing the content of psychological concepts by means of study of the objective activities in which the corresponding psychic processes arise and appear. But the problems cannot be solved by this method alone. Sometimes the result has been a one-sided, artificial scheme; as when Leontiev [38] attempted to remove such concepts as 'recognition' and 'consciousness' from the theory of the structure of activity. Elsewhere, arguments have been inconsistent, objective signs being marshalled together with subjective signs that are quite independent of them and have been drawn from introspective evidence;

[1] Teplov, *Text-book of Psychology for Middle Schools*, 5th ed., p. 72.
[2] Kornilov, *Text-book of Psychology for Teachers' Training Colleges*, p. 131. These text-books are not available in translation.

such, for example, is my description of such concepts as 'sensation of musical pitch', or 'aural conceptions in music' [65]. The nature of psychological concepts is a very important aspect of methodology in psychology. Objectivity of method is determined not only by the investigator's material and his means of obtaining it, but even more by the concepts which he brings to its analysis.

QUESTIONS OF PSYCHOLOGICAL THEORY [1]

BY

S. L. RUBINSTEIN

O NE OF THE MOST IMPORTANT conditions for the successful development of psychology is a profound and penetrating analysis of theoretical questions.

The theoretical ideas of the last generation of foreign psychologists are not outworn, but there is no sign of new theoretical generalizations, summing up the discoveries of experimental investigation from new standpoints, and so setting a course for future work. This situation in psychology is one aspect of the crisis in world science; a crisis which is due, in part, to neo-positivist influences on methodology. In the U.S.S.R., the position is very different; there are exceptional opportunities for the development of psychological theory because psychology relies on its own achievements and on all that is most progressive in world science. Soviet psychology has firm methodological and philosophic bases, new perspectives have opened out as a result of more profound study of higher nervous activity, and there is much positive work upon which to build. Nevertheless, Soviet psychologists have not made full use of their opportunities. We still do not pay sufficient attention to questions of psychological theory. As a result there are over-simplified sociological tendencies and tendencies towards mechanism, which are totally divorced from Marxism and put brakes on the development of psychology. [2] In sum, the reconstruction of psychology on the scientific foundation of Pavlovian physiology has raised theoretical problems which have not yet been solved.

The task of working out these problems cannot be deferred. In this connection it must be stressed that theoretical work cannot be

---

[1] *Voprosy Psikhologii*, No. 1, 1955, pp. 6–18 (translated by H. Milne).

[2] These trends have been commented upon in *Voprosy Filosofii*, No. 4, 1954. They are clearly shown in an article by V. M. Arkhipov, 'The Material Nature of the Psyche and the Subject Matter of Psychology', *Sovetskaya Pedagogika*, No. 7, 1954; the author reduces the psychological to the physiological, i.e. in effect, he denies the existence of the psyche.

counterposed to experimental work. There can be no doubt that the broad development of experimental work is of vital importance and essential to the development of psychological science; without it, psychology can neither live nor grow. Bu texperimental investigation is blind unless its course is illumined by theory. If theory is despised it always takes a cruel revenge; the abandonment of theory usually means the dominance of bad theory. Serious attention must, therefore, be devoted to problems of psychological theory. What is needed is a deepening of theoretical investigations.

In this article an attempt, but only an attempt, is made to draw attention to some of the more pressing problems, and to indicate, in the most general terms, a possible approach to their solution.

I

Of recent years, Soviet psychologists have embarked upon the task of reconstructing psychology on the scientific foundation of Pavlovian teaching. The question naturally arises: what is the relation between this task and the construction of psychology on the basis of dialectical materialism?

The reconstruction of psychology in the light of Pavlovian teaching means its reconstruction on the basis of the theory of reflexes. But an analysis of the conception of reflexes as a scientific theory compels us to distinguish its specifically physiological content from those philosophical principles of which it is a special form of manifestation. In fact, this differentiation is not always made; which means that the particular form of manifestation of philosophical propositions may be substituted for those propositions themselves, so concealing their essential philosophical meaning. For example, the materialist principle of determinism is now frequently regarded by psychologists as one of the propositions of the reflex theory;[1] whereas, in fact, the reflex theory must be regarded as a particular expression of the dialectical materialist principle of determinism.

The danger of replacing a general philosophical principle by the special form in which that principle is manifested in a particular science, is that this substitution places allied sciences in a false position. In this particular case, psychology is faced with a false choice: either to accept the general principle in that special form in which it is manifested in another science or totally to reject it. But the real task of psychology is to find, for this same philosophical principle that

---

[1] This way of treating the principle of determinism is widespread; it has even penetrated the *Prospectus for a Textbook of Psychology*, edited by Leontiev, Rubinstein, Smirnov and Teplov (1953).

underlies the theory of higher nervous activity, *a new, specifically psychological* form of manifestation. If this were done, and the principles manifested in the theory of higher nervous activity and in psychology were identical, this alone would be a reliable foundation for the 'marriage' of psychology and physiology; only then could there be a fusion without the loss of that which is specific to each of these sciences.

What do we understand by the 'reflex' nature of psychic activity? This means that psychic activity is an externally conditioned, response activity of the human brain; that psychic phenomena are determined by the interaction of a person, as subject, with the objective world. This proposition contains, in an undeveloped and specific form, the idea that is given developed and generalized expression in the dialectical-materialist conception of the determined nature of phenomena, as their objective, regular interconnection and inter-conditioning.

In the history of scientific and philosophical thought, determinism originated in connection with a mechanistic world view. It was originally a theory of causation, conceiving of an external impulse which directly defined the end result of an external action. It is easy to see the worthlessness of this conception of determinism; scientific facts and daily observation tell against it. At every step, we see that one and the same action can cause differing reactions in different people; and that one and the same action can cause different reactions in the same individual under different conditions. All phenomena, not only of an organic but also of an inorganic nature, confirm this. The effect of any cause depends, not only on the nature of the object which acts as cause upon another object, but also on the nature of this second object. According to dialectical-materialist determinism any change in one phenomenon is reflected in all others and is itself a response to the action of another phenomenon; this is the basis of the interconnection and inter-conditioning of all phenomena. The response is conditioned, not only by the nature of the active phenomenon, but also by that of the phenomenon acted upon. The same general principle may be expressed in another way; in the proposition that external causes act through the medium of internal conditions which are the basis for the development of phenomena.

This general principle is realized in forms as many and as various as the phenomena that enter into interaction. As a general philosophic principle, it relates not to a specific class of phenomena but to all phenomena. Therefore, in each specific class of phenomena it must have a particular form of manifestation, corresponding to each particular form of interaction. If psychology is to be constructed on the basis of dialectical materialism, it is necessary to find the specific form of manifestation of determinism in psychic phenomena. To solve this problem, it is first necessary to clarify the relation of the physiological to the psychological.

II

As the reflex activity of the brain develops, there arise new—psychic—phenomena: sensations, perceptions, and the like. Consequently, there also appears a new subject for investigation, setting new tasks for study—the tasks of psychology.

The reflex activity of the cortex is activity that is at once nervous (physiological) and psychic, insofar as one and the same activity is regarded from different standpoints. Therefore, the task of studying it is twofold; it must be studied as nervous activity governed by the physiological laws of neurodynamics (the processes of stimulation and inhibition, the irradiation, concentration and mutual induction of these processes); second, it must be studied as psychic activity (the processes of perception and observation, memory, thought, and the like).

Each science studies the phenomena of reality in those specific relations with which it is concerned. For physiology, reality appears as a combination of stimuli which act on the analysers in the brain; for psychology, reality appears as *objects* of cognition and action with which *man, as subject*, interacts. It is here that the specific sphere of interaction which defines the subject matter of psychology is revealed. The specific tasks of psychology commence when the psychic activity taking place in the brain of man is studied. Psychology, which studies the psychic activity of human beings, is one of the human sciences.[1] It is a science which discovers the laws governing the psychic activity that goes on in man's brain.

Since psychic activity is activity which goes on in the brain, it is

[1] Those who attempt to deal with this question usually complicate matters by postulating that the natural and social sciences are opposed, so excluding communication between them. Moreover, by using the term 'social sciences' they obscure the finer shades of difference between sciences dealing with society and those that deal with socially determined phenomena. It is to this latter group that the psychology of man and the other human sciences belong. The traditional antithesis between the natural and the socio-historical sciences, which presupposes an objective antithesis between nature and society, inevitably falls to the ground—as Marx has shown—when the subject of man is approached; for man is both a product of the development of nature and the subject of history. It is impossible, therefore, to find a place for the human sciences in general, and psychology in particular, if the starting point is the *antithesis* between nature and society. Psychology, as one of those sciences dealing with the *nature* of man which is the product of *history*, has special connections with sciences that deal with nature (primarily the physiology of higher nervous activity) and with socio-historical sciences.

subject to all the laws of neurodynamics; without bringing in these laws it is impossible fully to explain psychic phenomena. Therefore psychological investigation cannot be regarded as opposed to and isolated from the physiological study of neurodynamics, but as the natural continuation of this study, preserving and utilizing all its findings for the explanation of psychic phenomena. At the same time, the product of neurodynamics—the new, psychic phenomena which arise as a result of nervous activity—condition the new plan of psychological investigation; here those very processes which are the object of study for physiology appear in a new, specific form. Studied in this form, these processes are determined by relationships from which physiology has been abstracted.

For example, from a physiological standpoint, learning by heart—that is, recollection organized in a specific way—is the organization of a system of stimuli acting on the brain; it is, therefore, subject to all the laws of neurodynamics that govern the cortical processes. But to explain the result of learning by heart solely in terms of these laws is to leave out of account a whole series of interrelationships which are characteristic of learning by heart as a special type of psychic activity. In this new form of psychic activity, new dependencies inevitably appear; dependence on the nature of the individual's activity, on the relations into which he enters in the course of activity, on his attitude towards what is being recalled (e.g. towards the material he is learning, towards the teacher, his classmates and so on). Psychology studies the process in the framework of these new dependencies, and each psychological investigation discloses one or other of these dependencies, from which physiology is divorced. It is precisely the discovery of these dependencies, and the regularities to which they are subject, that is of key importance to an understanding of the organization of a man's activity. The task of discovering them falls upon psychology.

Since psychic phenomena obey the physiological laws of higher nervous activity (the laws of neurodynamics), they appear as the effect of the operation of physiological laws; similarly those physiological and biological phenomena which obey the laws of chemistry appear as effects of the operation of chemical laws. But physiological processes represent a new, unique form of manifestation of chemical laws, and it is precisely this new specific form of manifestation that is covered by the laws of physiology. In the same way, the physiological laws of neurodynamics find in psychic phenomena a *new, unique form of manifestation which is expressed in the laws of psychology*. In other words, psychic phenomena remain psychic phenomena, even though they appear as a form of manifestation of physiological laws; just as physiological phenomena remain physiological, though as an outcome of biochemical investigation they also appear as a form of manifestation of the laws of chemistry. Such, in general, is the interrelationship of the laws governing the lower and higher forms of movement of matter, the relationship between 'lower' and 'higher' regions of scientific investigation. The fact that the more general laws governing the lower regions spread to the more specialized regions does not exclude the necessity of discovering the specific laws of these higher regions.

The discovery of the biochemical nature of physiological phenomena has resulted, not in the disappearance of these as specific phenomena, but in a deepening of our knowledge of them. However far-reaching the discoveries of biochemical regularities controlling the formation of cortical connections, reflexes will not cease to be reflexes; and the same must be said about all other physiological phenomena. With advances in the biochemistry of digestion, for example, our knowledge of this process becomes more profound; but though it may appear as the specific effect of chemical reactions, it remains *a specific form* of manifestation of these reactions—a process of digestion characteristic of living beings, and not a process of reaction of chemical elements.

In the same way the regular dependencies established by psychological investigation, as a result of neurodynamic analysis, appear as the effect of the operation of neurodynamic laws governing the reflex activity of the brain. But this does not mean that psychic phenomena cease to be specific. The fact that psychic phenomena appear as the effect of the operation of the laws of higher nervous activity does not mean that laws established by psychological investigation lose all importance. Indeed, physiological investigation itself, which aims to give a neurodynamic explanation of psychic phenomena, starts out from the data of psychology. Sechenov's discovery of central inhibition resulted, as he himself says, from an attempt to solve by physiological means, problems posed by psychology; the relevant problem was the 'restraining' character of volitional behaviour, and central inhibition was Sechenov's answer. Pavlov, as the reports of his 'Wednesdays' show, continually 'measured up' his physiological ideas against psychic phenomena, and 'tested' their usefulness by their success in explaining these phenomena. This is a general law regulating the interrelationships between different disciplines in the system of sciences: the higher regions pose problems to the lower and the lower regions furnish the means for their solution; the former delineate phenomena which require explanation, the latter serve to explain them. The interrelationship of psychology and the physiology of higher nervous activity fits into this general framework.

If the relationship between physiological and psychological laws, between physiological and psychological characterizations of the brain's activity, is understood in this light, it becomes clear that certain definitions which have recently gained currency are invalid.

It is obvious, in the first place, that to represent the psychic and the physiological as two coordinated sides of a single process, is incorrect. This formulation conceals the hierarchy of primary and derivative, of the basis and the form of its manifestation, which expresses the essence of the relationship between physiological and psychological characterizations; it erroneously represents the two as related on equal terms, as coordinated, parallel. The mistake is that various 'sides' are indicated but not the interrelationship of these 'sides'.

Another proposition, which is sometimes opposed to that cited, is also invalid. According to this, physiological and psychological characterizations are consecutive 'components' of psychology's characterization of psychic phenomena, physiology being limited to a partial (physiological) characterization of these phenomena. This proposition expresses the theoretical conception of the old 'physiological psychology', at once mechanist and idealist. Unfortunately, it also expresses (though not as a consciously elaborated, theoretical, conception) the actual state of affairs in some of our psychological work, which consists of a conglomeration of consecutive, imperfectly correlated, physiological and psychological data. It is impossible to justify this method of constructing investigations, which gives practical expression to a theoretically false conception. To give physiological and psychological descriptions separately and consecutively, or to include the first in the second, means that the physiological characterization of phenomena loses its effectiveness; insofar as in this framework, psychic phenomena do not appear in their specific role as that *new, original* form of manifestation of physiological laws, which finds expression in the laws of psychology. Therefore, when an attempt is made to discover specific psychological laws, from this initial standpoint, a false *antithesis* between psychological and physiological laws arises. This antithesis, and the isolation of one set of laws from the other, is simply an expression of the falsity of the external, consecutive combination of the physiological and the psychological in the original proposition.[1]

Another view, very generally held but no less erroneous, is that the laws of neurodynamics have to do with the material basis of psychic phenomena; while psychological laws relate to the psychic phenomena which form a 'superstructure' on this material, physiological

[1] Cf. the article by N. P. Antonov, 'Dialectical Materialism—the theoretical basis of psychology', where, in an attempt to establish the independence of psychology, just such a false antithesis is made between psychology and the physiology of higher nervous activity; *Voprosy Filosofii*, No. 1, 1953.

basis. This formulation is particularly misleading because, by describing the laws of higher nervous activity as the 'basis of psychology', it seems to approach a genuine understanding of the relationship between physiological laws and psychology. But, in fact, the real tendency, the inner sense, of this formulation is towards dualism. It establishes, in a 'vertical' direction so to speak (from the physiological 'basis' to the psychic phenomena which are 'constructed on top' of it), the same external, consecutive picture as was presented by the preceding proposition in a 'horizontal' direction. According to this view the laws governing higher nervous activity have no bearing on psychic phenomena, but relate only to their physiological 'basis'. Psychic phenomena, seen in this light, do not appear as a form of manifestation of neurodynamic laws; the links have been broken. This, once more, means a restoration of the old schema, which is both mechanist and idealist.[1] The whole content of Pavlov's teaching on higher nervous activity, the whole course of development of science, refutes this conception.

III

The direction of scientific investigation is always determined, whether consciously or not, by theoretical conceptions; and the theoretical standpoint determines the structure of investigation. What should be the direction, and the structure, of psychological investigation?

The decisive factor here should be the dialectical-materialist principle of determinism; the proposition that external causes operate through internal conditions is a direct expression of this principle. It is not difficult to show that it was precisely this proposition that shaped Pavlov's 'model' investigation during his study of higher nervous activity. It is usually stressed, quite rightly, that Pavlov regarded the activity of the brain as activity which embodies the external interrelations of the organism with the conditions of its life. But it is no less important to emphasize something else: Pavlov was able to reveal the regularity of these external relations only because, in studying them, he discovered the *internal* laws of the neurodynamics of the cortical processes, the laws which govern the movement of these processes (the laws of irradiation and concentration) and their interrelation (the law of induction).

In the absence of a knowledge of these internal laws it is only possible to state, in a roundabout way, that such and such an external

---

[1] This is clearly demonstrated in the article by B. V. Beliaev, 'The Basic Law of Psychology' (*Sovetskaya Pedagogika*, No. 9, 1953); the author reaches the stage of completely divorcing the image from the activity of the brain.

influence produces such and such a reaction (linking them directly according to the schema: stimulus—response); or it may be possible to indicate groups or types of influences, linking with them groups or types of reactions. As is well known, this is the method of behaviourism. In contrast to Pavlov, behaviourism follows the mechanist schema: stimulus—response. Its description of external connections between stimulus and reaction is in keeping with the pragmatic, generally positivist methodology which provides the starting point of behaviourism. This course does not lead to the disclosure of real laws. In the course of the Pavlovian investigations, the phenomena studied (the secretion of saliva in response to a stimulus, the formation of a conditioned connection) became 'indicators' of the laws which lay behind them. Refracted through internal interrelationships, through the internal laws governing the activity of the brain, the external relations of the organism with its conditions of life appeared (in Pavlov's work) in their true regularity. Only this course leads to genuinely scientific knowledge.

Psychological science cannot be built in a different way, on the basis of another 'model'. The radical weakness of psychological theory is apparent when it is realized that psychological investigations have not, up till now, been consciously constructed in this way.

The study of thinking may be taken as an example; in particular, studies relating to schoolchildren. Here there is frequent mention of cases of transfer, or lack of transfer, of the methods of solving one problem to a similar problem. This phenomenon, which the teacher constantly comes across in his work, is very important to the evaluation of thinking activity. The usual reason given for transfer or nontransfer is the variation in conditions when the problem is presented. A rough, schematic, and consequently oversimplified summing up of such investigations, is the statement that transfer depends on the variation in conditions. But 'transfer' is, properly speaking, a metaphorical description of some external event which does not disclose its inner psychological content. *Psychologically*, transfer is *generalization*. On the other hand, to speak of variation of the conditions in which the problem is presented to the pupil, is to describe the action, not of the pupil, but of the teacher. To link transfer and variation is to bring into direct relation an external influence (the teacher's action in varying the conditions) and the result of the thinking activity of the pupils, while at the same time ignoring this activity; in other words, an explanation has been constructed according to the schema stimulus—response, which does not reveal the inner content of the thinking activity, its inner laws.

What does variation of conditions mean in relation to the thinking activity of a pupil? Only one thing. Variation creates favourable conditions for *analysis*, for the separation of relevant and irrelevant conditions; that is, for the separation of the conditions of a problem in the proper, exact sense, from accessory circumstances attending it in any particular instance. Behind the dependence of transfer on variation of conditions, therefore, there appears another instance of dependence, that of generalization on analysis.

Another example may be quoted, indicating another current trend. Thinking is often treated as a combination of intellectual operations, and the intellectual operations themselves as a series of methods of solving intellectual problems, socially elaborated in the process of development of scientific knowledge, and assimilated in the process of education. (This trend of thought is outlined in the same simplified, rough, and schematic manner as was the first.) This theory of thinking places in the foreground the *assimilation* of knowledge and skills (methods of solving problems) in the process of education. There can be no question that the assimilation of knowledge and skills is a matter of first importance; without it, thinking is impossible. But what precisely does assimilation in the process of education mean? It is a pedagogical fact. If investigators are content merely to study this fact, they naturally confine themselves to the task of describing the stages of assimilation, and the necessary conditions for successful assimilation. The investigation runs the danger of remaining essentially in the sphere of pedagogical problems. For a proper psychological investigation it is necessary to make clear what is the psychological significance of assimilation; that is, to disclose the inner psychological content, the inner laws, of the pupil's thinking activity as a result of which assimilation takes place. *Psychologically*, assimilation of knowledge is the thinking activity which takes place during learning, and consists of analysis, synthesis, abstraction and generalization.

To say, when describing the stages of mastering mental operations, that initially the operations are conducted at the practical level (counting with the fingers) and later at the mental level (counting in the head), is only to give a description of a certain phenomenon, one which undoubtedly takes place and is very important. But this process must be analysed in psychological terms. *Psychologically*, the shift from 'external' to 'internal' operation is a process of abstraction, the movement of which must be traced out.

Thinking activity is directly revealed in the form of a multitude of various operations. Each of these must be subjected to a special study and explanation which takes account of its peculiarities. If all these particular explanations of particular operations are finally to fuse into one general theory of thinking, it must be demonstrated that all particular operations, without losing their specific character, are acts of

273

analysis and synthesis, of generalization and abstraction, performed in various conditions, on various material, and at various levels. Analysis and synthesis represent, as it were, the 'common denominators' of all thinking activity and thus permit of a generalized treatment; with their derivatives, abstraction and generalization, they are concepts essential to a general theory of thinking and in the study of thinking their movement must be traced. To describe any intellectual activity psychologically means, in the final count, to show it as derived from the activity of analysis, synthesis and so on.

In sum, analysis itself, synthesis and generalization take on various forms and give various results, depending upon the particular system of thinking activity in which they appear; their regular interrelations make up the basic internal laws of thinking. Psychological investigation must reveal these basic internal laws, which, though they do not comprise all that is necessary to explain thinking activity, are yet essential to such an explanation. The starting point in the study of thinking activity must, of course, be the external interrelations formed by the individual in the process of education, his relations with the tasks he meets in the course of social life and study. But unless the internal laws and relations, through which these external interrelations are refracted, are disclosed, it is impossible to understand these very interrelations in their regularity, to understand man's thinking activity.

There are not, then, two ways of constructing a psychological theory, one resting on the internal relations of thinking activities, and the other directed towards the external relations of thinking and the object of thinking. There is one, and only one, way of investigating thinking psychologically and constructing a theory. This consists in discovering the inner laws governing thinking activity by studying the external interrelations of thinking activity with its object, and in understanding these external interrelations themselves in their regularity by refracting them through the inner laws of thinking activity. For example, in the light only of the inner laws governing generalization, it is impossible to determine *what* precisely will be generalized, and by what signs. This depends on the individual characteristics of the objects themselves and the external interrelations between subject and object. But unless the inner laws of generalization are known, it is impossible to understand how a generalization will be effected and what result it will give. External interrelations are seen to obey laws only after the laws governing internal interrelations are disclosed.

The task of psychological theory may, then, be formulated in the following general terms. It is necessary to express the phenomena of life in psychological concepts which separate out those aspects that comprise the special subject matter of psychological investigation; it

274

is necessary to express the interdependence of these aspects by means of inner psychological laws, and thus to come to a psychological understanding of the laws governing the external interrelations of an individual with the objective world and with other people, his relations to social experience and to the system of knowledge he acquires in the process of education, and so on.

IV

The structure of psychological theory has been outlined in general terms. It is now necessary to outline its content, even if only schematically.

The central place must be occupied by the psychic as a *process*, as *activity*. This proposition of Sechenov remains valid. By the psychic as activity, we understand a psychic process, or combination of processes, which satisfies some vital human need and is directed towards a definite end more or less directly connected with the satisfaction of this need. We have, therefore, to do with the activity of a *man*, a *subject*, a *personality*, not simply the activity of some organ or other (even though it be the brain); we have to do with a man's activity brought about through his brain. Examples of such activity are aesthetic perception, or thinking, since they satisfy an aesthetic or cognitive need and are directed to this end; a psychic process which is not a human activity in this sense, always enters into and depends upon some other activity. This, then, is the first task of psychology, study of the psychic as a process or activity. This includes the study of consciousness as a process, as the activity of perceiving the world.

Every psychic process is included in man's interaction with the world and shares in the regulation of his actions, his conduct; each psychic phenomenon is, then, both a reflection of the mode of life and a link in the regulation of men's conduct and actions. Therefore, the sphere of psychological investigation extends to men's movements and actions; i.e. it covers not only 'psychic' mental activity, but also the practical activity whereby men change nature and remake society. But psychology studies only the specifically psychological content of practical activity, its motivation and regulation, whereby actions are brought into conformity with the objective conditions in which they are performed as these are reflected in sensation, perception and consciousness.

A psychic process, a psychic activity, is always a link between the individual and the world. In psychic activity something always occurs which produces a reflection of objective reality, i.e. its image. An image in itself, apart from a psychic process or activity, is not, and

275

cannot be, a subject for psychological investigation. An image cannot exist apart from a process, though under certain conditions it appears to *the subject* to do so because the process itself, in which the image is formed, is not perceived by the subject. In these cases, psychological investigation, by changing the conditions of the stream of perception and by concentrating on the formation of the corresponding activity, must reveal the whole process. In complex conditions, as in the first stages of formation of the corresponding activity (e.g. the visual perception of an object or situation), there occur visual analysis, synthesis, generalization, and, on this basis, interpretation; in a word, all the psychological elements of the process of perception. The image, therefore, as the object of psychological investigation, is indissolubly linked with psychic activity. The specific character of psychic processes and activity can only be understood if they are considered in close connection with the image which arises in the course of their functioning. Visual perception, for example, stands out specifically only in connection with the image that appears in the process of visual perception.

On the other hand a psychic process, which finds concrete expression in an image reflecting the objective world, presupposes a subject who, again, is always connected with the objective world. Psychic processes and psychic activity must, therefore, be regarded as one of the forms of connection between the subject and the objective world. This means that theories relating to psychic processes must be linked with the theory of man's psychic properties, that these processes find expression in the characteristics of the subject as well as in the image of the object.

The question of the relation between man's psychic activity and psychic properties is fundamental to psychological theory. It is the connection of man's psychic properties with his activity that opens the way for the formation of these properties. Only if it can provide a correct answer to this question can psychology make a significant contribution to knowledge; and, in addition, its own specific contribution to the great cause of education. At present the theory of abilities, of psychological properties of personality, the psychological characterization of personality in general, is the most undeveloped part of psychology. In this sphere, in particular, there are attempts to 'materialize' the psychological; these are made to appear scientific by means of a crude psychomorphology, which directly links abilities with the morphological structure of the brain while ignoring the dynamics of reflex activity.

The reflex conception of the psychic relates not only to psychic processes but extends also to psychic properties. A psychic property is an ability, under known conditions, to respond with a specific psychic activity to influences generalized in a definite way. The extension of the reflex conception to psychic properties necessarily leads to a linking of the theory of psychic properties with the theory of psychic processes.

According to the traditional point of view, properties of personality are simply traits of character, or the ability to perform complex types of professional activity (e.g. that of a musician, a mathematician); these properties are treated as individual peculiarities distinguishing one man from another. It is impossible, however, to divorce consideration of outstanding individual peculiarities from a study of the elementary 'ancestral' properties common to all men. If there is such a divorce, the outstanding capacities of certain individuals inevitably become a mystery, and the guiding line to their study is broken. In contradistinction to such an approach, all the properties of man must be considered in their interconnection, and the starting point must be the 'ancestral' properties common to all men.

A common property of this kind is sensitivity in all the variety of its forms and levels, understood, not as a dimension inversely proportionate to its thresholds, but primarily as the ability to respond with sensations and perceptions to specific influences under specific objective conditions. Underlying this property is a combination of unconditioned and conditioned connections. Any activity that is at all complex—for instance, visual perception of the spatial properties and relations of objects—always functions as a whole, including its conditioned-reflex components. Therefore, the formation of psychic properties and of the corresponding psychic activities takes place *simultaneously* and represents, essentially, a single process. Psychic properties, which appear physiologically as a system of nervous connections, exist only in the form of regularly ensuing psychic activity.

To complete the general picture one more point should be added. It is clear that the psychological characterization of a man's personality cannot consist merely of the sum of its properties, each of which may be expressed psychologically as a specific response to a stimulating factor directed towards the subject. This means the splintering of personality, and leads to the harmful mechanist theory that each stimulus acting upon a man determines its own effect, independently of the general dynamic situation, brought about by other stimulating factors, in the content of which it operates. Here is the central link in 'the psychology of personality', the starting point and end point for a completely adequate theory of motivation. To disclose the internal laws governing these dynamic relations, through which are refracted all the external forces which act upon man, is the most important of the many important tasks of psychology.

The many problems involved cannot be analysed here. They will only be solved in the course of a whole series of systematic theoretical and experimental investigations. This article is intended only to chart the direction of such investigations.

APPENDIX I

PSYCHOPATHOLOGICAL RESEARCH IN THE U.S.S.R.[1]

BY

A. R. LURIA

WORK IN THE FIELD of pathological or clinical psychology is an essential part of Soviet psychology.

In developing this complex field of inquiry, Soviet psychologists maintain a very close liaison with those working on the pathophysiology of higher nervous activity, and set themselves a double aim. On the one hand, by bringing the exact methods of psychological experiment into clinical practice, they try to put the diagnosis of nervous and psychic ailments on a scientific basis, and to elaborate scientific methods of restoring impaired functions. On the other hand, they try to use their knowledge of pathological modifications of psychic processes to reach a better understanding of the general laws of human psychology. Pavlov indicated that 'the pathological, by breaking down and simplifying what is hidden, fused and complicated in the physiological norm, often reveals it to us'.[2] This proposition underlies the importance of investigations into pathological processes for the science dealing with the normal structure of all human psychic activity.

I

An important aspect of psychopathological research consists of clinical studies designed to assist the exact definition of the concrete mechanisms underlying nervous and psychic ailments.

This field of work is one of the oldest in Russian psychology. In the 1890's a psychological laboratory was founded in the psychiatric clinic of the well-known Russian psychiatrist, S. S. Korsakov; a

[1] This article was specially written for this volume (translated by H. Milne).
[2] Pavlov-Anrep, 301.

similar laboratory was founded a little later in the clinic of the famous neurologist and psychiatrist, V. M. Bekhterev, in the neurological clinic of A. I. Rossolimo and others. The founder of Russian physiology and scientific psychology, I. M. Sechenov, often spoke of the application of psychology to the solution of the main problems of medicine. It was under the influence of the ideas of these great doctors and experimentalists that Russian clinical psychology developed; this clinical psychology carried through a large number of experiments devoted to the psychological study of the disturbance of psychic processes in a number of nervous and psychic ailments.

Important advances in the field of pathological psychology were made by L. S. Vigotsky, a remarkable Soviet psychologist who worked in this field from 1927 to 1934, and died prematurely. Vigotsky questioned the expediency of investigating psychic functions (memory, attention, and so on) in isolation. He took as his starting point the notion that psychic activity develops in the process of reflecting the external environment, and that this reflection is mediated through language. Vigotsky carried out important researches into the changes that take place in the forms in which the real world is consciously reflected in subjects with pathological cerebral conditions. He used a number of methods which permitted him to study how a human being, at different stages of development, generalizes his perceptions, and to study the concomitant changes in the meaning of language, the main instrument of abstraction and generalization.[1] He was thereby able to show how the meaning of words is disturbed where there are pathological conditions of the brain (aphasia, schizophrenia), as well as the changed forms which the generalized reflection of the external world assumes in cases of abnormal development (deaf-mutism, mental backwardness). Vigotsky's researches enabled him to attempt a description of the main characteristics of the thinking, and, more generally, of the consciousness of subjects suffering from diseases of the brain, and to subject some of the most important clinical symptoms of nervous and psychic ailments to psychological analysis. These studies were the beginning of a whole series of investigations by Soviet psychologists in different fields of clinical practice,[2] and struck out new paths in Soviet psychopathology.

These investigations led to the complete rejection of the use of superficial and formal psychometric tests for giving a clinical diag-

[1] The experimental methods which Vigotsky proposed for the study of thinking have been exhaustively described in psychological literature. In particular they were expounded and popularized in J. Kasanin's book *Language and Thought in Schizophrenia* (University of California Press, 1944).

[2] Luria, Bein and Kogan in neurology; Zeigarnik, Lebedinsky and others in psychiatry; and Levina, Boskis, Zankov, Soloviev, Shif and Vlasova in defectology.

nosis of mental illness, for defining the degree of mental under-development or for defining the extent of defect. The main task of psychological investigation was considered to be the more precise definition or *characterization* of a defect—the concrete study of the qualitative change in the *structure* of psychic processes which ensues as a result of a pathological condition of the brain. This is particularly necessary because the external symptoms are seldom sufficient to allow an immediate judgment about the physiological mechanisms which lie behind them, and a simple superficial description of the symptoms without their psychological definition can lead to serious clinical errors. Thus, simply to point to the symptom of a disturbance in writing which occurs in cases of pathological conditions of the brain, gives no basis for reaching a conclusion about the mechanisms which have produced it; a psychological analysis, however, can show how the nature of this symptom varies in different cases. In certain cases a disturbance in writing is the result of a previous disturbance of aural analysis and synthesis (as a result of which the individual loses the power of analysing the phonic composition of a word, and cannot write it); in other cases it results from a defect in the exact articulations which enter into phonic analysis, which are also required for correct writing; in a third group the disturbance is due to defective preservation of the series of consecutive phonic traces, whose order must be preserved for correct writing; in a fourth group it is due to a profound disturbance of the general dynamic of the nervous pro-cesses; this leads to the loss of the regulating influence of the initial intention, and its replacement by an inert perseveration of separate elements in the writing. It follows that, if the origin of the pathological symptom is to be correctly appreciated, and if scientifically sound in-structions are to be given for its removal, there must be a careful analysis of the structure of this defect and a search for the initial disturbance which led to the emergence of this or the other symptom and its consequence.

Such a definition of the symptom and the determination of the mechanisms behind it can only be achieved on the basis of *a careful psychological analysis of the construction of the 'function'*, whose nor-mal operation is disturbed by the pathological process. A careful analysis of the way in which the 'function' is formed in the course of development, the stages it goes through, and the manner in which it operates in normal psychic activity has, therefore, become the essen-tial prerequisite of the application of psychological methods to the analysis of clinical symptoms. Soviet psychologists have made a large number of studies on these lines.[1] These are all based on the premises

---

[1] The breakdown of perception and recognition has been studied by Soloviev, of recall by Zankov and Leontiev, of the speech processes by Luria, Bein, Boskis

outlined above, and, with the help of careful psychological experiment, have assisted in the definition of psychic changes observed in the mentally ill.

This approach to the psychological definition of a symptom, which must necessarily precede its physiological explanation and anatomical localization, has enabled Soviet psychologists to study the principal forms of nervous and psychic illness from new positions. A series of books which have appeared during the last ten years [1] have generalized the results of a large number of investigations conducted by psychologists who have introduced experimental psychological methods into the analysis of breakdowns of human activity, and who, refusing to confine themselves to a superficial description of pathological phenomena, have aimed at analysing their substance. This work has made possible a substantially accurate definition of the syndromes of aphasia, apraxia, agnosia, and mental breakdowns, and the introduction into clinical practice of a number of new principles in the analysis of mental illness.

II

The principles outlined above, involving a careful qualitative analysis of the genesis of a pathological syndrome and its mechanisms, enabled Soviet psychologists to do a great deal of work on the restoration of functions disturbed by a pathological condition; this work was widely developed during the second world war.

It is clear that such disturbed functions can only be successfully restored if the investigator is thoroughly acquainted with their construction, and can qualify the peculiarities attendant upon their breakdown with sufficient clarity. Ignorance of the construction of a disturbed function has frequently disarmed doctor and educator in their efforts to restore it; in addition, a primitive notion of psychic activity as the direct result of the operation of some group of cerebral cells (a notion which sprang from the views of Virchowian cellular physiology, and the concepts of formal genetics) has often led to the false conclusion that functions which have broken down as a result of organic injury of the brain cannot be restored.

Soviet psychologists have reached radically different conclusions

and Kogan, of reading and writing by Ananiev, Levina and others, of counting by Rudenko, of thought and purposive action by Zeigarnik, Rubinstein, Shubert, Vasilevskaya, Pevsner and others.

[1] Luria's *Traumatic Aphasia* (1947) and *Essays on the Psychophysiology of Writing* (1950); Boskis's *Peculiarities of the Development of Speech in Children whose Aural Analyser has broken down* (1953); Soloviev's *Peculiarities of the Cognitive Process in Pupils of Special Schools* (1953); Levina's *A Study of Children who have lost the Power of Speech (suffering from alalia)* (1951), and others.

from those just mentioned, enabling them to find new scientific methods of restoring disturbed functions.

Investigations conducted by Soviet psychologists, and described in a number of works issued in the post-war years,[1] show that every concrete activity which has broken down as a result of organic disease or injury (e.g. wounds of the brain or of the peripheral nervous system) cannot by any means be regarded as the direct function of a particular limited group of cells. In the vast majority of cases it is a *complex functional system* which is formed during a man's life according to the laws of temporary connections, and rests on the most complex constellation of conjointly operating parts of the nervous system. In this respect Soviet psychologists have only developed the views of the leading Russian physiologists, Pavlov (who introduced the principle of systematization into the analysis of the work of the cortex) and Ukhtomsky (according to whom any cerebral function is a result of 'the joint operation of a constellation of centres'). The very fact that functions which have broken down as a result of disease or injury are constructed in this way points to their high degree of plasticity, and to the possibility of restoring them or compensating for them by their reconstruction.

Investigations by Soviet neurophysiologists and especially by Anokhin [2] have shown that even the simplest and inborn functions, such as breathing, sucking, and swallowing, are really very complex 'functional systems', which rest on an elaborate complex of conjointly operating parts of the nervous system; it has been shown experimentally that when some link in the chain of this functional system breaks, the activity in question breaks down, but this breakdown is not fatal, and, if this functional system is reconstructed under certain conditions, the disturbed function can be restored. The basic mechanisms of this restoration have been attentively studied, and the conditions under which it can be most successfully realized have been established in the works of noted Soviet physiologists, Asratyan [3] and Anokhin.[4]

[1] *The Restoration of Movements* (1948) by Leontiev and Zaporozhets; *The Restoration of the Functions of the Brain after War Wounds* (1948) by Luria; *Psycho-pedagogical Problems of the Restoration of Speech in cases of Cranial-cerebral Trauma* (1945) and *Speech Disorders and Speech Restoration in cases of Cranial-cerebral Trauma* (1948), ed. Zankov, etc.

[2] *The Problem of the Centre and the Periphery in the Physiology of Nervous Activity* (1935), and *Problems of the Physiology of Higher Nervous Activity* (1949).

[3] *The Physiology of the Central Nervous System* (Moscow, 1953).

[4] A summary of Anokhin's latest investigations is given in his articles 'Peculiarities of the Afferent Apparatus of the Conditioned Reflex and their Significance for Psychology', in *Voprosy Psikhologii*, No. 6, 1955, and 'General Principles governing Compensation of Disturbed Functions and their Physiological Basis' in the report of a session of the Institute of Defectology of the Academy of Educational Sciences, January 1956.

If such comparatively simple functional systems as the inborn acts of breathing and swallowing, which mature in the later stages of embryonic development, are so plastic, and can, under certain conditions, be restored, then a much greater degree of plasticity is possessed by the more complex functional systems which are formed during the life of a man and rest on a most elaborate complex of conjointly operating areas of the cerebral cortex.

The investigations which Soviet physiologists and psychologists conducted after the second world war confirmed the proposition that injuries to the brain or the peripheral nervous system give rise directly to two kinds of functional disturbance which are different in nature and can be remedied by different means. On the one hand, the injury leads to temporary shock or inhibition of the functions, and this can be removed by special protective or disinhibitory therapy; the employment of pharmacological substances (e.g. prostigmin) which act on the mediatory processes, and are a powerful means of freeing a function inhibited by injury, gave very good results in the treatment of the after-effects of war wounds; this practice has become firmly established in the clinical treatment of nervous disorders. On the other hand, a bullet wound destroys the brain or nerve tissue, and produces irreversible results. This does not mean, however, that the function lost as a result of such a wound cannot be restored.

Observations of physiologists and psychologists have shown that in these cases the sole means of restoring the disturbed function is to rebuild the functional system which produced the activity. This rebuilding proceeds primarily along the lines of changing the afferent connections on which this function rests, a process which can, under certain conditions, ensure that the same function is performed by a new undamaged system of nerve centres.

Thus, an attentive study of hand movement in the performance of work operations, conducted by Leontiev and Zaporozhets,[1] showed that in conditions of partial injury to the peripheral nerves (e.g. to the plexuses), the disturbance of the movements is not of an efferent but principally of an afferent nature.[2] It also showed that if the instructions given to the subject are changed and he is asked not 'to raise his hand', but 'to grasp some object', then the displacement of the afferentation from the kinaesthetic to the visual, and the inclusion of the motor act in a system of object-based action (performed through a much more complex system of cortical connections), bring about a

[1] *The Restoration of Movements* (1948).
[2] The proposition concerning the role of afferent systems in motor acts, which Pavlov introduced into physiology, was reflected in the works of Orbeli, *Lectures on the Physiology of the Nervous System* (1935), and Bernstein, *The Structure of Movements* (1947).

considerable extension of motor possibilities. The reorganization of the system of therapeutic re-training of patients suffering from injury to the peripheral nervous system on these lines has produced very valuable results, and had considerably increased the speed with which lost functions have been restored.

Luria, Zankov and their collaborators applied a similar principle in their work on the restoration of speech, writing and reading after brain injuries. In many cases a correct definition of the symptoms appearing after injury to the temporal, occipital and pre-motor areas of the brain brought a better understanding of the mechanism of the disturbance of these functions, and led to the rejection of incorrect and useless methods of training which were often practised in clinical treatment; the restoration of a disturbed activity could then be correctly organized on the basis of a knowledge of its construction. By tracing out a considerable number of cases in which the practical and gnostic functions of speech, writing, reading and counting were restored, the investigators were able not only to discover methods effective for different kinds of derangement, but also to penetrate much more deeply into the mechanisms of the disturbances themselves, and to come near to providing a theory of the restoration of functions which have broken down.[1]

The achievements of physiologists and psychologists have not been limited to the treatment of war wounds; they have also embraced questions of compensation for defects met with in peacetime, and especially in the different departments of defectology. Psychologists have done a great deal of work in this field. The investigations of Sokolyansky into pedagogical methods of training blind deaf-mutes are of very great interest (one of these blind deaf-mutes, Skorokhodovaya, has herself described the work done on her in her two remarkable books, *How I Perceive the World*, and *How I Conceive the World*. A large group of studies on compensation for defects of blindness has been described by Zemtsova in her monograph *The Problem of Compensation for Blindness* (1956). Boskis, Morozova, Korsunskaya, Zykov and others have described their experiments on the restoration of speech and thought to deaf-mutes. Levina has contributed to the theoretical basis of logopedics, which is concerned with establishing rational methods for restoring speech, writing and reading in various cases of abnormal speech development. All these investigations, which are united by one common idea, the reconstruction of functions by forming new systems in the process of re-training, make up an important chapter in Soviet psychopathology and defectology.

[1] The basic principles of this theory have been given in the books mentioned in previous notes.

III

The work of Soviet psychologists in defining the main pathological symptoms, and working out a scientific basis for the restoration of disturbed functions, for long did not advance beyond a careful study of the types of activity which were upset by the pathological process, and of the way the restoration of these functions proceeded in the process of compensation. This work has gone further only in recent years, linking up with investigations into the physiology and pathology of higher nervous activity, and setting itself the task of discovering the precise physiological mechanisms which lie behind the corresponding pathological conditions of the brain.

Every shock to the brain—including organic shock—produces a certain change in the condition of the main nervous processes—stimulation and inhibition; it changes their strength, equilibrium and mobility. The physiological characteristics of the work of a pathologically modified cerebral cortex were carefully studied by Pavlov's school,[1] but they were not at the centre of attention of psychologists. While psychological investigations provided valuable descriptive material, and were of great assistance in making possible an exact definition of the symptom and in determining scientific methods of compensation, they were for this reason incomplete and sometimes even one-sided. This lack of contact with physiological analysis, which is characteristic of almost all the investigations mentioned above, made a more profound treatment essential. Most of the work on psychopathology done in recent years has, therefore, been characterized by the great attention given to analysis of the physiological mechanisms which lie behind the changes in functional systems in pathological conditions.

Ivanov-Smolensky, who used a variant of the conditioned-reflex method for the study of the pathology of higher nervous activity in man, showed that pathological conditions lead to a lowering of the power of nervous processes, to a significant lowering of all forms of active inhibition, to an increase in the importance of the part played by external inhibition, to negative induction, to noticeable inertness of the nervous processes, and, most important of all, to dissociation of the two signal systems which produces a disturbance in the conscious activity of the patient, and a disturbance in the normal regulation of his behaviour. These changes in higher nervous processes take place not only in cases of focal shock to the brain, but also with diffuse cerebro-asthenic syndromes and in various cases of defect in psychic development. Soviet psychologists in recent years have devoted their

[1] By Petrova, Krasnogorsky, Ivanov-Smolensky and others.

attention to a careful study of all these changes lying behind the well-known forms of defect.

One of the most important signs of this movement was the appearance of a large number of studies using physiological methods for analysing the psychological data obtained; in this way the physiological and psychological lines of investigation were brought together.

Myasishchev studied certain important physiological mechanisms underlying the derangement of the affective processes in pathological conditions of the brain. On the initiative of Ivanov-Smolensky very extensive work was undertaken on the breakdown of the interaction of the two signal systems in various pathological states.

Luria and his collaborators made an intensive study of the peculiarities of higher nervous activity in various cases of mental backwardness—cases of oligophrenia, cases with cerebro-asthenic syndromes, and cases of local shock to various lobes of the brain. The main point here was to study the breakdown in the interaction of the two signal systems which accompanies these conditions. Gershun and Sokolov revealed the peculiarities in the structure of the sensory processes which appear in pathological conditions of the brain. Sokolov and Vinogradova studied disturbances in the orienting reflexes which make up the central part of a sensory act. Schmidt, Bein, Bassin and others made special investigations into the derangement of higher nervous activity which underlies aphasia, with the aim of rendering the conception of this derangement more precise. Zeigarnik, Lebedinsky, Soloviev, and others directed their painstaking investigations towards disclosing the neurodynamic basis of disturbance of the intellectual processes in pathological conditions of the brain.

The work of Soviet psychopathologists at the present time is mainly directed to the study of pathological change in the dynamics of the nervous processes which lie behind disturbances in psychic activity. There is every reason to suppose that such a rapprochement between the psychology and the physiology of higher nervous activity will be extremely fruitful. In the course of scientific development many important results have been achieved in the border regions where the meeting of two sciences guarantees the emergence of new lines of scientific investigation. It is just such a development that is now taking place in the sphere of pathological psychology in the Soviet Union.

APPENDIX II

THE FOURTEENTH INTERNATIONAL
CONGRESS OF PSYCHOLOGY [1]

BY

A. V. ZAPOROZHETS AND E. N. SOKOLOV

THE PROGRAMME of the Fourteenth International Congress of Psychology included a wide variety of problems which are being developed in various directions and from sharply divergent theoretical standpoints. The reports presented at the Congress differed widely in scientific importance.

Among the papers given at the session on 'Mechanisms of Motivated Behaviour', special mention should be made of the paper of H. F. Harlow (Wisconsin) on 'Exploratory Drives in Primates'. Pavlov laid great stress on the high degree of development of orienting reflexes in the anthropoid apes, and this has been studied by the Soviet psychologists Ladygina-Kots and Voitonis. In his experiments, Harlow developed complicated differentiations in primates by using the following method of reinforcement: when the ape made a correct choice a small window opened through which he could see everything that was going on outside the experimental room. The 'curiosity' of the animal was so great that this reinforcement was quite sufficient for the development of complicated differentiations.

Another line of investigation into reflex activity concerned the development of conditioned reflexes in monkeys by applying a direct stimulus to the brain by means of an electric current.

The introduction of electrodes directly into the brain for the investigation of conditioned reflexes in mice was demonstrated by the collaborators of Hebb (Montreal), who is engaged in studying the higher nervous activity of animals.

---

[1] *Voprosy Psikhologii*, No. 1, 1955, pp. 116–20 (translated by H. Milne). The proceedings of this Congress, which was held at Montreal in 1954, have been published by the North Holland Publishing Co., Amsterdam, 1955.

Cortical processes lying at the basis of human behaviour was the theme of lectures by W. Penfield and his collaborator, the electrophysiologist H. H. Jasper (both Canadians). Penfield's report was devoted to a review of the data obtained in the course of neurosurgical operations when the cortex is stimulated by an electrical current. Penfield uses such stimulation, and the simultaneous registration of the electrical activity of the brain, to pinpoint the centre of pathological disturbance in cases of epilepsy and other pathological conditions of the brain. The verbal answers of the patient (being operated on under local anaesthesia) as various areas of the brain were stimulated provided a large amount of information about the part played by separate areas of the brain in different psychic processes.

H. H. Jasper, in his paper 'Correlates between Psychological Processes and the Electrical Activity of the Brain', elucidated a number of questions connected with the role of encephalography in the investigation of psychic processes. He gave a sober warning against being led astray by a simple comparison of psychic processes and the data of electrophysiology. He pointed to contradictory facts concerning the frequency of the electrical oscillations (the main characteristic of the electrical action of the brain), stressed the prospects opened out by new methods of investigation (the microelectrode technique), and indicated the inaccuracy of existing psychological terms which hinder research. But in his own communication Jasper himself did not use the physiologically exact concept of the conditioned reflex, but the descriptive concept of 'learning'. While correctly pointing out the inadequacy of the concepts of subjective psychology, he attempted, as did Penfield also, to connect the data of electrophysiology directly with a descriptive characterization of psychic processes, without analysing the processes of higher nervous activity which lie at the basis of these psychic processes.

A special session was devoted to motor abilities. M. Ponzo (Rome), in his paper 'The Motor Factor from Perception to Action', summed up the investigations of motor functions which were conducted in Turin and Rome. Many of these researches were of a practical nature and were concerned with the study of work habits. The paper dealt principally with the theoretical significance of the investigations. Having analysed the results obtained, the author concluded that the motor factor plays an important part not only in the effector, but also in the receptor and central parts of the action. Facts were quoted showing how perception of weight changes, and how the body scheme changes in dependence on the nature of the movements being performed. The author of the paper emphasized that the central part of the action consists of mental actions which in principle do not differ from external actions, and which include motor components.

A. T. Welford (Cambridge), in his paper 'Timing and Organization of Manual Skilled Performance', dwelt on the significance of the central factor in movements, and on the important role in the central organization of manual movement played by the special features of both exteroceptive and proprioceptive afferentation. Specific difficulties in the isolation and discrimination of signals lower the speed of movement. This accounts for the increase in the duration of reactions among old people and among subjects who are in a condition of fatigue. The increase in speed which follows practice is connected with a change in the central organization of movements. When a series of movements is frequently repeated, the subject gradually ceases to perform each movement separately, and forms more complex motor 'units' which make it possible to perform a motor task more rapidly.

It is important to notice that the general direction of investigation into habits now being carried out abroad departs from the mechanistic theory of habits advanced by orthodox behaviourists. Attempts are being made to give a psychological analysis of motor training in human beings, and to explain the part played by perception of the conditions of the problem, verbal instructions, and so on. However, as the well-known English psychologist Bartlett justly observed during the discussions, work on the study of habits has still a very fragmentary character, and has not been unified round central psychological problems. The investigations are largely confined to the statement of facts, and do not give any really deep psychological analysis of the process of formation and transfer of habit. In this connection, Bartlett showed a very favourable attitude towards Soviet investigations into the special features and role of orienting-exploratory activity in the formation of motor habits.

It should be observed that the positivist, phenomenalist character of many investigations is bound up with the fact that many American and West European psychologists hold the wholly mistaken view that the theory of conditioned reflexes is useful only in explaining the simplest forms of training, and cannot be applied to the analysis of the formation of higher processes.

Much of the work of the Congress was devoted to sensations and perception. H. Pieron (Paris), in his paper 'The Problem of the Role of the Receptor, the Conductor and the Interpretative Processes in Colour Vision', dwelt on the interrelation of the receptor, conductive, and cortical mechanisms in the emergence of a sensation; in his opinion the most important problem is the investigation of the processes which take place at various stages in the transmission of nervous excitation. He referred to the presence of conditioned-reflex mechanisms in colour vision, but, in his opinion, their role lies in the 'interpretation' of the signals entering the cortex. R. Granit (Stockholm), in his paper 'Brain Control of the Sense Organs', drew an analogy between the organ of vision and the organs of movement. Referring to earlier data concerning the part played by the brain in changes in the electrical activity of motor neurons, he pointed out that similar phenomena also take place in visual reception. Granit introduced microelectrodes into separate gangliar cells of the retina, and established that the stimulation of the centrifugal paths leading to the retina from the cortical and subcortical centres of vision causes substantial changes in the form and frequency of the impulses arising in the gangliar cells of the retina.

The report given by R. Gunter (London) dealt with the interrelation between the data furnished by electrophysiological investigation of the potentialities of the visual receptor, and the data concerning the use of these potentialities in the behaviour of the animal. According to his information, there are three systems of receptor-mediators in the peripheral organ of sight of a cat, each of which reacts when it is selected; this suggests that a cat possesses three-component vision. However attempts to develop colour differentiation in cats (brightness being equal) were unsuccessful. Thus a discrepancy exists between the potentialities of the peripheral receptor apparatus and the corresponding processes in the central nervous system, and for this reason these potentialities are not made use of in the animal's behaviour. Gunter's report shows that the forms in which nervous impulses are transmitted have not yet been sufficiently studied. It is impossible not to agree with Pieron when he referred to the importance of investigating the nature of the signals which transmit differences in the radiation acting upon the eye.

The paper of H. K. Hartline (United States) on 'The Excitation of Visual Receptors and the Patterns of Nervous Activity in the Eye' was based on material obtained from the study of the work of the visual receptors of *Limulus*. He spoke of the complex integration of impulses which is effected by the optical nerve, as a result of which the separate ommatidia of *Limulus* do not work in isolation. The excitation of one of the groups leads to the inhibition of another, neighbouring group. These dynamic interrelations take on a still more complex character in the functions of the eye of vertebrates, where complicated signalling takes place as a result of change in the illumination and displacement of the representation of the object on the retina.

Ivo Köhler (Innsbruck) in a paper, 'Experiments with Prolonged Optical Distortions', told of the results of experiments where the subjects wore glasses with one blue lens and one yellow lens for two or three weeks. The subject saw objects as blue or yellow depending on the direction of his glance. When the glasses were worn for a long period a gradual adaptation to these conditions took place, so that when grey objects were presented to the subjects they began to experience sensations of grey in spite of the presence of the chromatic filters. After the glasses were removed the subject seemed to see colourless objects as either blue or yellow according to the direction in which he looked. Analysis of Köhler's data shows that here we have an interesting case of the formation of sensory conditioned reflexes, which have already been studied systematically for many years in the physiological and psychological laboratories of the Soviet Union.

In considering the situation in foreign psychology with regard to the problem of sensation and perception one cannot but notice a certain disillusionment with Gestalt psychology, which until recently was supreme in this field, and an eagerness to stress the role of experience and training in the processes of perception. A number of investigators, abandoning their one-sided interest in the peripheral receptor apparatus alone, are going over to the study of the central mechanisms of perception. Several are beginning to incline to the reflex conception of sensory processes. But this progressive tendency is advancing slowly, and is far from consistent. The majority of foreign psychologists, when speaking of the role of individual experience in perception, use the purely descriptive term 'learning', and neglect the strictly scientific concepts of the theory of higher nervous activity.

The transition from direct perception to ideas and concepts was the theme of the lecture delivered by J. Piaget (Geneva—Paris). Piaget explained the results of his investigation into the part played by perceptive and intellectual components in the development of spatial ideas in children from 5 to 12 years. He showed that although children of pre-school age find their bearings quite successfully in spatial relations as they perform different actions, they have not yet formed ideas of homogeneous geometrical space. For the formation of these more complex ideas of geometrical space direct perception is insufficient, a certain level of development of intellectual operations is necessary.

Piaget's lecture, which contained many very illuminating examples to illustrate his arguments, deserves profound study. It included an examination of the important problem of the age levels at which the child directly perceives and understands reality, and the connection between the child's age and the degree of complexity of his actions.

As distinct from his former work where he opposed elementary sensory processes to intellectual acts, Piaget has here taken a step forward in the sense that he now recognizes their connection and interaction. Unfortunately this positive tendency was insufficiently developed in the report, so that it appears that the author still imagines sensory experience and mental operations to be independent factors which only interact in the formation of spatial ideas. Piaget's collaborator B. Inhelder made an interesting contribution on the development of children's thinking from 5 to 16.

The general problems of consciousness were discussed at a special session on the theme 'Consciousness: Revised and Revived'. The programme notes of this session drew attention to the need for a review of the negative attitude to the problem of consciousness which characterizes behaviourism, and which arose as a reaction against introspectionism.

J. Nuttin (Louvain), in his report 'Consciousness, Behaviour and Personality', advanced the proposition that the world as it is perceived represents the world in itself, and the perception of it is a direct contact with what surrounds us. Consciousness signifies, therefore, primarily an entry into the real world, and is not shut into the internal world of ideas. Consciousness makes up an important aspect of behaviour and personality. The structure of personality represents the unity 'I—the world', and not at all an internal organization 'I'.

S. S. Tomkins (Princeton), in a paper dealing with the relation between the conscious and the unconscious, developed the idea that consciousness represents a special case of 'doubling' in nature ('one part of space duplicates itself in another part of space'). The role of consciousness consists in making it possible for us to perform our actions in a 'more informed' manner. It is the most important quality of man.

F. Heider (Kansas), in his paper 'Consciousness, the Perceptual World, and Interaction with Others', spoke of the role of consciousness in society. He elaborated the proposition that human intercourse depends on the subject's perception of another person, and the perception by both of one and the same surrounding world.

Thus alongside a crudely mechanist denial of consciousness and various kinds of false idealist interpretations of consciousness, we find several Western European and American psychologists striving to formulate the problem of consciousness and its role in human life in a positive way.

The session devoted to the topic 'Recent Advances in the Study of Conditioned Reflexes' attracted a good deal of attention. At this session the Soviet delegates, A. N. Leontiev, B. M. Teplov, E. A. Asratian and E. N. Sokolov, gave their papers.[1] J. I. Lacey (of the United States) and H. Eysenck (of England) also gave papers. This session attracted a large audience. All the seats were filled and also all the passages in the great auditorium of McGill University, where

[1] Cf. pp. 226, 92 (Ed.).

the meeting took place. The local press reported that this was one of the most crowded sessions. The unanimous applause with which the audience greeted the Soviet investigators bore witness to the sincere interest of a large number of West European and American scientists in Soviet psychology, and in the development of psychology on the basis of the teaching of Pavlov.

J. I. Lacey communicated the results of his investigations in a paper entitled 'Conditioned Autonomic Reflexes in the Experimental Study of Anxiety'. He developed in his subjects conditioned emotional reactions to words spoken by the experimenter. Certain words were reinforced with an electric shock to the hand (during the experiment the subjects were pressing a hand on a key in a given rhythm). The changes in the reactions of the heart and blood vessels and the electrical resistance of the body were recorded.

All the subjects were divided into two groups: one group was warned that certain words would be accompanied by an electric shock; the subjects belonging to the second group were given no such warning, and right up to the end of the experiments did not know which words would be accompanied by an electro-cutaneous stimulus. Conditioned reflexes were developed in the subjects of both groups, but the reflexes of the 'unwarned' subjects differed significantly in character from those of the 'warned' subjects. In the 'unwarned' group the indices were even higher than in the 'warned' group. It is interesting to note that in their case a broader generalization of reflexes in response to words of similar meaning was also observed.

Lacey also found that the 'warned' subjects as it were adapted themselves to the expected electric shock: objectively this was expressed in a tendency towards a lowering of the indices of their affective reactions, in spite of the continuing action of negative reinforcement.

The title of the paper presented by Eysenck (London) was 'Conditioning and Personality'. On the basis of his psychopathological investigations the lecturer came to the conclusion that Spence's theory of hysteria, current in the West, is not supported by experimental data, and that his own results confirm the conception of hysteria advanced by Pavlov.

Lively discussions followed. The official leaders, P. Fraisse (Paris) and E. L. Kelly (Michigan), spoke on the Soviet reports. They emphasized the value of the investigations described, and made a number of concrete observations on certain individual propositions. One of those who took part in the discussions, Maria Nieto (Montevideo), spoke of investigations into conditioned-reflex activity being conducted in Uruguay. Amid this fruitful exchange of opinions, the speech of G. Razran (Brooklyn) struck a sharply discordant note. He expounded a series of scientifically unfounded and radically false views on Pavlov's teaching and its psychological significance.

The papers given by both Soviet and foreign psychologists devoted to the conditioned-reflex bases of the psyche, and the great interest in these reports shown by many members of the Congress, bear witness to a strengthening of the progressive tendency among foreign psychologists, shown in their striving to investigate psychic processes in close connection with the study of their physiological mechanisms. But many transatlantic investigators are still inclined to approach the facts of 'conditioning' in the descriptive manner of the behaviourists, and to underestimate the necessity of studying the concrete peculiarities of cortical dynamics in the formation of temporary connections.

We have only touched on a few papers of scientific interest, without, of course, exhausting them. It must be said, however, that some reports were presented to the Congress, which had no scientific significance whatever. Among these were, first, many papers dealing with so-called social psychology. In this field, instead of genuine investigation, superficial inquiries, principally by means of questionnaires, are widely used. It would be possible to quote examples of investigations in other branches of psychology which are far from objective science. It is not the task of this short article to give a critique of them.

The work of the International Congress of Psychology shows once more that personal intercourse and creative discussion of scientific questions is a most important means of establishing and developing scientific links and mutual understanding, and of combining the efforts of scientists from various countries in the interests of the progress of science and of peaceful cooperation between nations.

As we left Canada, we, the members of the Soviet delegation, carried away with us a profound regard for the Canadian people and the advanced Canadian scientists who welcomed us so hospitably in their country.

BIBLIOGRAPHY

(i) *English Editions of the Works of Pavlov*

PAVLOV-GANTT i: *Lectures on Conditioned Reflexes*, translated and edited by W. Horsley Gantt (London, 1928). This is the third edition of the collection of articles and lectures first published in Russia in 1923 under the title *Twenty Years of Objective Study of the Higher Nervous Activity (Behaviour) of Animals*. Five papers are added, so that the period covered is 1903–28.

PAVLOV-GANTT ii: *Conditioned Reflexes and Psychiatry*, translated and edited by W. Horsley Gantt (New York, 1941). This is a collection of articles and lectures dating from 1928 to Pavlov's death in 1936.

PAVLOV-ANREP: *Conditioned Reflexes: An Investigation of the Physiological Activity of the Cerebral Cortex*, translated and edited by G. V. Anrep (London, 1927). This is an edition of the series of lectures delivered by Pavlov at the Military Medical Academy in Petrograd, where he was professor of physiology, in 1924. It was first published in Russia in 1926 under the title *Lectures on the Cerebral Hemispheres*.

Selected Works (Moscow, 1955). A selection of lectures and papers published by the Foreign Language Publishing House of the U.S.S.R. It includes early works on the circulation of the blood and digestion, as well as papers included in the above editions. In addition, there is a short selection from *The Pavlovian Wednesdays*; this consists of reports of the weekly meetings of the research workers in Pavlov's laboratories which took place on Wednesday mornings. Some of the papers include references to the Russian edition of this work. It should, perhaps, be noted that these reports were compiled from a stenographic record and a student's notes, which were never read, checked nor initialled by Pavlov himself; the style is, therefore, colloquial and since the record may include inaccuracies it is only used with caution.

Though page references are given to these volumes throughout, the translation of quotations from Pavlov's works in the text will be found to differ. In every case, there has been a most careful translation of the original Russian with the aim of ensuring the greatest possible accuracy.

Another volume referred to is a translation of the main reports and resolution of the *Scientific Session on the Physiological Teaching of I. P. Pavlov* (F.L.P.H., Moscow, 1951).

Other relevant works in English are E. A. Asratian, *I. P. Pavlov: His Life and Work* (F.L.P.H., Moscow, 1953), and A. G. Ivanov-Smolensky, *Essays on the Patho-Physiology of Higher Nervous Activity* (F.L.P.H., Moscow, 1954).

296

(ii) *Russian Sources*

1. ANANIEV, B. G. Psychology and the problem of the twin operation of the cerebral hemispheres. *Pavlov's Theory and Philosophical Questions of Psychology* (1952).

2. ANDREEVA, E. K. Breakdown in the formation of the system of semantic connections in cases of injury to the frontal lobes. *Thesis*, Moscow University (1951).

3. BERNSTEIN, N. A. The nature of dynamic coordinating functions. *Scientific Notes of Moscow University*, 90th issue (1945).

4. BYCHKOV, M. S. The electro-physiological investigation of motor impressions in the light of Pavlov's teaching. *Thesis*, Leningrad University (1951).

5. BYKOV, K. M. The cortex and the internal organs. *Selected Works*, ii (Moscow, 1954).

6. BYKOV, K. M., & SPERANSKY, A. D. A dog with a severed corpus callosum. *Researches of the Physiological Laboratory of I. P. Pavlov*, Vol. I, No. 1 (1924).

7. DENISOVA, M. P., & FIGURIN, N. L. On the first food reflexes in infants at the breast, *Questions of Genetic Reflexology*, ed. N. M. Shchelovanov (1929).

8. DENISOVA, M. P. Stages in the development of child behaviour from birth to one year. *Ibid.*

9. DENISOVA, M. P. An experimental study of the reaction to novelty in children up to one year. *Ibid.*

10. EGOROV, T. G. *The Psychology of Mastering the Habit of Reading* (Moscow, 1953).

11. FADDEEVA, V. K. Peculiarities of the interaction between the first and second signal systems in children. *Journal of Higher Nervous Activity*, Vol. I, No. 3 (1951).

12. FADDEEVA, V. K. The formation of conditioned connections by means of orienting-testing reactions. *An Approach to the Study of Higher Forms of Neurodynamics in the Child* (1934).

13. FILIPPYCHEVA, N. A. Inertia of the higher cortical processes in cases of local injury to the cerebral hemispheres. *Thesis*, Moscow University (1952).

14. GURIANOV, E. V. Habit and Action, *Scientific Notes of Moscow University*, 90th issue (1945).

15. HARTSTEIN, N. G. Age characteristics of conditioned inhibition in children. *Experimental Research into the Conditioned-reflex Activity of the Child*, ed. A. G. Ivanov-Smolensky (1930).

16. IVANOV-SMOLENSKY, A. G. *A Method of Investigating Conditioned Reflexes in Man* (1928).

17. IVANOV-SMOLENSKY, A. G. Concerning the study of the joint activity of the first and second signal systems. *Journal of Higher Nervous Activity*, Vol. I, No. 1 (1951).

18. IVANOV-SMOLENSKY, A. G. An approach to the study of higher forms of neurodynamics in the child. *Proceedings of the Physiological and*

BIBLIOGRAPHY

Pathophysiological Laboratory for the Higher Nervous Activity of the Child, Symposium IV (1934).

19. IVANOV-SMOLENSKY, A. G. New facts from experimental research into the higher nervous activity of the child. *Archives of the Biological Sciences*, Vol. XLII, Nos. 1–2 (1936).

20. IVANOV-SMOLENSKY, A. G. The interaction of the first and second signal systems in certain normal and pathological conditions, *Physiological Journal of the U.S.S.R.*, Vol. XXXV, No. 5 (1949).

21. IVANOVA, M. P. Breakdown in the interaction of the two signal systems in the formation of complex motor reactions in cases of injury to the brain. *Thesis*, Moscow University (1953).

22. KAPUSTNIK, O. P. Differentiation of inhibition and its age and typological characteristics. *Experimental Research into the Conditioned-reflex Activity of the Child*, ed. A. G. Ivanov-Smolensky (1930).

23. KAPUSTNIK, O. P. Interaction between direct conditioned stimuli and their verbal symbols. *Ibid.*

24. KAPUSTNIK, O. P., & FADDEEVA, V. K. Extinction of conditioned reflexes in children aged five to twelve. *Ibid.*

25. KARIMOVA, R. S. The part played by the mastery of elementary grammatical structure in the development of the child's thought. *Thesis*, Leningrad University.

26. KASATKIN, N. I. *Early Conditioned Reflexes in Human Ontogenesis* (Moscow, 1948).

27. KHOZAK, L. E. The formation of conditioned connections in the child by cross-coupling on the basis of past experience. *An Approach to the Study of Higher Forms of Neurodynamics in the Child* (1934).

28. KOLTSOVA, M. M. On the rise and development of the second signal system in the child. *Researches of the Laboratories of I. P. Pavlov*, Vol. IV (1949).

29. KOSTOMAROVA, N. M. Certain breakdowns in the organized activity of the cortex in cases of brain injury. *Isvestia of the Academy of Educational Sciences of the R.S.F.S.R.*, Vol. LIII (1954).

30. KOTLIAREVSKY, L. I. The neurodynamics of conditioned couplings which arise suddenly in complex situations. *An Approach to the Study of Higher Forms of Neurodynamics in the Child* (1934).

31. KOZIN, N. I. Age peculiarities of the automatization of motor reflex reactions. *Experimental Investigation of the Ontogenetic Development of the Dynamics of the Human Cortex*, Symposium V, ed. A. G. Ivanov-Smolensky (1940).

32. KRASNOGORSKY, N. I. *The Development of the Study of the Physiological Activity of the Brain in Children* (Moscow, 1935).

33. KRASNOGORSKY, N. I. The same, in the symposium *Basic Cortical Mechanisms in Children* (1939).

34. KRASNOGORSKY, N. I. Some age characteristics of the physiological activity of the cerebral cortex in children. *Report of the Session on the Tenth Anniversary of the Death of I. P. Pavlov* (1948).

35. KRESTOVNIKOV, A. N. *Essays in the Physiology of Physical Exercises* (Moscow, 1951).

BIBLIOGRAPHY

36. KRESTOVNIKOV, A. N. *The Physiology of Man* (Moscow, 1938).
37. LAVROVA, Z. G. Orienting trace reflexes in children. *Experimental Research into the Higher Nervous Activity of the Child* (1933).
38. LEONTIEV, A. N. Psychological questions of consciousness in learning. *Isvestia of the Academy of Educational Sciences*, No. 7 (1947).
39. LEONTIEV, A. R., & ZAPOROZHETS, A. V. *Rehabilitation of Movement* (1945).
40. LUBOVSKY, V. I. Breakdown in the interaction of the two signal systems in cases of oligophrenia. *Researches of the Department of Psychology, Moscow University*.
41. LURIA, A. R. Peculiarities of the interaction of the two signal systems in the formation of a motor reaction in normal and abnormal development. *Reports to the Conference on Questions of Psychology* (1954).
42. LURIA, A. R. Clinical study of injuries to the cortex in the light of Pavlov's teaching. *Journal of Higher Nervous Activity*, Vol. II (1952).
43. LURIA, A. R. *An internal picture of illness and disease* (Moscow, 1942).
44. MESHCHERIAKOV, A. I. Breakdown in the interaction of the two signal systems in the formation of simple motor reactions in cases of local injury to the brain. *Thesis*, Moscow University (1953).
45. NARODNITSKAYA, G. D. The formation during childhood of new conditioned connections without preliminary elaboration. *An Approach to the Study of Higher Forms of Neurodynamics in the Child* (1934).
46. NECHAIEV, N. V. (ed). *Methods of Industrial Training* (Moscow, 1951).
47. PARAMONOVA, N. P. The development of the interaction of the two signal systems in the formation of motor reactions in children of pre-school age. *Thesis*, Moscow University (1953).
48. PAVLOV, I. P. *Collected Works*, Vol. III, Book 1 (1951).
49. PAVLOV, I. P. *The Pavlovian Wednesdays*, Vol. I.
50. PAVLOV, I. P. *The Pavlovian Wednesdays*, Vol. II.
51. PAVLOV, I. P. *The Pavlovian Wednesdays*, Vol. III.
52. PEN, R. M. The formation of new conditioned connections by means of imitation. *An Approach to the Study of Higher Forms of Neurodynamics in the Child* (1934).
53. PLATONOV, K. I. *Language as a Physiological and Curative Agent* (Kharkov, 1930).
54. PUNI, A. TS. *Theory and Practice of Physical Culture*, No. 1 (1953).
55. RYKOV, N. A. Concerning the Formation of a Skill, *Sovetskaya Pedagogika*, No. 10 (1953).
56. SECHENOV, I. M. *Selected Philosophical and Psychological Works* (Moscow, 1947).
57. SECHENOV, I. M. *Reflexes of the Brain* (1942 ed.).
58. SECHENOV, I. M. *Elements of Thinking* (1943 ed.).
59. SHCHELOVANOV, N. M., & AKSARINA, N. M. (ed.). *The Upbringing of Infants in Children's Institutions* (1949).
60. SKIPIN, G. V. On the systematization of the functioning of the cerebral hemispheres, *Researches of the Physiological Laboratories of I. P. Pavlov*, Vol. VIII (1938).

BIBLIOGRAPHY

61. SMIRNOV, A. A. *The Psychology of Memory* (Moscow, 1948).
62. SMOLENSKAYA, E. P. Concerning the verbal symbols of conditioned and differentiating stimuli. *An Approach to the Study of Higher Forms of Neurodynamics in the Child* (1934).
63. SOKOLOV, A. N. Speech mechanisms of mental activity. *Işvestia of the Academy of Educational Sciences of the R.S.F.S.R.*
64. SPIRIN, B. G. The breakdown of the mobility of nervous processes after an operation on the brain. *Thesis*, Moscow University (1951).
65. TEPLOV, B. M. *The Psychology of Musical Abilities.*
66. TRAUGOTT, N. N. Interrelations between direct and symbolic projections in the formation of conditioned reflexes. *An Approach to the Study of Higher Forms of Neurodynamics in the Child* (1934).
67. USHINSKY, K. D. *Man as the Object of Education* i (1881).
68. ZINCHENKO, P. I. The problem of involuntary recollection. *Scientific Notes of the Kharkov Educational Institute*, Vol. I (1939); Involuntary recollection, *Sovetskaya Pedagogika*, No. 3 (1945); Involuntary and voluntary recollection, *Scientific Notes of the Ukrainian Institute of Psychology*, Vol. II (1950).
69. ZAPOROZHETS, A. V. Changes in the interrelations of the two signal systems during the development of the pre-school child. *Reports to the Conference on Questions of Psychology* (1954).

INDEX

Abilities, 189, 223, 251, 258, 276; inborn, 25-6, 30, 184-5, 228 ff.; research on, 39, 42

Academy of Education Sciences, 22-3

Activity: and consciousness, 6-9, 24, 184, 249, 251, 253; and formation of connections, 165 ff.; and intellectual development, 186 ff.; and knowledge, 6, 218, 239-40; purposive, 241; and memory, 163, 164 ff., 187; and sensation, 133; with objects, 111, 193, 206 ff., 215 ff., 230

Adaptation, 10, 14, 85, 89, 234, 240-1, 244-5, 292

Adolescence, 186-7, 194

Analysers, 132 ff., 155 ff., 159, 200; auditory, 93-4, 149, 156; and differentiation, 52-3, 149; functions of, 14-15, 53; interaction of, 31; motor, 16, 38, 125, 134, 146, 156, 200; skin, 94; visual, 15, 32, 40, 93, 95, 97, 100 ff., 146; work of, 30

Analysis and synthesis, 15, 18, 35, 67, 72, 136, 145, 197, 273-4, 281

Animation, complex of, 54

Apes, 71-2, 164, 288

Aphasia, 280, 282, 287

Association, 1-2, 18, 66, 69 ff., 76-8, 81, 132, 150, 153, 164 ff., 195

Attention, 84 ff., 187, 244, 280

Automatization, 221, 224, 230, 236-8, 240, 245

Behaviour, 48, 118, 152, 184, 234, 248-9, 254, 288-9, 293

Behaviourism, 4, 21, 236, 238, 258-9, 272, 290, 293, 295

Blindness, 41, 285

Brain: compensating ability of, 147, 187-8, 283, 285; electrical activity of, 32, 92 ff., 289; extirpation of part of, 15, 86, 147; injury of, 125 ff., 282 ff.; localization in, 11, 15, 86-7, 155-6, 282; motor area of, 15-16, 146; see also Reflex activity of brain and Cerebral hemispheres

Cerebral hemispheres, 58, 87, 125-6, 156, 164, 240-1; frontal lobes, 67, 125; function of, 19; twin activity of, 31, 146 ff.

Child development, 47 ff., 54 ff., 116 ff., 139, 160, 183 ff., 197 ff.; stages in, 62, 186 ff.; see also Mental actions

Children: backward, 25, 41; deaf-mute, 41; defective, 22, 33, 110-11, 124 ff.; dullness in, 186, 205 ff.; retarded, 224, 231-2; tone-deaf, 228-9

Cognition, 33, 133, 204, 213

Collective, 43, 185

Comparison, 199-200

Compensation, intra-system, 227

Concepts, 78, 81-2, 214, 231, 250, 262, 292; formation of, 35-6, 76-7, 191 ff., 219 ff.

Conditioned reflex: advantages for investigation, 16, 272; age differences in formation of, 57, 118-19, 198; and analysers, 50-1, 135, 198; and association, see Association; complexity of, 12; dependence on unconditioned,